The reimagined party

Manchester University Press

The book is dedicated to the women who have informed my life. My mother, sister, grandmothers and aunts have been a powerful influence on my thinking, fuelling my curiosity and passion to write. They have given me the faith to find my own voice, and the courage to think about problems in a different way.

The reimagined party

Democracy, change and the public

Katharine Dommett

Manchester University Press

Published by Manchester University Press
Altrincham Street, Manchester M1 7JA

www.manchesteruniversitypress.co.uk

British Library Cataloguing-in-Publication Data
A catalogue record for this book is available from the British Library

ISBN 978 1 5261 4751 6   hardback

ISBN 978 1 5261 4752 3   paperback

First published 2020

Typeset in Baskerville and Myriad Pro
by R. J. Footring Ltd, Derby, UK
Printed in Great Britain by TJ International, Padstow

Contents

Figures

Tables

List of tables

Acknowledgements

This book was forged of failure. After spending over a year and a half trying to write a book, I was forced to admit that the idea just didn't work. For any writer, the realisation that you simply don't have enough to say is difficult to face. And yet, in the grips of failure, I conceived a new project and idea that inspired this book. In this text, I hope to cast a new light on debates about political parties. Too often our discussions of party politics can be dominated by the events of the day and it is difficult to find the space to step back and consider how it is that we would like to see politics work. This book aims to facilitate such a debate, providing new insight into public views of parties by testing and exploring perceptions and desires in a range of different ways. The results show that, far from rejecting parties, these organisations are still valued, but there are areas where they do not live up to many citizens' ideals.

The research and writing process has been supported by numerous individuals and by a lifetime of investment and support from family and friends. Particular thanks go to Luke Temple for his work on this research. His enthusiasm, patience and love of crisps have been a constant companion throughout the project. When I started this research my knowledge of statistics was fairly basic, and Luke has provided support throughout on quantitative methods. He helped to build the regression models presented in the appendix of this book and has made invaluable contributions to the analysis.

We have co-authored a number of articles building on this work, and this book would not have been possible without his support, so I owe him a debt of thanks. The project has also been supported by a number of other people. I particularly want to thank Simon Burall, Sarah Allan and the staff at Involve for their work on the deliberative workshops, as well as Todd and Kristen Hartman, Robin Hughes, Indra Mangule and Alex Hastie. I also want to thank all the individuals who participated in the surveys and workshops conducted for this research.

I have also been fortunate to find an environment at Sheffield University in which thinking and research can thrive. I have been surrounded by friends and colleagues always eager to exchange ideas and unendingly generous in their time and support. I particularly want to thank Charles Pattie for his love of marginalia and invaluable critique, Colin Hay for his mentorship, Pat Seyd for his endless support and Andy Hindmoor for his advice. More broadly, I owe a debt of thanks to Clara Sandelind, Jonna Nyman, Sam Power, Warren Pearce, Tom Stafford, Ruth Blakeley, Holly Ryan, Holly Snaith, Brenton Prosser, James Weinberg, Nikki Soo, Liam Stanley and many others for innumerable discussions and distractions from this book. I would like also to thank the ERSC for funding this research, and acknowledge the support of grant ES/NO1667X/1.

Finally, I would like to thank my family for their investment and support. I owe a particular debt to my grandfather, who, with a twinkle in his eye, kept me constantly asking questions and striving to know more. I could also not have written this book without the unending support of my husband, James, whose generosity and patience are unparalleled.

Introduction

Political parties are an established feature of contemporary democratic politics. For decades, parties have organised government,
competed in elections and influenced the way society is run. Yet
despite their importance, parties' position in society is presently
unclear. As has been documented over successive decades, there is
wide-ranging evidence of discontent with traditional party politics,
with mainstream parties witnessing declining popular support and
being described in almost uniformly negative terms. But, simultaneously, there are also signs that the public have not entirely renounced
party politics, with newer parties and unconventional party leaders
achieving support and success. In such a climate it is not clear how
citizens view political parties and what it is that people desire from
these organisations.

   In this book, I use a range of methods to explore what citizens
ideally want from parties, and then probe how parties are currently
seen to measure up to these desires. Given that many parties are
seeking to generate public appeal through innovations such as the
creation of registered supporters' networks, the adoption of community organising principles and even the use of data mining, this book
provides important insights into the kind of reforms that may be able
to bring parties in line with citizen desires. Probing citizens' views,
I explore different influences upon public perceptions of parties in
an attempt to determine what it is that citizens like and dislike, and

where and how people would like to see parties change. To do so, I direct attention to the way parties represent, provide opportunities for participation, govern and conduct themselves. Through this analysis I demonstrate that there is no simple cure for parties, but neither is there a rejection of partisan politics; rather, what many people appear to desire is an expansive reimagination of the way that parties operate.

The reimagined party

The idea of a reimagined party captures the desire for a wide-ranging change in party politics. But it does not signal the rejection of established ideas of party democracy in favour of more technocratic or populist ideas. Rather, I argue that people want existing aspects of party politics – such as aggregation and mediation, responsive and responsible governance, and partisan leadership – to be performed in a slightly different way. People therefore call for more open and inclusive parties, ones that listen to different views but that also advance principled visions of the national interest. They want to see established principles of party democracy reimagined to reflect new norms and ideas.

To think about what this means, it is useful to consider an analogy from the car industry, where the idea of 'reimagined' cars is often found. Car manufacturers frequently claim to 'reimagine' classic car designs and models, drawing on the best from the past to create new models equipped with the latest mod cons. Take the example of the Mini, which was relaunched in 2001. Whilst the classic Mini had been successful in its day, for modern customers the car no longer had appeal. Although originally praised for its go-kart-like handling and simple interior and mechanics, these features and style were no longer viewed as desirable. In part this was due to technical functionality. The old Minis lacked air conditioning, heated seats and an efficient engine, meaning that most people – with the exception of a number of classic car enthusiasts – were unlikely to buy the car. But it wasn't just this – there was also a sense that the 'feel' of the car no longer chimed with modern buyers and that it wouldn't be enough to simply add integrated satnav or parking sensors to the old Mini body. What was required was a reimagining of the car that, recognising the growing popularity of SUVs and larger, safer cars, created a new Mini that was playful, practical and that, whilst recognisable as a Mini, was undoubtedly new. The new, reimagined Mini therefore did not just add new functions or change how existing features performed, but also signalled a step-change in how the car was viewed and felt to drive. Without these changes the Mini would have continued to wane, becoming the preserve of devoted classic car fans.

Political parties are somewhat like the old Mini design. Whilst essential for politics, many parties have become somewhat tired and out of kilter with modern practices and desires. Although all the essential ingredients are there, parties need to be updated. Like Minis, this does not just mean adding new functions, capacities or processes to the existing shell: it requires a more thorough re-evaluation of what a party looks like, how it behaves and what kind of emotional response it provokes. Only if parties adapt in this way can their longevity be secured.

This kind of change is something that is not new to parties. Parties have long had to evolve and transform to remain relevant. Whilst once the preserve of a small elite, parties have expanded and adapted, adopting new structures, procedures and policy ideas to remain abreast of modern trends (Budge et al., 1987; Katz and Mair, 1994; Mair, 1997). What is at present unclear, however, is what form of evolution or change citizens now desire. To offer answers to this question, in this book I explore people's desires for parties and how current practices measure up to these ideals. Whilst finding that people do not have uniform preferences, I show that many people from different backgrounds, who support a range of parties, voice an unrealised desire for parties that are more open and inclusive, responsive and responsible, and that offer principled leadership.

Presenting these insights, I consider whether and how parties wish to respond to citizens' views, and argue that whilst it is not possible to identify a single initiative or set of reforms that will guarantee positive perceptions, it is possible to highlight the types of change that many citizens desire.

The value of parties

In calling for parties to be reimagined, I build on an extensive body of theoretical work about parties. This scholarship outlines parties' position as seminal democratic institutions that have helped to bridge the gap between rulers and the ruled by providing mechanisms through which the people can engage in politics and political institutions can be run. In thinking through the traits that define systems of party democracy, a number of ideas and principles can be identified, but it is common to see emphasis placed on parties' representative capacities, their ability to deliver responsive and responsible governance, and the provision of political choice.

As democratic organisations, much emphasis has been placed on parties' capacity to facilitate democratic linkage (Figure 0.1). As Lawson (1980, p. 3) illustratively outlines, political '[p]arties are seen, both by their members and by others, as agencies for forging links between citizens and policy-makers. Their raison d'être is to create a substantive connection between rulers and ruled.' This capacity to combine and execute representative and governing functions simultaneously renders parties unique and pivotal organisations because, unlike other bodies, they are able to identify, articulate and enact

Figure 0.1 Parties' role as linkage organisations

citizens' desires. Whilst alternative systems of governance may be capable of replacing certain party functions, no alternative has yet emerged that is able to balance the varied roles that parties simultaneously perform (Dommett and Rye, 2017).

As representative organisations, political parties act as key institutions through which citizens can channel their ideas into the political system and exert some influence (however small) over the way societies are run. In systems where hundreds of thousands of people hold opinions and are given a say, parties provide a mechanism through which many different voices and ideas can be aggregated and transformed into coherent agendas that inform how the country is governed. By performing functions including facilitating participation, integrating and aggregating different views and managing conflict, Sartori (2005) argues that parties are able to identify and represent the views of the people. This makes parties key mediating organisations that collect and integrate many different views.

In addition to acting as representative organisations, parties also perform key governing roles. As Mair (2009, p. 5) has outlined, parties develop policy programmes, select governors and implement agendas, helping to bring about change in society and deliver governing outcomes. Many of these activities can be conditioned by the representative desires citizens outline, with parties, in Sartori's (2005, p. 24) terms, 'communicating the demands of society to the state, as the basic link or connector between a society and government'. And yet parties are not simply vehicles for transmitting public demands; they are also agencies of the state and therefore play a role in shaping and managing competing demands. Parties have to balance these pressures by being *responsive* to citizens' demands and also *responsible* in recognising 'internal and international systemic constraints and compatibilities' (Bardi et al., 2014a, p. 236; see also Birch, 1964, p. 13). This means that parties can act contrary to public demands, being influenced by factors such as material pressures, the need to balance long-term needs and short-term demands, and systemic constraints. What is key to maintaining legitimacy is that parties deliver publicly acceptable outcomes, meaning that people accept instances in which their desires are not executed (Keman, 2014). Parties are therefore judged on multiple fronts, suggesting that it is not only their capacity to channel citizens' views into the political system that matters, but also their ability to realise publicly acceptable political outcomes (Rothstein, 2009, p. 313).

In addition to their functional roles, parties also enable democratic politics by providing political choice. Operating within electoral systems, parties are authorised and held to account through competitive elections that give citizens equal opportunity to grant or withdraw a political mandate (Lipset, 1959). When parties obtain the support of a plurality of voters they are authorised to act as citizens' representatives (Pitkin, 1967), giving them governing authority. It is on this basis that parties claim that their exercise of power is rightful, and why, as Beetham (2004, p. 107) argues, those subject to party authority have a duty to obey. It is also key that citizens have the opportunity to object to party practices by being able to choose an alternative regime (Pitkin, 1967).

Political parties therefore need to provide voters with choice. Although choices can be made on many different bases – such as evaluating the relative competence of different parties or the physical attractiveness of different political candidates (Milazzo and Mattes, 2016) – historically choice has been offered through the provision of different political agendas. As argued by Edmund Burke in the eighteenth century, parties exist as 'a body of men [sic] united for promoting by their joint endeavours the national interest, upon some particular principle in which they are all agreed' (Burke, 1998 [1770], p. 271). Given that people do not share uniform conceptions of the national interest and prioritise different principles, different parties form and compete to win power, providing a vehicle through which those with shared beliefs and objectives can come together to promote their common vision of society. It is these ideas that underpin the principles of the 'responsible party model' proposed by the American Political Science Association (1950), which argues that, amongst other traits, parties offer different partisan positions that allow citizens to exercise choice (Kitschelt and Wilkinson, 2009).

Cumulatively, these traits define parties' role as democratic institutions. Parties have historically been understood as representative institutions that balance responsive and responsible governing imperatives, and that provide citizens with political choice.

The relationship between parties and citizens

Interestingly, the principles of party democracy leave a number of questions about how parties actually enact each of these ideas. Rather than there being one benchmark for how all parties should and do connect with people and the state, the past and present practices of parties show that these organisations can operate in very different ways. In regard to representation, for example, it is possible for parties to connect with citizens using different styles of representation and different organisational structures. Parties may also focus on different representative constituencies, and demonstrate different degrees of responsiveness to citizen demands. These alternatives (and many others besides) mean that parties can come in many different forms (Scarrow et al., 2017) and that their practices can vary over time. Far from being settled institutions, the dynamics of party politics can therefore vary and adapt.

In thinking about the history of political parties, it appears that the form of party organisation has evolved. Whilst they were once small, elite-led organisations, over time parties became mass-membership bodies in which ordinary citizens could become involved. The evolution of parties has been prompted by a range of pressures and impetuses, but attention has often been paid to the significance of how parties are seen. Over previous decades, therefore, it has been common for scholars to diagnose popular discontent with parties and to call for them to adapt and change. Indeed, scholars have used survey data to identify negative views

(Clarke et al., 2016; Hay, 2007; Stoker, 2006) and to raise concerns about 'the viability of party democracy' (van Biezen and Saward, 2008). Many of these calls have seemed particularly pressing because whilst mainstream parties are viewed negatively, there have been signs that new political parties and unconventional politicians are achieving support. Far from signalling a flaw within the very idea of partisan politics, these dynamics suggest that certain attributes or practices are not garnering public appeal and could be beneficially changed. What is not presently clear, however, is what precisely it is that citizens want and whether established mainstream parties can adapt to meet these desires. For this reason, there is a need for empirical analysis that explores how parties are viewed and what it is that citizens desire.

In this book I evaluate and explore our understanding of parties by looking in detail at how they are viewed by citizens, largely through an empirical mixed-methods study (detailed later in this chapter, under 'Empirical data collected in this book'). Distilling citizens' views of representation, participation, governance and party conduct, I discuss different facets of how parties are perceived, to argue that there is a desire amongst many citizens for parties to be reimagined. Outlining the form of public desires and the challenge of realising these ideals, this book is intended to help scholars and practitioners alike understand citizens' views of parties and consider avenues for possible response.

Analytical approach

In examining the connection between citizens, parties and the state, this book is of course by no means unique and it is possible to find many existing studies of parties. However, unlike past work, which has tended to ask 'what is the problem with parties?', in this book I ask 'what do people want from parties?' This subtly different question has important implications, as it focuses attention on public perceptions and ideals.[1]

Studies of public perceptions are often conducted in political science. In addition to established survey methodologies, scholars utilise focus groups, interviews, deliberative discussions and many other methods to generate insights into how citizens think about and engage with politics. In the party context, a study of public perceptions is particularly appropriate because parties themselves are inherently concerned with what the public think. Whether acting to represent citizens or to secure their own electoral success, parties seek new ways to discern and interpret the public's ideas, using, for example, focus groups to test policy positions or the resonance of political campaigns. In this book, a wider lens of analysis is adopted by examining citizens' views of parties in general (rather than of a specific party), asking how people view current practices and what they ideally desire from these organisations.

A study of public perceptions is particularly valuable in the context of debates around how parties are viewed. Whilst much attention has been devoted to how the public think and feel about parties, many of the claims made in existing studies – and especially those diagnosing party decline and the growing illegitimacy of parties – have relied on proxies to infer public opinion. Scholars have used data outlining declining party membership levels or falling levels of party affiliation as indicators of how parties are viewed. Whilst there may be a connection, there is no guarantee that these metrics capture public views. Indeed, it is possible that falling engagement may reveal more about changing patterns of participation than views of parties per se. This suggests the value of asking citizens about how they perceive parties, and of directly probing their desires and perceptions of the way parties currently perform. Whilst these views may not always be the most informed, it is important to see how citizens understand parties. I therefore agree with Dalton and Weldon's (2005, p. 932) assertion that '[b]ecause parties are central to democracy, public orientations toward political parties are an important research question'.

In studying public perceptions, it is important to consider from the outset what is meant by the idea of public opinion and what implications these ideas have for the claims made in this book. The idea of public opinion is widely encountered and it is common for academics and political commentators to talk about what the public think, often using single methods (and often survey data) to support their claims. Such analysis is highly insightful, but within this book I argue that there are important limitations to such techniques that often go unacknowledged. These limitations concern the kind of data provided by measures of public opinion, and have implications for the way methods were selected for the empirical study reported in this book. To unpack these ideas, it is useful to think about two questions often implicit in discussions of public opinion: first, does 'the public' exist; and second, what do we mean by 'opinion'?

Beginning with the question of whether the public exists, and the associated query as to what it is we study when we refer to this idea, it is important to note that in this book I do not argue that the ideas of all the people can be captured and described. Understanding the term 'the public' to refer to the collective of people within any given jurisdiction, it can often be the case that analysts (unwittingly) give the impression that they know precisely what percentage of the people accept the principles of democracy, favour capital punishment or like a particular soap opera (amongst many other topics). Without careful reporting, such claims can suggest that the views of *all* of the people have been observed, collected and distilled into relatively homogenous descriptive categories, belying the impossibility of measuring the ideas of each and every member of the population. In practice, any description of public opinion is a generalisation based on samples and indicative inquiries that are used to construct an account of what the population as a whole are likely to think. This is because no method can capture what every individual person thinks, and even if it could, analysts would be unlikely to uncover sufficient similarity in views to allow them to produce a singular account of what the public as a unified entity think. As such, descriptions of public opinion are not capturing something that exists and that can simply be observed, but are, rather, highlighting patterns to offer a narrative of what might be said about collective views based on individual responses (Zaller, 1992).

Recognising the constructed nature of public opinion and analysts' role in constructing accounts of what the public think, it is useful to think of the observation of public opinion as an art rather than a science. Even the most robust, demographically representative sample relies on assumptions about the representativeness of individual views and constructs an account of what the public think. Whilst some methods of generalisation are, of course, more robust than others, public opinion should not be viewed as something that can be simply observed, but rather as something that we construct. For this reason, in this book I explore different data sources to build up a picture of what people think. By observing patterns in how those who participated in the empirical study think about parties, and exploring explanations for these beliefs, I build a deeper understanding of public ideas. To do this, different methods are used, examining and testing the resonance of ideas uncovered through an online survey and in deliberative workshops to build up a rich picture of what people think.

In adopting this approach I argue that it is important to think about public opinion towards parties not as a homogenous thing, but something that contains important nuances and variations. Highlighting different trends in how the public think and talk about parties, I show that people often don't think in the same way, and that there are important gradations and differences in public ideas that make it difficult to talk about public opinion as a uniform thing. For this reason, I highlight major trends in public attitudes, discussing the extent to which certain ideas are held, and the degree of agreement around those ideas.

Adopting this approach, in this book I conduct analysis in accordance with a specific answer to the second question – what it is we mean by 'opinion'. Public opinion can be evoked as a homogenous entity just waiting to be 'discovered' by academics and politicians, but it is deeply complex and often diverse. Whilst frequently discussed as something that is fully formed and which can simply be tapped by questions that probe citizens' thoughts, a wealth of research has shown that, in practice, people's views are tentative, changeable and sometimes even entirely contradictory (Converse, 1964). Indeed, studies have shown that when the same people are asked the same question in repeated interviews, only about half give the same answers (Zaller and Feldman, 1992, p. 580). This insight may suggest that any attempt to measure public opinion is doomed to fail, but within this book it is simply seen to reveal the importance of understanding the *kind* of insight that studies of public opinion offer.

What researchers encounter when they conduct opinion polls, surveys, focus groups or interviews are often answers that do not reflect concrete, long-held positions (although this can be the case) but that frequently represent a more unpredictable collection of ideas and views, triggered and shaped by different question wording, circumstances and environments. Public opinion observed through research therefore exists as one account of a set of ideas and opinions that guide citizens' responses. These opinions can, of course, change, but even at a single point in time, an individual is likely to present her or his ideas in different ways. A respondent can therefore at one instance indicate support for a more egalitarian society and economic redistribution, whilst at another argue that the benefits system is defunct and rewards the feckless and idle. These two views, whilst appearing contradictory, call upon different ideas and associations that prompt the individual to make two very different responses. Expressions of public opinion are therefore contingent upon a range of shifting and varied contextual factors. This means that survey responses or workshop findings should not be seen to offer an unshakable picture of public attitudes or indeed to capture a given sample's fixed preferences. Rather, these methods provide contextually contingent insights into public views on particular subjects, views that can be compared and contrasted to test and explore the resilience of these ideas.

In line with this understanding, public opinion is not something that can be easily or precisely measured to produce concrete facts. Rather, it is capricious and complex. This conception may appear to undermine the very agenda I pursue in this book. If, after all, public opinion doesn't exist as an observable phenomenon, and if all opinions uncovered are contingent, then how is it possible for a book such as this to offer insight into people's views of parties? This question goes to the heart of the knowledge claims presented in this text. Far from striving to discover people's fixed ideas and views, I am interested in exploring how different groups of people understand and make sense of the world. Using a mixed-methods approach, I build up a picture of how people think about parties, how fixed their ideas are and whether there are patterns in how different types of people answer the questions posed. This means that, rather than focusing on single data points, I am interested in using findings to identify recurring themes and ideas that underpin people's responses.

Contribution

This book sets out to make two contributions: first, it offers empirical insight into how parties are viewed; and, second, it interrogates these findings to unpack their implications for parties. Whilst parties are a familiar component of contemporary politics, there have been few studies focused on attitudes towards these organisations as a component of the democratic system. There have been many studies of democracy, parliaments, political representatives and government, but less attention has been devoted to parties as discrete organisations (Martin, 2014). By focusing attention entirely on parties, this book therefore adds new insight into how politics is viewed.

In looking at parties, this book also takes another distinctive approach. Previous analyses of public attitudes have tended to examine attitudes towards *specific* parties, for example in the British context generating findings about Labour, the Conservatives or Liberal Democrats that highlight, say, the way a particular party's performance affects its electoral success and appeal. In this book I instead think primarily about parties at the regime level, generating insights of relevance to all political parties. This approach reflects a desire to identify their common challenges; however, it is important to recognise that previous studies have shown differentiations in how specific parties are viewed. An extensive literature on partisan influences has shown that people tend to speak more positively about their favoured party than about opposition parties (Campbell et al., 1960). Whilst partisan attachments have been shown to be weaker today than in the past (Dalton, 2004), party affiliations and identities can nevertheless be a powerful influence on how people think about parties.

In line with this insight, it might be expected that people will view the party they support favourably, whilst arguing that other parties violate important ideals. This dynamic means that there are some instances in which parties may be doing everything a citizen says they want, but still be seen to be acting contrary to those desires. Acknowledging this possibility, I am nevertheless interested in seeing whether there are certain core principles and ideals that people want from all parties. For this reason, throughout the Party Survey and workshops that formed the empirical basis to this study, participants were prompted to think about parties as a classification of organisation, and were presented with prompts such as: 'These questions are about political parties in the UK. When answering, please try and think about your views of parties in general, rather than a specific political party.' It should be noted that many respondents did find it challenging to disaggregate their views, despite being given numerous prompts and reminders. Participants in one workshop had the following exchange:

> I think it depends on the party, because the party in government at the moment is definitely more focused on governing than representing, so it depends on which political party you're thinking about. I don't think they are all the same.
> I think it is very valid to say that it depends on the party.

Comments in other workshops included:

> It's difficult, because it depends on which party. If I think of that party I'd give that answer. If I think of that party I give that answer.

> I think words apply differently to Conservative and Labour, but I'm not sure about the smaller parties.

These difficulties are acknowledged and addressed in the analysis in different ways. First, to explore whether differences in partisanship informed how parties in general were viewed, multivariate analysis was used to look at trends in people's responses. Statistical methods were used to explore whether the supporters of specific parties and strong/weak partisans answered questions in similar ways (amongst other variables), making it possible to determine whether partisans had different views and desires of these organisations. Interestingly, significant variations in response were not found, suggesting that partisanship does not drive different attitudes towards parties in general.

It may also, however, be the case that people judge specific parties differently from how they judge parties in general. To assess this possibility, it may have been preferable to ask participants about their views and desires of every specific party; however, issues of cost and survey fatigue meant that this approach was not adopted.[2] Instead, in the Conclusion, I present a supplementary analysis, of a follow-on survey done in April 2019 (Party Survey 2), that tests the degree to which different parties are seen to live up to the ideals this book identifies. Asking about Labour, the Conservatives and the UK Independence Party (UKIP), I explore the degree to which these specific parties are seen to align with identified ideas. Employing these two strategies I interrogate the differences between views of parties in general and views of specific parties, offering new insight into the dynamics of people's views.

Thinking about attitudes towards parties in this way, this book offers an important corrective to some existing debates. When speaking about the public's views of politics, commentators and academics often talk in sweeping terms about widespread malaise and unrealistic demands, but data collected in this book reveals interesting gradations of public opinion. Whilst it is undoubtedly the case that people are often instinctively negative about parties, I show that people's views are nuanced and that, for many citizens, parties are realising their ideals. Moreover, I show that many citizens are not simply negative, but can identify and articulate a set of principles and beliefs that parties would do well to take seriously. This book therefore offers an important extension to our understanding of citizens' attitudes towards parties.

Whilst a study of public perceptions of parties is in itself valuable, this book also explores the practical implications of these findings for party politics in present-day Britain. In focusing on public perceptions and asking 'what do people want from parties?', I am inherently interested in how parties may wish to respond. A key part of this book is therefore highlighting citizens' desires in order to discuss how parties may wish to change. It is important to clarify, however, that this does not lead me to identify specific policy reforms that will result in more positive views. As the idea of the reimagined party communicates, citizens do not simply want parties to add new functions or processes to their existing structures; rather, there is a desire for a wide-ranging re-evaluation of what a party looks like and how it acts. This means that specific initiatives such as supporters' networks or open primaries are not guaranteed to advance the type of change that citizens' want to see. Instead, there is a need for parties to implement reforms in accordance with the type of ethos that I show many citizens to desire. This dynamic prevents me from offering a roadmap for reform, but in the Conclusion I do identify some options for change that parties may want to consider.

In thinking about parties' response, it is, however, important not to assume that parties – established or new – will be interested in embarking on programmes of reform designed to enact public desires. Whilst parties are important vehicles for democratic linkage, there are many reasons why they may want to disregard public views and act in their own regard. Indeed, factors such as the capricious nature of public sentiments (discussed above), the influence of the media and the seemingly inexhaustible nature of public demands (Flinders, 2009, p. 343; Hatier, 2012; Kimball and Patterson, 1997; Naurin, 2011; Stoker, 2006) may incentivise parties to ignore public desires. In line with this claim, the Conclusion of the book considers how parties may wish to use this data, outlining the potential for parties to *reform* in line with citizen views (by acting to bring themselves in line with citizen ideals), *re-educate* public views (by highlighting how the party already exemplifies desires) or *recalibrate* citizen views (by promoting alternative benchmarks for party success). These possibilities suggest that, whilst parties may not all want to reform in line with public views, they can benefit from gaining a more detailed understanding of how parties are viewed.

By entwining theory and practice in this way, I seek to contribute to debates on the future of political parties. To ground this discussion, a study of Britain is used. Whilst the findings of this book will offer important insights for countries elsewhere, it is necessary to focus on just one country in order to generate detailed, multifaceted insights into the public's perceptions of parties. Given the range of methods used, it is challenging to do justice to the data from just one country, let alone present a cross-country comparative analysis. For this reason, I use this case study to think about lessons for elsewhere, offering a benchmark for scholars to extend and test these ideas.

Empirical data collected in this book

In this book, a combination of data from two nationally representative surveys and three deliberative workshops are used to understand what the public think, and to map the possible responses of political parties.

To test public attitudes towards parties I commissioned a survey with YouGov – the Party Survey – to examine citizens' views of parties in general, specifically interrogating ideas around representation, participation and governance. Given the complex nature of these ideas, questions were extensively tested and refined to ensure that respondents would be clear about what they were being asked (a challenging task when dealing with multifaceted concepts such as representation).[3] Responses were also tested to ensure their reliability, and if reliability was called into question they were not included in the analysis. For example, data from individuals who had conducted the survey in less time than it would take the average person to read the questions, let alone answer them, was removed. Valid responses were gathered from 1,497 people between 17 and 21 November 2017. The data presented are weighted in accordance with YouGov measures to extrapolate a nationally representative sample from respondents. The figures presented in the book show the percentage of respondents rounded up to the nearest whole number to avoid spurious accuracy in the reporting of public opinion.

In addition, a second, shorter survey (Party Survey 2) was fielded via YouGov between 8 and 9 April 2019. This survey gained 1,692 valid responses and was used to test the findings of the book and, specifically, their implications for judgements of specific British parties. Importantly, respondents to this survey were not from the same group as the Party Survey and hence this sample was not used to test changes in respondents' views.

Throughout the book, survey results are mainly presented using descriptive statistics and diagrams. Some regression analysis is conducted, the output tables for which are presented in Appendix 3, in order to make the presentation in the main text more accessible to those unfamiliar with statistical tools. Regressions were used specifically to determine whether factors including age, gender, educational level, previous voting behaviour, knowledge about how parties work, strength of partisanship, party affiliation and trust in parties predict people's responses. This allowed me to see whether public preferences are uniform, or whether they vary in accordance with certain common traits and ideas held by different groups. Where interesting trends emerged, these are highlighted in the text.

In introducing the statistical analysis within this book, it should be noted that the results presented contain 'Don't know' responses. Although it is common for analysts to remove 'Don't know' responses in presenting their results, the decision was made to report this data because of the relatively high number of instances in which 'Don't know' was selected. Given the abstract nature of many of the questions asked, it is perhaps unsurprising that this option was frequently chosen (Bourdieu, 1979, p. 128). Nevertheless, I believe it is important to report this data in order to make it abundantly clear that a large proportion of respondents do not have clear ideas. Where preferences for party linkage and conduct can therefore be discerned, it is important to remain cognisant of the large number of people who do not report favoured ideas and who may or may not support the conclusions presented here. Far from undermining the argument of this book, this approach allows me to reflect in more detail on the challenge any party faces in seeking to respond to public views.

To complement the use of survey data, I also utilise deliberative workshops to generate insight into citizens' ideas. A mixed-methods approach is valuable because studies have shown that surveys in particular are vulnerable to producing contingent knowledge. Contextual prompts and question wording have been shown to affect how individuals respond to questions and responses can vary if questions are asked in a different way. Survey data therefore offer an important glimpse into the ideas that individuals hold on complex and unfamiliar topics, but I argue that they are most fruitfully viewed alongside other indicators that allow respondents' ideas to be tested, probed and understood. Indeed, in my own analysis, many puzzling survey responses became comprehensible only when viewed in the context of more expansive qualitative data. In line with this belief, additional data was gathered at deliberative workshops.

Deliberative workshops can come in different forms and generate different kinds of data, hence it is important to clarify the form of knowledge generated here and the precise mechanism used. Within this study, three deliberative workshops were held in Sheffield in January and February 2018. In each workshop, five smaller groups were facilitated simultaneously, with four or five individuals undertaking common tasks introduced by a facilitator. This allowed more data to be collected within the budget confines of the project. The workshops themselves had different compositions:

- Workshop 1: party activists and campaigners,
- Workshop 2: people with no formal engagement with political parties,
- Workshop 3: a 50/50 split of the above two groups.

In total, 68 people participated in these workshops, with an average of 22 people in each session.[4] In the text, the first two groups are respectively referred to as 'activists' and 'non-activists'.

These deliberative workshops differed in important ways from more traditional focus groups. Focus groups are traditionally used to provide insight into citizens' opinions, helping scholars to understand how and why views are formed. Usually composed of homogenous groups of strangers (Morgan, 1996), they reveal how a 'particular population or group process and negotiate meaning around a given situation' by observing how meaning is constructed and how different ideas and social norms affect the opinions groups come to hold (Stanley, 2016, p. 237). For this study, the focus group method was adapted in workshops to generate insight into what and how people think about parties, but also how they want these organisations to behave. Given that participants often do not have fixed ideas, in the workshops respondents were given the opportunity to discuss and reflect on their priorities, after being presented with additional information and scenarios designed to test and develop their thinking. This mirrors the tenets of deliberative theory, which suggests that '[r]esponses manufactured on the spot are not necessarily what respondents would say in answer to the same questions if they had had some information and time to think or discuss with others what was involved' (Fishkin et al., 2000, p. 658). When people encounter new ideas, hear different perspectives or are encouraged to grapple with potentially competing ideas, it is argued that different kinds of knowledge emerge. Given that my interest is in not only what citizens think, but also how parties may want to respond, these workshops generated important insights, as they allowed detailed scrutiny of the attributes participants believed to be essential for parties, and revealed the trade-offs they were willing to make when led in a task to design their ideal party. This method therefore allowed the project to move beyond collecting a simple list of what respondents said they wanted in regard to representation, participation, governance and conduct, to tease apart priorities and desires. The sessions therefore differed to conventional focus groups, but were also distinct from deliberative forums, as the objective was not to promote good deliberation or produce a consensual view amongst participants, but rather to allow participants to confront and discuss different ideas.

Returning to the idea of what different methods can capture in relation to public opinion, these sessions were not conducted in an attempt to identify generalisable conclusions that could be extrapolated to explain how the wider public think. Participants were selected on the basis of their engagement with parties, as well as their gender, age, ethnicity and partisan support to ensure that a cross-section of society was represented, but it is not claimed that they represent a microcosm of society. This means that these sessions were used to identify different explanations, discuss rationales and observe patterns in responses, providing rich insight into why citizens view parties as they do. Data drawn from these workshops is therefore discussed in two ways to examine how participants responded and reacted to prescribed tasks. First, content produced by participants in response to pre-defined tasks (such as being asked to list three words or short phrases associated with parties) is aggregated to examine the extent to which common views emerged across the different groups. Second, the workshop discussions (over 60 hours in total) were recorded and analysed using NVivo software to detect common explanations, processes of rationalisation and shifts in position. Through these means, it becomes possible to explore existing theories around linkage, but also to diagnose a desire for certain kinds of party conduct and, more widely, for reimagined parties. Presenting this data, the book uses tables and quotations. In places, passages of discussion are reproduced. It is worth noting that these passages and quotes were not transcribed verbatim; rather, an intelligible transcript was produced that accurately captured the ideas but also the language that an individual used. Specific participants are not distinguished by name or identifying marker, but it is specified, where relevant, which workshop that participant was in. One notable finding of this analysis was that participants often varied only marginally in their views – with activists and non-activists alike commonly expressing the same frustrations and ideas.

A mixed-methods approach allows findings to be tested and explored in different contexts and ways. However, it is important to note that the surveys and workshops did not recruit the same individuals. Survey respondents were recruited by YouGov, whilst workshop participants were identified by a local company in Sheffield (see Appendix 2), hence there is no overlap in respondents. To evaluate the comparability of findings, all participants in all parts of the study were asked to answer the same set of questions covering some basic demographic and political characteristics (see Table A.1 in Appendix 1). This exercise revealed similarities and differences that in many ways reflect the challenges of recruiting research participants; however, these differences do not hinder the task of asking (and answering) 'what do people want from parties?'

Book structure and findings

In introducing the idea of a reimagined party, this book comprises seven main chapters. Each of these can be read in isolation to identify valuable insights about citizens' views of and ideals for parties, but they are most informative when considered collectively, as this reveals the presence of recurring reimagined ideals.

In Chapter 1, I review existing evidence on public attitudes towards parties in the UK and beyond to understand what we know about the public's views of parties. Presenting data from cross-national and UK-based surveys, I demonstrate that, far from parties uniformly being seen as negative, there are important nuances in people's views. Seeking to gain greater insight into what citizens want from parties, I argue that there is a need to look at current perceptions and desires. Outlining this approach, I argue that there is value in looking at two facets of party organisation to understand citizens' views. The first is connected to the idea of democratic linkage, whilst the second focuses on party conduct. Introducing these ideas, I set out an agenda for the remainder of the book, outlining the value of inquiry that explores citizens' desires for and perceptions of parties today.

Chapter 2 is the first of three chapters that explore citizens' perceptions of democratic linkage and begins by interrogating citizens' views and desires for representation. Exploring three aspects of representation – parties' style of representation, their representative source and their degree of responsiveness – this chapter shows that there is a gulf between citizens' perceptions and ideals. Rather than indicating a desire for a move away from traditional partisan principles of representation, the analysis instead suggests that citizens want parties to represent a more expansive range of ideas and views. There is, accordingly, evidence of support for an open and inclusive party ethos, and for a mediating approach. Looking at current perceptions, it appears, however, that, for many people, parties are seen to fall short of these ideals.

Chapter 3 turns to examine a second aspect of citizens' relationship with parties by exploring perceptions of participation. The chapter reviews citizens' perceptions of participatory opportunities, requirements, rights and mediums to argue that whilst there is a desire amongst citizens for more opportunities for participation, there is little desire to engage personally. This suggests that reforms are unlikely to improve public engagement, but that there are still areas in which participatory opportunities are currently seen to be out of kilter with public ideals. Specifically, it is argued that many citizens ideally want engagement opportunities where they can make a clear impact, and are attracted to the idea of 'multi-speed' parties where they can get involved with different levels of commitment and via different mediums.

Chapter 4 considers a final aspect of democratic linkage, concentrating on perceptions of parties' connection to the state. The chapter specifically explores views on governance, timeframes and motivations, and finds that performance in government is a vital dimension of how political parties are evaluated. Unpicking what citizens desire, I argue that there is a wish for parties that are reliable, trustworthy and that deliver their promises, take advice and act to promote the national interest. At present, however, parties are seen to be self-interested, electorally focused, unreliable organisations that focus on short-term demands rather than long-term interests. This suggests, once again, a gap between ideals and current practice. However, it does not indicate a desire for parties to become more technocratic, administrative organisations akin to businesses, but rather suggests a wish for parties to rebalance responsible and responsive governing imperatives.

Chapter 5 turns to consider party conduct. Reviewing existing theories of party conduct, I present evidence that people have specific desires for how they would like parties to behave that cluster around seven principles, evident with remarkable uniformity in the data gathered for this book. I argue that there is a desire for parties that are transparent, communicative, reliable, principled, inclusive, accessible and that act with integrity. However, when looking at how parties are currently viewed, it appears that these ideals are often not manifest in the way parties are seen to conduct themselves. Once again, therefore, there appear to be significant differences between citizens' ideals and perceptions of parties.

Chapter 6 explores the evidence presented in the previous four chapters. Although these chapters can offer valuable insights when read in isolation, in this chapter I argue that they also reveal cumulative insights about what citizens want. Reviewing quantitative and qualitative data, I challenge the idea that parties are seen in uniformly negative terms and show variation in the demand for, and desired form of, change. Using this data, I argue that there are certain areas where there is a greater incentive for parties to respond to citizens' views. Highlighting these areas, I do not focus on specific data points to outline discrete policy reforms, but instead look for patterns within this data that, I argue, show the presence of certain recurring principles and ideals. I go on to identify three clusters of ideas that relate to unrealised desires: a wish for parties that are more open and inclusive, more responsive and responsible, and that offer principled leadership. These principles are of interest because, far from challenging the tenets of party democracy, they instead suggest a desire to reimagine well established principles. Offering this diagnosis, the chapter closes by reflecting on the challenges faced by any party seeking to respond to public opinion. Discussing issues of universality and reliability, I show why efforts to enact reimagined ideals may not be greeted favourably or improve how parties are viewed.

The final chapter concludes the book by revisiting the idea of the reimagined party and exploring what this idea means for parties in the UK and around the world. Extending existing analysis, I consider the insights these findings offer for *specific* parties, considering how the Conservative Party, Labour Party and UKIP measure up against these ideas. Equipped with these insights, the chapter then explores the different ways in which parties may want to respond to this data. Three types of potential response are identified and discussed: parties might wish to reform, to re-educate or to recalibrate citizens' desires. Reviewing these options, that concluding chapter discusses the implications and limitations of this work.

Chapter 1

Public attitudes towards parties

The relationship between citizens and parties is central to the health of party democracy. Parties need to gain public consent in order to have the authority to govern, and they need to be seen as legitimate in the eyes of those they represent. These dynamics mean that parties are often conscious of how they are perceived and are eager to respond to public views.

In this chapter I review existing data on public attitudes towards parties to make the case for a more detailed analysis of how parties are viewed and what the public desire. Noting an established trend for scholars to highlight evidence of party disengagement and negative citizen views, I argue that public attitudes are not actually as negative as often depicted. Indeed, far from rejecting partisan politics, I argue that many citizens continue to support parties and the ideals of party democracy. Yet, what does emerge from data on public attitudes is evidence that citizens are attracted to certain party traits and disillusioned by others. For parties interested in continuing to evolve in line with public desires, this suggests the importance of determining what citizens want to see from parties and the extent to which parties currently live up to these ideals.

In offering this analysis I consider different aspects of party democracy to explore the various influences on citizens' views. First, in line with theories of democratic linkage I examine the possibility that citizens' views of parties are influenced by judgements of party representation, participatory opportunities and party governance. Tracing changes in how parties are organised, I discuss the possibility that citizens may view certain types of representation, for example, in more positive or negative terms. By exploring the dissonance between desires and current views I argue it is possible to see where desires are unrealised. In addition, I engage with a second area of scholarship on political conduct. Recognising recent insights from studies focused on political integrity and corruption, I argue that citizens' views may also be accounted for by variations in how parties behave. In much the same way, therefore, it is possible that people want to see certain forms of party conduct that parties are currently not seen to be delivering. Identifying the potential significance of these two different realms, I call for a new analysis that investigates people's desires and how these match up to current perceptions.

How are public attitudes towards parties currently depicted?

Political parties have been the subject of much attention in political science scholarship, and one particularly prominent aspect of this literature has been the tendency for academics to highlight evidence of what has variously been termed a 'crisis' or 'decline' in parties (Daalder, 2002; Dogan, 1997; Drummond, 2006; Everson, 1982; Ignazi, 2017; Norris, 2011; Pharr and Putnam, 2000; Wattenberg, 1986; cf. Reiter, 1989). Mobilising data on public attitudes and political engagement, it has been contended that contemporary parties 'could scarcely be less liked or respected' (van Biezen, 2008, p. 263) and that 'contemporary publics seem increasingly sceptical about partisan politics' (Dalton and Wattenberg, 2002, p. 3). Others have noted that parties are seen to be 'unresponsive, untrustworthy, and unrepresentative' (Dalton and Weldon, 2005, p. 937) and that '[v]oters distrust political parties, see them as out-of-touch and think them incapable of making a difference in government' (Driver, 2011, p. 210). Such negative depictions are epitomised in the following statement:

there is ample evidence and growing literature testifying that we now live in an age characterized by increasing popular disenchantment with political parties, and by growing distrust with the political class more generally. The evidence here is wide-ranging but also fairly consistent: a declining sense of party attachment and partisan identification; diminishing public confidence in parties in general; falling party memberships; reduced electoral turnout; increasing support for new parties, small parties, and 'antiparty' parties – and, more generally, for anti-establishment organizations of the extreme left and the extreme right – as well as for autonomist, regionalist, and populist movements. All of this evidence clearly points to a declining capacity on the part of traditional parties to maintain solid linkages with voters, and to engage these voters and to win their commitment. Above all, the evidence points increasingly and unequivocally to the decline of parties as representative agencies. (Bartolini and Mair, 2001, p. 334)

These claims are based on a wealth of survey data collected in cross-national studies such as the World Values Survey (WVS), the Eurobarometer survey, the European Social Survey (ESS) and the Comparative Study of Electoral Systems (CSES). More particular to Britain – the case study examined in detail in the rest of this book – insights have also been gathered by the British Social Attitudes Survey (BSA), the British Election Study (BES) and the Audit of Political Engagement. Reviewing this data, it appears that there is ample evidence to support these claims.

Beginning with attitudinal data at the cross-national level, a range of different survey measures have routinely found low levels of confidence and trust in parties, and shown that parties are viewed in less favourable terms than other institutions. Looking at reported confidence in parties, the WVS, for example, has shown that across 58 countries between 2010 and 2014, most respondents answered that they had not very much or no confidence at all in parties, with just 29% saying that they had a great deal or quite a lot of confidence in parties. This survey has also shown there to be less public confidence in parties than in other types of institution (see Figure 1.1). Despite the idea of 'confidence' being a vague and often ambiguous term,

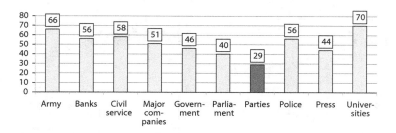

Figure 1.1 World Values Survey (WVS), 2010–14: percentage of respondents saying they have a great deal or quite a lot of confidence in different institutions

such findings have led scholars such as Dalton and Weldon (2005, p. 936) to argue that 'negative views of political parties are a general feature of contemporary public opinion. Voters lack confidence in parties across this range of large and small nations, strong and weak economies, majoritarian and proportional electoral systems, and other systemic characteristics' (see also Pharr et al., 2000).

Similar findings have emerged in questions asking about citizens' trust in parties. In 2017, the Eurobarometer[1] survey found that, on average across the 28 member states of the European Union (EU), only 22% of respondents said that they tended to trust political parties.[2] Once again, distrust appears to be particularly pronounced when comparing parties with other political institutions (Figure 1.2). Further insights have also been provided by the CSES, where analysis across 13 countries found that only 30% of respondents tended to agree or strongly agree with the statement that 'political parties in [a given country] care what ordinary people think', suggesting that many people do not feel that parties listen to ordinary views.[3] Similarly, the ESS in 2017 found that – across the 21 countries surveyed – when asked '[w]ould you say that politicians are just interested in people's votes rather than in people's opinions?', 61% said that nearly all or most politicians were just interested in votes.[4]

In addition to these attitudinal survey measures, cross-national surveys have often used what Dalton and Weldon (2005) describe as

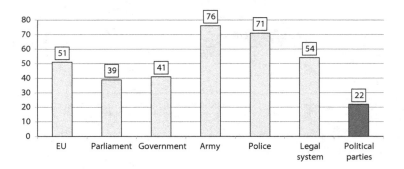

Figure 1.2 Eurobarometer, 2017: percentage of respondents who trust in different types of political institution

'indirect measures' of public views of parties, such as data on electoral volatility, party membership, turnout and party identification. These indicators have painted a similarly dismal picture of public engagement with parties. In terms of party attachment, for example, Dalton (2004) found that across nearly all advanced industrial democracies, the proportion of the public expressing a partisan attachment had declined. Moreover, the strength of that attachment had also weakened, signalling a substantial change in the way parties (and, indeed, other institutions) are viewed (and engaged with). Similarly, in terms of party membership, cross-national studies have produced evidence that parties no longer possess the mass memberships that were seen to demonstrate public support and democratic legitimacy. For instance, van Biezen and Poguntke (2014, p. 207) showed that across 27 countries, 'the average [party] membership ratio is just 4.7 per cent', signalling a fall from the 20-country mean of 5.0 reported for the late 1990s. This trend means that those involved in parties are now a 'relatively unrepresentative group of citizens, socially and professionally if not ideologically' (van Biezen et al., 2012, p. 38). Such trends have led falling party membership to be proclaimed by scholars such as Paul Webb (1995, p. 306) to be '[p]ossibly the most clear cut indication of the growth of popular alienation from political parties'. These collective indicators of parties' health and societal standing have therefore been used to show that parties are not viewed in positive terms. Indeed, scholars such as Enyedi (2014, p. 195) have argued that '[t]endencies in electoral turnout, electoral volatility, party membership, party identification and anti-party sentiment indicate a decline in the popular legitimacy of parties'.

UK trends

Turning to look in more detail at data available within the UK context, more detailed insights are found. Firstly, data from the cross-national studies cited above shows that general trends are more pronounced in the UK. In particular, the lack of confidence in parties appears more acute, with 77% of UK respondents to the 2017 Eurobarometer survey saying that they have not very much or no confidence in parties. Similarly, in terms of trust, 83% of respondents indicated distrust, a result surpassed by only a few other countries (see Figure 1.3). Longitudinal analysis has also shown that distrust is on the increase in the UK. Indeed, Dalton and Weldon (2005, p. 934) have argued that 'the British public has become significantly

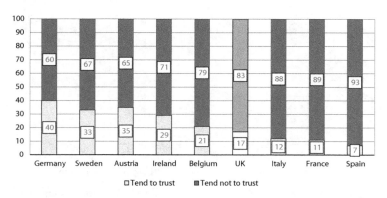

Figure 1.3 Eurobarometer, 2017: percentage of respondents indicating trust in political parties across the EU

less trusting of political parties over the past two decades' – a trend that they show to be new and significant for political engagement (Dalton and Weldon, 2005, p. 938).

In addition, studies conducted only in the UK have offered a dismal picture of how parties are viewed. The Audit of Political Engagement, conducted annually by the Hansard Society, has shown that parties are rarely seen to perform different functions well. Asking respondents to rate parties' effectiveness at 'providing a way for ordinary people to get involved with politics', 'providing capable politicians to run the country', 'telling voters about the issues they feel are most important in Britain and how they will work to solve them', 'ensuring that their candidates for elections represent a cross-section of British society' and 'creating policy ideas that are in the long-term interests of Britain as a whole', never more than a quarter of the public said that parties were good at each respective function (Hansard Society, 2018, p. 25).

Looking more specifically at the attributes parties are seen to possess, negative indicators are also found. The BSA reported (Figure 1.4) that, in 2011, 76% of respondents felt that 'parties are

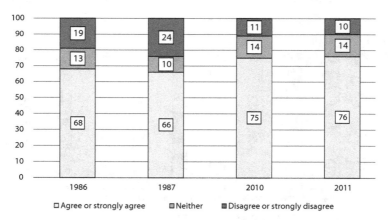

Figure 1.4 British Social Attitudes Survey (BSA), 1986–2011: extent of agreement that 'parties are only interested in people's votes, not in their opinions'

only interested in people's votes, not in their opinions', a figure that had increased from 68% in 1986. Similarly, in 2010, 85% agreed or strongly agreed that 'there is often a big difference between what a party promises it will do and what it actually does when it wins an election', suggesting evidence of distrust. The BSA also found in 2015 that 68% of respondents felt that '[p]arties and politicians in the UK are more concerned with fighting each other than with furthering the public interest' – a finding that echoes a similar question in the BES in 2010, which found that 79% agreed or strongly agreed that political parties spend too much time bickering with each other. On these metrics, it appears that British respondents have a range of concerns about the motivations driving party behaviour.

Data from a more in-depth study on the future of political parties conducted in 2014 by the Electoral Reform Society also shows evidence of discontent. Whilst people felt that parties should be performing key functions when it came to elections, government and policy-making, many of the respondents felt that political parties did not live up to the ideal. The study found instead 'widespread concern about the power of vested interests and cronyism' and a belief that parties were 'purely in it for themselves' rather than interested in serving wider democratic functions (Garland and Brett, 2014, p. 13).

Evidence of discontent can therefore be readily found, helping to explain the prominence of theories of crisis and decline.

An alternative depiction of public attitudes

In thinking about public attitudes towards parties and public desires for these organisations, it should, however, be noted that the data is by no means uniformly negative. In reviewing cross-national and UK-focused attitudinal data there is, in fact, evidence that the idea of party democracy is supported and that certain types of party behaviour are viewed in more favourable terms.

When asked about parties' role in democracy, most citizens believe that parties are central to democratic politics. Between 1996 and 2001, the CSES found that across 13 countries surveyed, on average 76% of respondents felt that parties were necessary.[5] This finding echoes Ignazi's (2014, p. 164) belief that 'citizens are still almost unanimous in the opinion that parties are necessary instruments for a democratic system' and suggests that, whilst many people are despondent, parties remain, as Linz (2002) argued, a 'necessary evil'. For Martin (2014, p. 13), who explores views of parties and democracy, this finding (alongside the negative attitudes reviewed above) means that 'democratic principles coexist next to negative perceptions of parties', suggesting that it is not a problem with democracy as a whole that citizens diagnose, but rather more specific concerns that appear to relate to parties themselves.

In Britain, trends are also not uniformly negative. The Audit of Political Engagement found that half of respondents were happy with the choice of political parties available to them at the general election in June 2017 (Hansard Society, 2018, p. 22), with those who were strong party supporters, interested in politics and older (amongst other factors) more likely to give this response. The Audit more recently found that 34% would describe themselves as a strong supporter of a political party (an increase on previous years) (Hansard Society, 2019), suggesting that a third of people are not alienated from the political system but continue to align themselves.

Thinking about the potential for more positive views, there is also evidence that parties with organisational practices and agendas that differ from those of more traditional or established parties can be viewed more favourably. This idea is supported by a wealth of scholarship that has traced the emergence of new political parties. Evident across the ideological spectrum in different countries, parties such as Podemos, En Marche, the Pirate Party, the Five Star Movement and Ciudadanos have entered the political scene and achieved public support. Indeed, En Marche, Five Star and Ciudadanos have the highest levels of favourability within their country (Simmons et al., 2018). For some, the success of these parties is often premised on the use of digital media to extend and deepen political participation, disintermediating politics and offering more authentic forms of political leadership (Gerbaudo, 2019, pp. 15–16). The appeal of such attributes has also been seen in the case of more established parties. In Britain, for example, there was widespread interest in the Labour Party's 2010 'registered supporters' scheme, which allowed people to pay just £3 to become a supporter and gain the right to vote in leadership elections (a significantly lower fee than to become a party member and gain the same rights) (Audickas et al., 2018, p. 14). In this way, greater opportunities for participation are seen to foster citizen engagement.

There are signs that events or leadership change can affect people's willingness to get involved in parties (Seyd, 2020). Looking in more detail at party membership figures in the UK, it appears that, beyond the headline message of decline, there are often interesting variations which suggest that people can be willing to get involved. Between 2009 and 2018, for example, the Labour Party reported a rise in membership from 156,205 to around 540,00 (Audickas et al., 2018, p. 4). Meanwhile, the Liberal Democrats have seen fluctuating membership, moving from over 100,000 in the 1990s to 49,000 in 2011 to recover to 99,200 in 2018 (Audickas et al., 2018, p. 11). The Scottish National Party (SNP) and Greens saw membership surges around the time of the Scottish independence referendum in 2014 and the 2015 general election, respectively.

These trends suggest that citizens are willing to engage, and yet there has been little analysis of what, precisely, it is that citizens are attracted to and how they would like to see parties behave. For this reason, I argue there is a need to consider citizens' perceptions and desires for parties in more detail, to determine where, if anywhere, people have unrealised desires.

Explaining public perceptions of parties

In thinking about the influences on citizens' views of parties I draw inspiration from a literature that has focused on the 'dissonance between what citizens want and what parties are delivering' (Martin, 2014, p. 13). Often inspiring studies of what Kimball and Patterson (1997) described as 'expectation–perception discrepancies', this work has explored citizens' expectations to argue that they are significant for how politics is viewed (Dommett and Flinders, 2014; Morgeson, 2013; Seyd, 2015). It suggests that citizens' views and behaviours are not just a product of their upbringing or demographic traits, but are shaped and altered by expectations and desires. Developing this idea, I argue that to understand current views of parties it is useful to consider, first, what citizens want from parties and, second, how parties are currently perceived to operate. To do so it is necessary to identify different aspects of party activity that could be influential in shaping people's views. In the analysis that follows, I focus on two different lines of thinking, considering, first, the relevance of perceptions of democratic linkage and, second, party conduct.

Democratic linkage and public views

The idea of democratic linkage is an established feature of party theory. As outlined in the Introduction, linkage theory argues that parties exist as mediating organisations that connect with citizens and the state to perform legitimate democratic governance. In their book on the topic, Dalton, Farrell and McAllister argue that 'political parties emerged as the primary linkage mechanism for facilitating the representative process' (Dalton et al., 2013, p. 5), whilst Lawson (1980, p. 3) argues that '[p]arties are seen, both by their members and by others, as agencies for forging links between citizens and policy-makers. Their raison d'être is to create a substantive connection between rulers and ruled'. This idea offers an important way to understand the position of parties, but has also emerged as a powerful explanation for citizens' apparent dissatisfaction with parties. In this line of thinking, when democratic linkage operates effectively then parties can deliver legitimate democratic governance; conversely, if linkage is not performed in a satisfactory manner then parties' legitimacy and democratic credentials can be called into doubt (Lawson, 2005, p. 163).

Perceptions of democratic linkage are seen to be particularly interesting within this book because many scholars have argued that parties have changed the form of linkage they provide. These changes could be seen to affect public perceptions, with past or present practices viewed with different degrees of favourability. To understand the alternative wishes that citizens may have for democratic linkage, it is useful to understand how parties are seen to have evolved. This section therefore outlines three models of party organisation – mass parties, catch-all parties and cartel parties – that have been offered by scholars seeking to map how parties link to citizens and the state. Whilst by no means the only forms of party organisation that are seen to have emerged, these models are particularly important as they highlight the potential significance of changes in representation, participation and party governance.

In thinking about democratic linkage, many scholars evoke an image of party politics that is closely tied to the idea of the 'mass party' (Duverger, 1954). Cited as the 'prototype of "The" party' (Ignazi, 2014, p. 162), this model describes a system in which parties offer socio-economic cleavage-based representation (Duverger, 1954, p. 417), with multiple opportunities for citizen participation. In the UK, mass parties are specifically associated with the post-war period, which exhibited high levels of party membership and partisan identification, and strong social communities around parties (Beer, 1982). These representative and participative dynamics not only provided citizens with a choice between alternative regimes, they also informed the kind of governance that parties delivered. Parties' governing agendas and actions were therefore closely aligned with specific representative claims identified through direct citizen input, positioning parties as agents of citizens' representative claims. The significance of the mass-party model for those interested in public perceptions of parties is that parties are widely seen to have moved away from this ideal. Indeed, successive groups of scholars have argued that party organisation has adapted in ways that affect the form of representation, participation and governance that citizens can expect. The catch-all theory of party organisation emerged in the 1960s and is associated with Kirchheimer (1966) and, in the UK, Epstein (1967). This theory argues that parties changed in response to the decline of class divisions and the fragmentation and individualisation of social identities (Dunleavy, 1987), altering expectations of how parties should behave. From this perspective, as it became harder for parties to secure electoral mandates by representing mass-based social cleavages (Särlvik and Crewe, 1983), they adapted, becoming less focused on the representation of distinct interests and more on securing electoral success. Reflecting on this model, Diamond and Gunther (2001, pp. 185–6) have argued that:

> the overriding (if not sole) purpose of catch-all parties is to maximise votes, win elections and govern. To do so, they seek to aggregate as wide a variety of social interests as possible. In societies where the distribution of public opinion (on a left–right continuum) is unimodal and centrist, catch-all parties will seek to maximise votes by positioning themselves towards the centre of the spectrum, appearing moderate in their policy preferences and behaviour.

Parties' connections with citizens were therefore seen to become more instrumental, with parties *using* representative claims to secure electoral power. Indeed, 'electoral science' was commonly seen to allow parties to identify and mobilise 'a wider audience and more immediate electoral success' (Kirchheimer, 1966, p. 184), transforming parties' connections with citizens into interactions defined by 'simple electoral persuasion rather than partisan mobilization' (van Biezen and Poguntke, 2014, p. 205). Parties therefore engaged less directly with the public, relying on opinion polls, message testing and external consultants to identify citizens' desires and construct electorally viable platforms. This meant that opportunities for participation were scant, with citizens encountering parties as 'relatively remote, at times quasi-official and alien structure[s]' (Ignazi, 2014, p. 163). It also meant that the choice between political parties was less distinctive, as parties tended to compete over their credentials on a relatively small number of salient political issues. These changing dynamics were also reflected in parties' governing logic. In place of distinctive group-based agendas, parties' governing agendas altered to reflect a consumer logic whereby parties acted 'as a broker between state and society' and tried to sell party products to citizens, treating them as consumers of representative claims, often formulated without their direct input (Deschouwer, 1996, pp. 275–6). This model therefore suggests that linkage evolved to come in a different form to that within the mass-party system.

Building on catch-all theories, a third conception of party organisation has subsequently emerged to take account of new organisational changes. Advanced by Katz and Mair, the 'cartel' model argues that, in terms of representation, parties no longer act as 'associations of, or for, the citizens' (Katz and Mair, 1995, p. 22; see also Katz and Mair, 2009), but are, rather, self-referential, professional bodies that provide alternative administrations for state governance. This dynamic limits political choice, as parties have become 'orientated towards agreed goals rather than contentious means' (Katz and Mair, 1997, p. 115), presenting 'an "ideology" of managerial competence to replace the various ideologies of principle' as the basis for choice between parties (Blyth and Katz, 2005, p. 46). In addition, when it comes to participation it is argued that, in the cartel model, 'participatory linkage is not widespread', as parties now focus on state administration rather than citizen engagement (Lawson, 2005, p. 162). As such, parties are seen to be 'increasingly disconnected from society', resulting in weak (if any) representative or participative ties to citizens (van Biezen and Poguntke, 2014, p. 214).

Also when it comes to governance, cartel parties are seen to be distinctive from the models above. As Mair (2009, p. 7) argued, parties in this model 'can no longer be seen as purposive actors who seek to implement – or prevent the implementation – of a particular program … on behalf of a given electoral constituency'. Halpin (2010, pp. 6–7) has described how, instead, 'the major party organizations [have] put the imperative of survival (as measured by electoral success) ahead of sustaining a primary linkage function', resulting in a situation where parties govern by placing emphasis on their capacity to act as 'good governors, administrators and managers of the polity' (Mair, 2009, pp. 8–9) and to advance the public good (van Biezen, 2014, p. 186). Party governance is therefore focused on delivering 'results rather than policy' (Katz and Mair, 1995, p. 22), producing limited, if any, ties between governing outcomes and representative claims.

Theories of organisational change therefore describe an evolution in how parties operate. Far from remaining static organisations, parties are seen to have adapted to reflect a changing social environment. These developments are significant for attempts to understand public perceptions and desires for parties because they highlight different practices in terms of how parties represent, offer opportunities for participation and govern (summarised in Table 1.1). The changes in party representation, participation and/or governance captured in these models (or evident in other forms) may be more or less favoured by citizens. It may, for example, be that citizens want to see parties providing numerous opportunities for participation and hence see trends depicted by the catch-all and cartel models in negative terms. Alternatively, it could be that people desire a specific form of governance, with views of parties reflecting the perceived presence or absence of this ideal. From this perspective, it may be that preferences for democratic linkage are related to how parties are viewed.

In offering this explanation it is notable that, as outlined in the Introduction, existing survey questions and measures offer limited insight into what citizens desire when it comes to democratic linkage, and how they perceive parties to be performing in line with these ideals. It is therefore not clear how citizens would like to be represented, what opportunities for participation they want, or how they would like to be governed. On this basis, I argue that there is a need to interrogate citizens' views of these ideas, exploring perceptions and desires of representation, participation and governance to see

Table 1.1 Models of party organisation

	Mass party	*Catch-all party*	*Cartel party*
Representation	Cleavage-based representation; clear political choice	Representative claims used to secure power; limited political choice	Emphasis placed on administrative credentials not representative claims; limited political choice
Participation	Direct engagement between parties and citizens via membership and affiliate organisations; many opportunities for participation	Minimal direct engagement between parties and citizens; scant opportunities for participation	Minimal direct engagement between parties and citizens; scant (if any) opportunities for participation
Governance	Clear links between parties' governing and representative agendas	Governance focused on maintaining power and delivering electorally valuable goals	Governance focused on maintaining power and demonstrating administrative competence

whether these ideas can help explain how parties are viewed. This approach allows an examination of attitudes towards each component of linkage, but it should be acknowledged that citizens may have unfilled desires when it comes to all three realms. Far from being isolated concerns, democratic linkage is a multidimensional process, making it interesting to look at the range of citizens' perceptions here. For this reason, Chapters 2, 3 and 4 are devoted to unpicking citizens' desires for representation, participation and governance in turn.

Party conduct and public views

In thinking through public attitudes towards parties I also consider a second possible influence on citizens' ideas of parties: party conduct.

Whilst theorists of party politics have paid much attention to the nature and consequences of changing party organisation, a different branch of scholarship has focused on the possibility that political behaviour can shape public views of politics. Whilst less extensive than work on linkage, this literature offers an interesting additional lens through which to consider how parties are viewed and how this tallies with desires.

Existing work focused on political conduct has come from a range of disciplines, but in the context of politics has tended to focus on citizens' perceptions of politicians (as opposed to parties). Of particular interest to this book, many studies have explicitly examined the relevance of perceived political behaviour for citizens' views. In this manner, Jennings, Stoker and Twyman asked 'what it is that citizens object to about politics?' and found evidence that it 'is the behaviour of politicians that is the main cause of concern rather than the processes of the political system or belief in government as such (Jennings et al., 2016, p. 898). Their analysis showed that 'the most intense points of citizen disillusionment with the political class reside in perceptions of its flawed character, in particular its fixation with headlines and protection of its own interests and those of the already rich and powerful' (Jennings et al., 2016, p. 894).

This line of thinking is also found in scholarship on political integrity. Allen and Birch's book *Ethics and Integrity in British Politics* provides important insight into how politicians are viewed. They find that there is a 'pronounced gap between citizens' aspirations as to how their politicians should behave and their perceptions of how politicians actually behave' (Allen and Birch, 2015, p. 7). They also find that whilst citizens value honest, successful and hard-working politicians, in practice they see politicians as self-interested, careerist and often corrupt. These beliefs are shown to have important consequences for 'citizens' attitudes towards and engagement with public institutions and politics' (Allen and Birch, 2015, p. 173). Such studies suggest that citizens' views of politics are conditioned by beliefs about how actors *should* behave (that are not realised in practice).

This idea is of interest in the context of existing data on public attitudes towards parties because the survey data reviewed earlier in the chapter indicates that party conduct is often viewed in negative terms. In particular, the BES and BSA survey questions suggest that parties are widely seen to be interested only in people's votes, not in their opinions and to be more concerned with fighting each other than with furthering the public interest. The idea that people have a poor view of parties' current behaviour has also been voiced within existing literature evaluating public views. Dalton and Weldon (2005, p. 947) have observed that '[m]ost citizens believe that parties do not care what they think, are not sufficiently responsive to public interests, and cannot be trusted to represent the public's interests'. Hay (2007, p. 37) has similarly argued that 'citizens do not trust politicians and political parties, since they project on to them in-strumental motives', and Webb (2002, p. 455) has argued that it is likely that 'popular distrust of parties stems in part from the wide-spread perception that they are self-interested, unduly privileged and inclined to corruption'. Scholars have also claimed that judgements of parties can be multifaceted, with Ignazi arguing that '[p]arties are perceived as an indispensable tool channelling the voice and the demands of the citizenry but, at the same time, quarrelsome and costly machinery composed of *prime donne* and parasites, social climbers and rent-seekers' (Ignazi, 2014, p. 160). On this evidence it appears that the public's views of parties may be informed by per-ceptions of political conduct that do not match desires. This suggests an alternative or complementary explanation for citizen perceptions that has hitherto gained limited attention.

In identifying this possibility it is, however, once again apparent that there is limited data available about the kind of behaviour that citizens would like to see from parties. Whilst some insights have been offered about how party behaviour is currently viewed, there has not been a systematic analysis of public perceptions and desires able to cast light on what precisely it is that citizens want to see in this realm (and where parties may be out of kilter with these desires). For this reason, in addition to surveying the three aspects of democratic linkage – representation, participation and governance – I supplement this analysis with a review of public desires and perceptions of party conduct.

Investigating what citizens want

In identifying the above two possible influences on the public's views of parties, it appears that citizens' views and desires can be shaped by many different things. Whilst other foci of analysis could be adopted, within this book I focus upon democratic linkage and party conduct because these topics spotlight areas where politicians have demonstrated some interest in pursuing change. Recent years have seen parties adopting initiatives designed to change representative procedures by opening up policy-making processes, boosting participation by creating supporters' networks or online digital forums, emphasising governance in the national interest by changing their rhetoric, or altering their conduct by electing leaders renowned for personal authenticity and honesty. What is not clear, however, is whether citizens possess desires for parties in each of these realms, nor is it clear how they see parties to be performing against these ideals. By exploring these points I am able to consider whether certain areas of party organisation are deemed more important than others, or whether citizens want to see wide-ranging change.

In order to interrogate these ideas and build up a picture of what it is that people want, the next four chapters examine these explanations in turn, presenting survey and workshop data on perceptions of representation, participation, governance and conduct. Exploring citizens' desires and rationales in this way, I argue that people have complex views of parties and are not unswervingly negative about these organisations. Indeed, in the analysis that follows, I show that there are many areas in which parties are seen to be performing well. What does emerge, however, is that when it comes to certain practices and structures, large numbers of respondents are not having their desires fulfilled. Highlighting these unrealised desires, I argue that there is a wish for parties to be reimagined by rethinking behaviour in each of these four realms.

Chapter 2

Parties, linkage and representation

To determine what citizens want from parties and whether parties meet these desires, I begin with the idea of democratic linkage. This theory indicates that to remain legitimate, parties must connect to citizens and the state, acting as intermediaries that pursue and regulate citizen demands. If, as Pedersen and Saglie (2005, p. 361) argue, '[t]he main role of political parties is the creation of linkage between elected representatives and the mass public', then linkage is likely critical to how parties are viewed (Deschouwer, 2005; Lawson, 1980).

Within this chapter, citizens' views of *representation* are interrogated. Combining workshop data and responses to the Party Survey, I ask what it is that citizens want in terms of representation, and how they currently see representation to be performed. Looking at three aspects of representation, I argue that, at present, parties are not seen to realise many citizens' ideals. Specifically, I show that many respondents want parties to balance representative styles, but perceive them to neglect trustee and, in particular, delegate styles (whilst appearing to meet partisan desires). Similarly, there is a wish for parties to think about different actors as sources of representation, but a perception that parties think more than is ideal about electors and party members, and less than is ideal about special interests, experts and, particularly, the majority. Finally, whilst people want parties to react frequently (though, notably, not all the time) to public demands, parties are currently seen to be less responsive than desired. For many respondents, parties do not, therefore, currently live up to ideals.

In highlighting these trends in public opinion, it is interesting to note that they do not suggest a rejection of traditional partisan principles of representation. Instead, they indicate support for the idea of parties as *mediating* organisations that think about the views of different people within society and respond only *some* of the time. This suggests a desire to reimagine the way parties enact representation, rebalancing different imperatives and integrating different voices to see parties represent a more expansive range of views.

Parties, citizens and representation

The idea of representation can be understood in a variety of different ways (Önnudóttir, 2016; Mansbridge, 2003; Pitkin, 1967). When thinking in broad terms about the ideals of party democracy it is useful to think of parties as 'devices to structure the masses and to integrate them into the political system' (Koole, 1996, p. 512). Parties enable representation by 'articulating interests, aggregating demands, [and] translating collective preferences into distinct policy options' (Mair, 2009, p. 5). Through these activities, parties link civil society to the state, giving citizens a say in how the country is run (Pastorella, 2016, p. 958). As such, parties resolve 'the basic representational dilemma of articulating and aggregating otherwise disparate interests, so that electoral majorities [can] be welded together and countries [can] be governed' (Mudge and Chen, 2014, p. 310). Understood in this way, parties are seen as organisations that structure political choice, allowing a group of people to promote an agenda 'upon some particular principle in which they are all agreed' (Burke, 1998 [1770], p. 271). This requires parties to perform a range of different functions, including *integrating* voices, enabling *participation*, *aggregating* demands, engaging in *conflict management* by mediating between perspectives, and translating preferences into programmes of governance by *expressing* demands (Sartori, 2005; see also Dommett and Rye, 2017, p. 414). Although parties' execution of these functions can vary, these principles have provided key benchmarks against which to assess representation.

In identifying these components of party representation, it is notable that many scholars have argued that parties no longer operate as effective representative organisations (Mair, 2009). Importantly for this book, it has been claimed that these changes (and apparent failures) in representative style are connected to negative citizen views and indicators of party decline. Bardi et al. (2014b, p. 154), for example, have argued that parties 'have lost the confidence of the citizenry as a result of their detachment from society'. In thinking about citizens' preferences and views of parties, this suggests that people may have ideals for representation that are currently going unfulfilled. At one level, it may be that citizens desire the form of party representation outlined above. For others, however, there are signs that citizens are attracted to alternative forms of representation. Some attention has therefore been directed to the appeal of technocratic or populist models of democracy, which envisage representation in different ways. In technocratic conceptions, decision-making occurs in accordance with 'value-free, objective criteria' (Centeno, 1993, p. 311) and is undertaken by elites who focus on discerning 'a unitary, general, common interest' (Caramani, 2017, p. 60; see also Dommett and Temple, 2019; Font et al., 2018; Hibbing and Theiss-Morse, 2002). In contrast, in populist models, representation involves parties identifying the general will or handing power directly to the people to make decisions (Mudde, 2004, p. 543; Müller, 2017; Taggart, 1996). These different under-standings suggest that citizens may want parties to offer specific forms of representation, and yet it is currently unclear what it is that people want.

In considering citizens' desires and views of representation within this chapter, three aspects of representation are discussed:

- parties' style of representation;

- parties' source for representation;
- parties' degree of responsiveness.

These components have been regularly examined in studies of representative practices (Rehfeld, 2009) but little work has looked at these ideas in the context of parties. Treating each aspect as a separate component of representation – whilst acknowledging that these three dimensions overlap and intermingle – the chapter asks what form citizens' preferences for representation take and then explores how citizens view each of these ideas.

Parties' style of representation

There is no single template for how parties should channel the ideas of (groups of) citizens into the political process; rather, there are different styles of representation. These differences are most readily grasped by looking at the thinking of the eighteenth-century British Member of Parliament (MP) and political thinker Edmund Burke. In a speech to electors in Bristol in 1774, Burke argued in favour of a certain kind of connection between himself and his electors. Distinguishing between MPs who act as delegates (that is, simply as conduits for citizens' desires) and those who act as trustees, Burke argued that representatives should not seek simply to reflect and respond to citizens' whims, but should instead exercise their independent judgement and act as 'trustees' of citizens' interests (which might involve taking decisions which, though in constituents' and/or the national interest, would be opposed by citizens themselves).

This distinction between styles of representation has routinely been extended to identify a further representative style: partisan representation. Differentiating between these forms, Önnudóttir (2016) outlines how '[u]nder the trustee style, the source for decision-making is the representative themselves, under the partisan style it is the party policy and under the delegate style the source is the voters'. These ideas are of interest because they provide different ideal

49

Table 2.1 Styles of representation

Style of representation	Source for party action
Delegate	Voters'/citizens' preferences and beliefs
Trustee	Parties' judgement of what is in the interests of the people/nation
Partisan	Parties' goals and objectives and/or the views of those affiliated to a party

styles of representation (Table 2.1). Whilst often applied to examine citizens' preferences for individual representatives, studies have not looked at how they affect public preferences for parties. Given the rise of new forms of populist party, this typography proves useful as it allows analysts to determine whether citizens would like parties to act as delegates (in line with populist principles), to act as partisans (in accordance with favoured party agendas or the ideas of those affiliated to a party group) or as trustees (who focus on the good of the nation – somewhat akin to technocratic ideals).

Looking at existing studies, there is some evidence from work on attitudes towards MPs that citizens favour delegate modes of representation, and feel that representatives are failing to fulfil this ideal. In 2012, a survey by YouGov (Kellner, 2012, p. 14) asked whether an MP should vote in accordance to his or her judgement, or according to the majority view of his or her local electorate. The latter (the delegate style of representation) was favoured by 58% of respondents, while 29% supported the trustee model (with 13% 'Don't know') (for similar results, see Carman, 2006; Vivyan and Wagner, 2015).

And yet there is evidence from elsewhere that citizens' preferences may be more complex. In the Swedish context, a survey asked whether 'MPs should act in the best interest of the public using their common sense', should 'regularly find out voters' opinions and act accordingly' or 'should vote according to their own opinion independently of their group' (with additional questions about the substantive representation of certain groups) (Bengtsson and Wass, 2010, p. 63). The results interestingly showed clear support for all three propositions, with 94% strongly or partly agreeing with the idea of using common sense, 90% with finding out voters' opinions, and 73% with acting independently. Whilst some preference for delegate representation and populist ideas can therefore be found, citizens appear to value other forms of representation, making it problematic to draw simple conclusions here.

Considering these findings, the Party Survey asked participants about the representative practices of an ideal political party. Specifically, survey respondents were asked the following:

Now, think about how political parties should ideally behave. When parties develop their policy positions, to what extent do you agree or disagree that they *should* think about the following?

Their view of what is in the public interest

What the public say they want

Their party principles and objectives

[1 = Strongly disagree, 2 = Disagree, 3 = Agree, 4 = Strongly agree; Don't know]

Rather than asking respondents to select one of the options listed, the survey gathered views on the extent to which they agreed that parties should adopt each of these methods of representation.

Figure 2.1 reveals that citizens value different representative styles to a similar degree. Virtually the same proportions of respondents agreed or strongly agreed that parties should adopt delegate or trustee styles of representation (around 72% in each case), whilst a slightly smaller percentage (66%) agreed that parties should adopt partisan behaviours. Mirroring the results of the study by Bengtsson and Wass (2010), it therefore appears that different representative styles are simultaneously seen to have appeal. Looking at the patterns in the responses, it also seems that people do not unanimously favour one option at the expense of others. Indeed, if comparing respondent results across their answers, it appears that 78% of people agreed

The reimagined party

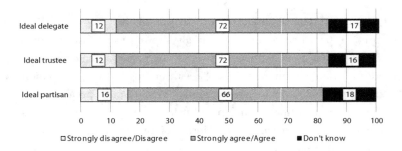

Figure 2.1 Party Survey: perceptions of ideal style of representation

or strongly agreed that parties should ideally act as trustees and delegates, 74% agreed that they should act both as delegates and partisans, whilst 72% felt the same abut partisans and trustees.

This finding also came through in the workshop discussions, where people voiced support for different styles and argued that an absence of certain representative traits was driving concern. Comments suggested that parties 'say a lot of stuff that they think people want to hear, not necessarily what they need' or that they are 'just looking to boost their popularity for the next election, over what the actual benefit is to the country'. When pressed on their priorities for representation, participants struggled to articulate clear preferences – but acknowledged the value of different types of representation. Indeed, discussions revealed people's desire to simul-taneously hold different views and their confusion about the virtue of different representative styles. For instance, one activist participant in workshop 1, having argued that an ideal party should allow party members to make policy, asked:

> What happens if … you are representing the people or representing the needs of the people, but if representing the needs of the people becomes contradictory to manifesto promises, then are your party members prepared to change the manifesto to fit in with what the people are telling you?

Elsewhere, participants questioned what parties should do when faced with different representative pressures, as captured by a discussion in workshop 3:

> If people [representatives] have a very strong opinion about something – are we saying they should ignore their own opinions or what they know about an issue?
> They should do what they are told by the voters to do....
> We appoint someone to represent us ... and therefore I think there are times when they should sacrifice what they actually think.

Such discussions show that people recognise the virtue of different styles of representation but struggle to prioritise between them – voicing support for different ideas whilst seeing the appeal of alternative views. These desires raise problems for parties, as it is possible for these styles to contradict each other. For example, a party may have an ideological commitment that stands in direct contrast to public opinion. In such instances it is difficult to determine which style of representation – partisan or delegate – should win out. Recognising the potential for such dilemmas, questions were included in the Party Survey that attempted to determine which representative style citizens prioritise. Trade-off questions were therefore used. First, looking at trustee and delegate representation, respondents were asked:

> Thinking about when political parties develop their policy positions, using the scale below – where 1 means political parties should use things like opinion polls to find out what the people want and then act on the results, even if this goes against what parties think is in the public interest, and 4 means parties should act on what they think is in the public interest, even if this might go against what opinion polls suggest the public want – where would you place yourself?[1]

In response, just under half of respondents (48%) indicated that they would prefer parties to use opinion polls to find out what the people want and then act on the results, even if this goes against what parties think is in the public interest. In contrast, 35% of respondents answered that parties should act on their view of what is in the public interest, even if this might go against what opinion polls suggest the public want (16% selected 'Don't know').

This is significant because it suggests a slight preference for delegate styles of representation, but workshop discussion showed ambiguity over what such preferences might mean in practice. As one discussion in workshop 3 (composed of party activists and non-activists) illustrates:

> What if you are representing your electorate, but what your electorate want, you don't think makes life better for all?
> Like Brexit.
> But we're talking about … if you had a conflict between what your view and what you voted.…
> What about if you came from some very nice Tory stronghold in Surrey, for example, and your electorate is largely people who have lots of very different issues to what we are worried about up here, and really are you making life better for all, or are you representing the interests of some people who don't want to make life better for all?
> I think the key word there is all … so, if you were elected by a majority of the posh people that live in your constituency, well do remember that although some of these other people didn't vote for you, you are still there to make sure that they are having a good deal.
> It is getting the right balance isn't it? Obviously you can't please everybody.

This discussion is illustrative of the perceived tensions between representing a group of individuals and acting in the wider public interest. In resolving these complexities, participants in different workshops argued that full delegate representation was unrealistic. In workshop 3, one participant therefore noted that delegate representation was not feasible because '[w]e're not able to say directly to the politicians, "this is what we want and please" … because there then has to be dialogue with other people who say they want the other thing and we are not speaking to those people'. An activist in workshop 1 argued that 'you can't get someone to represent you 100%, but it has got to be 70–80%'. A non-activist in workshop 2 directly spoke to the challenge of balancing these imperatives, reflecting that 'the trouble with representing well is that the people don't always know what is good for them!' These comments indicate that whilst delegate representation was perceived by many people to be highly attractive, it was not seen to be easy to realise or to entirely trump trustee imperatives. The workshops therefore helped to explain citizens' responses, showing that many people are simultaneously attracted to different representative styles.

Developing this finding, preferences for delegate as opposed to partisan ideals were examined. Respondents were presented with the following scenario:

> Some people say that it is more important to have political parties that stick to their principles, even if this means not following public opinion. Others say that it is more important to have political parties that follow public opinion, even if this means not sticking to their principles. Using the scale below – where 1 means it is more important to have parties that stick to their principles and 4 means it is more important to have parties that follow public opinion – where would you place yourself?[2]

The results show there to be very little differentiation between responses, with 41% answering that it is more important to have parties that stick to their principles, even if this means not following public opinion, and 43% arguing that it is more important to have parties that follow public opinion, even if this means not sticking to their principles. The distribution across the four scores is more or less equal on either side, with 14% strongly favouring principles (and 27% slightly favouring this option), and 17% strongly favouring public opinion (and 26% slightly doing so, with 16% selecting 'Don't know'). This suggests that there is not an unequivocal preference for either mode of governance, and that delegate and partisan representation both have appeal.

When seeking to discern what citizens want from parties in regard to representative style, these findings paint a confusing picture. Rather than showing support for a single representative style – be that partisan, trustee or delegate – they demonstrate that citizens value apparently contradictory modes of representation. When forcing individuals to choose between these options, there is a slight preference for delegate over trustee representation, but also recognition that there are limitations to this form of representation and that a balance of approaches is ideal. It therefore appears that people value alternative styles of representation and want parties to juggle a range of representative roles.

Reaching this conclusion, it is interesting to turn to current perceptions of party behaviour and to ask whether parties are seen to realise these ideals. In the Party Survey, respondents were asked:

> To what extent do you agree or disagree that when political parties develop their policy positions they consider the following things?
>
> Their view of what is in the public interest
>
> What the public say they want
>
> Their party principles and objectives[3]

Figure 2.2 shows that 61% agreed or strongly agreed that parties develop their policy positions by considering their own party principles and objectives, while 42% agreed or strongly agreed that parties considered their view of what is in the public interest, and 36% agreed or strongly agreed they considered what the public say they want.

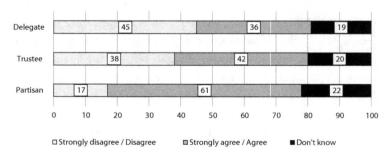

Figure 2.2 Party Survey: perceptions of current style of representation

These responses suggest that parties are not uniformly seen to be behaving in a way that mirrors public desires. Indeed, it particularly appears that parties are not seen to develop their policy positions by listening as much as desired to delegate and trustee imperatives. Instead, their representative behaviour is seen to be focused on partisan drives. Given that the previous question suggested that 66% agreed or strongly agreed that parties should think about partisan drives, it appears that these desires are being met. This makes it interesting to look at how this term was interpreted in the workshop discussions. When evoked in positive contexts, the idea of being partisan was associated with principled, value-led, authentic representation, but when thinking about how parties currently represent the public there was a wide-ranging belief that parties were self-interested and dogmatic. Even amongst party activists in workshop 1 it was argued that parties are self-serving and that 'the party system is fundamentally anti-democratic because it demands loyalty'. From this perspective there are reasons to question whether these findings actually show desires to be met.

Looking at the trustee and delegate types of representation, there is evidence that citizens' perceptions and desires are out of kilter. For both types of representation, the numbers of those strongly agreeing that these influences are thought about falls well below the ideal. However, it appears that people give a range of responses to this question, as there is a spread of respondents answering that they (strongly) agree (strongly) disagree or 'Don't know'. To think about these patterns further and to consider what they might show about unrealised desires, I examined people's answers to these two questions in more detail. To do this I, first, took responses to the question of how parties *should* be representing and simplified them. This involved merging the answers of those who said that they strongly agreed or agreed that parties should think about a given form of representation into a single category, and doing the same for those who said that they disagreed or strongly disagreed. This allowed me to identify two groups of respondents who either felt that, ideally, parties should or should not act in accordance with each of these representative styles. Then, turning to questions about perceptions, I again collapsed survey responses to identify respondents who felt that parties did or did not actually think about these representative influences. This resulted in four categories: 'parties should think about this', 'parties shouldn't think about this', 'parties do think about this' and 'parties do not think about this', with an additional option of 'Don't know'.

Equipped with these categories, it is possible to look at the patterns in question responses to see whether people tend to see their desires being met (answering either that parties should and do enact a given form of representation, or that they should not and do not), whether their desires are exceeded (answering that a party should not act in a certain way, but do), or whether their desires are being missed (stating that parties should act in a certain way, but do not). To present this data in the most accessible form, I use Sankey diagrams that show how responses changed. On the left of the diagram, the different blocks reveal the distribution of respondents who felt that parties should or should not act as partisans, trustees or delegates (with a separate diagram for each representative style). On the right, responses to questions about how parties are seen to actually act are recorded. Whilst the percentage of respondents giving each response is not given in the diagrams, it is possible to see the trends by looking at the relative size of the blocks that connect the left to the right of the diagram.

Looking at the first diagram, on partisan representation (Figure 2.3), this shows that the single largest group of respondents feel that parties should think about partisan representation and in fact do. Indeed, 51% of respondents fell into this category. Whilst qualitative analysis suggests that people may want parties to enact a slightly different form of partisan behaviour to that currently in evidence, from this diagram alone, it appears that many people are seeing their desires met. When looking at the trends depicted by the other lines in this diagram, it appears that some people have different preferences.

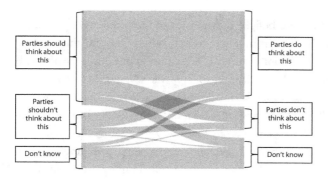

Figure 2.3 Comparing desires and perceptions of partisan representation

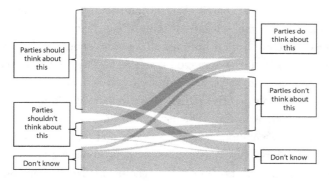

Figure 2.4 Comparing desires and perceptions of trustee representation

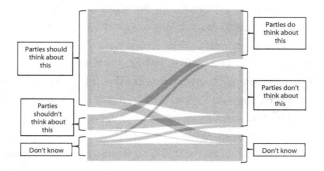

Figure 2.5 Comparing desires and perceptions of delegate representation

Whilst some believe that parties should think about partisan representation but in practice do not, others respond that parties should not think about partisan representation but do. Beneath these trends there are also indicators that people's views do not run in uniform directions. Indeed, the thinner lines in the diagram indicate that small numbers of people voice different desires and perceptions.

Looking at the three Figures (2.3–2.5) together, it is possible to draw a number of useful inferences. First, it is notable that within each diagram there is evidence that many people see their desires to be realised. In the partisan diagram (Figure 2.3) this is most obviously the case, but for trustee representation (Figure 2.4) the largest group of respondents (36%) also felt that parties did act in line with desires. Even in the delegate diagram (Figure 2.5), where the percentage of respondents who think that parties should and do think about this form of representation is smaller, 30% gave this response. This suggests that the picture is not entirely dismal for parties and that many people perceive parties to act in line with desires.

And yet, looking in particular at the diagrams on trustee and delegate representation, it is also evident that a sizable number of people do not perceive parties to be thinking about imperatives they deem to be important. Indeed, in relation to the diagram depicting trustee representation (Figure 2.4), 33% of respondents felt that parties should be thinking about trustee representation but were not. For delegate responses (Figure 2.5), the single largest group – 38% – felt that parties should be thinking about delegate imperatives but were not. This suggests that there is often a sizable (and sometimes majority) group of people who have unrealised desires.

Given the potential appeal (for parties) of responding to unrealised desires expressed by a sizable number of citizens, further analysis was conducted to determine the kind of people who gave this response. Logistic regression models were used to predict the sociodemographic and attitudinal characteristics of the respondents with unrealised desires for each of the three representation styles. The full results are given in Table A.2 (Appendix 3). By way of

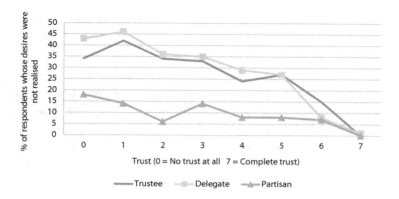

Figure 2.6 Party Survey: percentage of respondents whose desires for different styles of representation were not realised

summary, people who felt that parties should act as delegates or trustees but did not were diverse and did not belong to one party or display certain partisan views. The models tested for the significance of age, gender, education, voting behaviour, party knowledge, party trust, party identification and strength of partisanship; the only consistently significant predictors were age and party trust, with older voters and those reporting lower levels of trust more likely to report a gap between their desires and perceptions. Figure 2.6 shows that those with high levels of trust in parties (scoring themselves 6–7) were likely to say that their ideals were met in reality, whilst those reporting low levels of trust (0–2) were more likely to say that their desires were not met.[4] This was particularly the case when it came to delegate and trustee styles of representation, but party trust was statistically significant in each model.

Other traits emerge as statistically significant, but inconsistently or at a lower threshold of significance. Indeed, it was striking that there were few uniform trends, suggesting that it is not a specific kind of person who is likely to report that their ideals are not realised in practice.[5] Parties interested in responding to this data should therefore not envision a disgruntled set of party supporters or strong partisans to be alone in having unrealised desires, but rather consider this dissatisfaction to be held across the board.

Taking the findings collectively, this discussion reveals important nuances in public opinion. Far from being uniformly negative, it appears that many people think that parties are broadly acting in line with their desires. There are, however, a large number of people who are not seeing their desires reflected in practice, particularly when it comes to delegate and, to a slightly lesser extent, trustee styles of representation. It also appears from qualitative data that the type of partisan representation parties are seen to be offering is somewhat out of kilter with desires. On this basis it appears that parties may want to consider how they enact and depict represen-tation, recognising that many people do not want an alternative form of populist or technocratic representation, but rather desire a balance of representative styles.

Parties' source for representation

Related to the idea of parties' style of representation are questions concerning more specifically which groups or which individuals parties should be listening to. The act of representation is inherently discriminatory, as it involves the ideas and interests of some gaining representation at the expense of others (Urbinati and Warren, 2008, p. 393–4). In this way, parties promote the interests of their members as opposed to the wider population, they can consider expert voices rather than the general will, or they can focus on what electorally important voters desire. Competing ideas around what constitutes an appropriate source for representation can therefore be found, making it interesting to ask who citizens think should be the focus of parties' attention, and whether they perceive parties to realise their ideals.

Within representative systems, the precise individuals that parties focus upon can vary. In the era of mass-party politics (Duverger, 1954), parties were seen to represent a specific section of society, with party agendas aggregated to reflect the views of members and supporters. More corporatist accounts have focused on the ties between parties, businesses and/or special interest groups such as trade unions. Often viewed in negative terms and seen to connote concerns over the influence of groups rather than citizens, these constituencies are nevertheless of interest because of historic ties between certain parties and interest groups (such as the Labour Party and the trade unions, and the Conservative Party and business). Additionally, reflecting the narratives of catch-all party organisation, it is argued that parties have become preoccupied by the goal of 'increasing electoral support, winning governing positions and distributing the spoils of victory' (Caramani, 2017, p. 58). Attention has therefore moved away from socio-economic cleavages towards swing voters, whose support can be won by different parties over time. As such, three forms of source for representation associated with traditional party democracy can be identified and tested to explore citizens' preferences and views.

Once again, technocratic and populist theories of representation pinpoint other actors as the source of representative claims. These theories – whilst not devoted to the study of parties per se – pinpoint other actors as the source of representative claims. Technocratic parties are not reliant on popular consent and can therefore privilege expert knowledge and experience to determine the most appropriate form of action (Caramani, 2017, p. 58). As such, these parties can operate at one remove from the desires of specific groups or the wider population, using expert advice to determine the common good. In contrast, populist conceptions of democracy place primacy on interpreting the common good by listening to the voice of 'the people' (Mudde, 2004, p. 543; Müller, 2017; Taggart, 1996). This can require high degrees of responsiveness to public demands or an elite constructed narrative of the general will.

Derived from these different theories, the Party Survey examined which groups respondents felt should be represented by parties. Participants were asked:

Now thinking about how political parties should ideally behave, when parties develop their policy positions how often *should* they think about the opinion of each of the following groups?

The majority of the population

People whose votes they are trying to win

Party members and supporters

Experts

Business and special interest groups (such as trade unions)

[1 = Almost never, 2 = Less than half of the time, 3 = About half the time, 4 = More than half the time, 5 = Almost all of the time; Don't know]

Three of the options tested different partisan constituencies, whilst 'Experts' and 'The majority of the population' explored views of technocratic and populist ideas, respectively. Looking at the responses, presented in Figure 2.7, a clear desire for parties to act in accordance with more populist conceptions of democracy appears. Indeed, nearly two-thirds of respondents wanted parties to think about the majority of the population when forming policy positions. This was reflected in workshop contributions, where respondents argued that parties should be 'doing what the people want them to

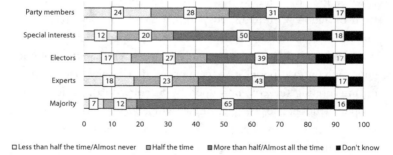

Party members: 24, 28, 31, 17
Special interests: 12, 20, 50, 18
Electors: 17, 27, 39, 17
Experts: 18, 23, 43, 17
Majority: 7, 12, 65, 16

0 10 20 30 40 50 60 70 80 90 100

□ Less than half the time/Almost never   ▣ Half the time   ■ More than half/Almost all the time   ■ Don't know

Figure 2.7 Party Survey: perceptions of how often parties should think about the opinion of different groups when they develop their policy positions

do' and should, 'regardless of the issues, put the public first', acting 'for the people not themselves'. And yet the majority were not the only group that respondents felt should be thought about: 50% gave the same response to special interests and 43% did for experts. Even the idea of the party membership and electors being thought about received support from around a third of respondents.

The idea that parties should think about different actors rather than just one representative source emerged forcefully in the workshops during an exercise where participants were asked to identify actors who should inform policy-making, and then prioritise the influence of those different actors. In this task, workshop participants were given blank pieces of card on which to write down their own suggested sources of policy. After 10 minutes, a series of cards were shown to participants with some predefined sources. Participants could then decide to discard or integrate these sources into their discussions.

Looking at Table 2.2, there was variation in how people responded to this question, as it was not the case that the same actors were listed by each group. What is notable, however, is that experts were widely supported as a source of policy (mentioned by each of the 15 groups of four or five participants across the three workshops). There was also support for a role to be played by the public, party members and the party leader.

When asked to prioritise the attention that should be given to these different actors, the participants in only three of the 15 groups were able to agree on a ranking. The vast majority wanted to give equal status to many or all of their chosen actors and asserted the value of including them all. Indeed, six groups rejected the need to prioritise entirely, making comments such as 'can't we reject that and say that they all have to be involved?' This suggests, as indicated in Figure 2.7, that many respondents do not believe that parties should rely on one source, but instead think that parties should mediate between the demands of different groups – performing the sort of aggregative function that defines party representation but is often

Table 2.2 Number of instances when workshop participants highlighted a desire to incorporate different groups as sources of policy

Source of policy-making	Total number of mentions (15 max.)	Workshop 1: Activists (5 max.)	Workshop 2: General public (5 max.)	Workshop 3: Activists and general public (5 max.)
Experts	15	5	5	5
Public/voters	12	4	4	4
Party members	11	4	3	4
Party leader	11	3	5	2
Party representatives	6	3	1	2
Interest groups	4	1	1	2
Party supporters	3	1	1	1
Activists/campaigners	3	0	3	1
Those affected	2	0	2	0
Community	2	0	1	1
Conference	2	2	0	0
Business	1	0	0	1
Cabinet	1	0	1	0

The shaded categories indicate the prompts participants were presented with.

seen to have declined (Dommett and Rye, 2017). An activist participant in workshop 1 illustratively articulated a desire for a multi-stage policy-making process that would allow different people to feed in:

> I would love to see panels of experts deciding where education should be headed based on evidence and then they give an option of 'we think these are four or five good options we should be pursuing', then throw that open to the electorate with the information that they need in order to make an informed decision on actually which of these directions should we be taking. So it is ultimately the people making the decision, I suppose, but the experts within industries are guiding that.

A number of different processes and procedures were envisaged, often involving large numbers of people. The practical implications of executing such approaches in terms of time and resource were recognised, as were issues of feasibility. Reflecting on the ability for parties to integrate and satisfy a range of different voices, participants acknowledged that:

> You would have too many people, you would have too many different ideas, wouldn't you?
> Yeah.
> So you've got to have a limit, you've got to have a main function to the party.

This discussion, and others like it, suggested that parties cannot simply act as neutral arbiters that blindly follow people's views, but rather need to actively shape and respond to different perspectives. A participant in workshop 3 reflected: 'Sometimes when they say, "we'll just listen to what people say", that is a bit disingenuous because they need to lead whilst they are having ideas that people want to follow as well'.

This connected to another idea around party agendas and principles, with one activist in workshop 1 stating that parties need to 'make clear what they stand for, what they represent, and what they want to bring forward to come into government' and another calling for parties to be 'leaders of thought'. Voiced regularly by party activists, it was argued that 'you can't please all the people all time and I think you have to stick with your aims and objectives of how to be the best party in order to help the most people'. However, it was not just activists who voiced such ideas, as non-activist participants in workshop 3 also called for parties to 'present a vision' and to 'set out what they think'. Integrating these two sets of ideas, it appears that participants want political parties to think about a range of voices, mediating between different ideas with reference to party-specific philosophies and aims. Although not all participants voiced this idea, this approach was not challenged when proposed in discussion, but was greeted in positive terms. On the basis of this discussion, it therefore appears that citizens are attracted to the idea that different people can have a voice and influence policy-making, but are aware of the need for parties to act as mediating organisations that work to reconcile the views of different groups.

Having interrogated citizens' representative desires, it is again interesting to examine how the behaviour of parties is perceived. To do so, participants were asked:

> In your opinion, when parties develop their policy positions, how often *do* they think about the opinion of the following groups (for each statement please tick one)?
>
> The majority of the population
>
> People whose votes they are trying to win
>
> Party members and supporters
>
> Experts
>
> Business and special interest groups (such as trade unions).[6]

Looking across the three theories, it appears that many groups are not seen to be thought about as much of the time as citizens desire. Indeed, Figure 2.8 shows that electors are the only group a majority of respondents (51%) believed to be thought about more than half the time. Using Sankey diagrams to look in more detail at

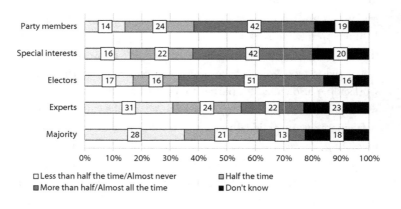

Figure 2.8 Party Survey: perceptions of how often parties think about the opinion of different groups when they develop their policy positions

68

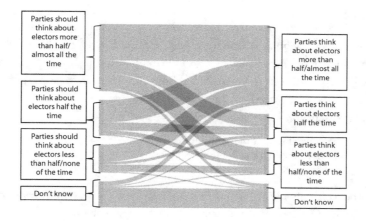

Figure 2.9 Comparing desires and perceptions of time spent thinking about electors

trends in people's responses, it appears that few people are having their desires for parties met, but also that there is little uniformity in preferences.

Beginning with partisan sources, Sankey diagrams show that people's views vary. Looking at 'think about electors' (Figure 2.9), it appears that some people do believe that parties think about electors as much as desired, some feel that parties don't think about them as much as desired, and many others feel that parties exceed desires (parties should think about electors half or less than half the time, but actually think about them more than half the time). Observing these differences, it is clear that responses run in very different directions, suggesting that there is little uniformity in what is desired or perceived here – a trend mirrored in the Sankey diagrams produced (but not shown) for other partisan sources.

When it comes to technocratic theories, 43% felt that parties should think about experts more than half the time, but only 22% felt that parties did this, suggesting that many people are not having their desires fulfilled. Workshop data echoes this idea as, across all three workshops (but in particular amongst non-activists in workshop 2), there was a belief that parties 'don't take on board, real solid, scientific information' and 'are not listening – they could go anywhere and get advice and information, but they don't'. Even where parties were seen to think about expertise, there were questions raised in workshops (see further Dommett and Temple, 2019). One discussion in workshop 2 ran:

> They do tell us that they consult experts.
> But they don't tell us who those experts are.
> Or what those experts really say?

And yet it should be noted that analysis (not shown) indicates that people do differ in the extent to which they feel that parties currently listen to experts, with relatively equal numbers of respondents viewing parties to listen to this group only half of the time, and others less than half the time.

In terms of populist ideas, most people – 65% – feel that parties should think about the majority of the population, but the Party Survey shows that only 13% felt that parties do so. The Sankey diagram (Figure 2.10) reveals that trends in responses are far more

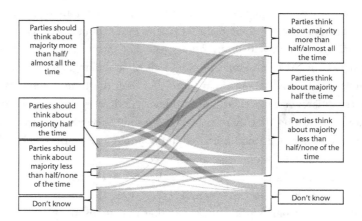

Figure 2.10 Comparing desires and perceptions of time spent thinking about the majority

uniform for this question. Indeed, a clear majority of respondents think that parties should think about the majority more than half or almost all the time but think that parties actually think about them less than half or none of the time.

This view was reflected in the workshops, where the idea that parties do not listen to 'the people' was often voiced. Participants often argued that parties 'don't listen to people's concerns', suggesting that people want parties to think about the majority more of the time than they currently do. And yet, when given time to discuss the idea of representing the majority, workshop discussions raised questions about the feasibility of this approach. Participants questioned how the majority view could be determined, asking 'who is the public ... constituents, voters...?' and 'representative of whom?' This suggests that whilst the idea of majority representation is attractive, and parties are not currently seen to be acting in accordance with this group's views, there was caution about the ability of parties to act as simple 'transmission belts' that convey citizens' views into politics (Sartori, 1976). Indeed, citizens appeared to recognise the need for parties to listen to, think about and mediate between different ideas.

In thinking about desires for the source parties represent, this data suggests that people want parties to think about different groups. Rather than favouring a shift in representative focus away from established partisan models to more technocratic or populist systems, there appears to be a wish for parties that think about multiple voices. Looking at differences between desires and perceptions, it appears that most people feel that the majority are listened to less than desired. This suggests that parties keen to think about aligning themselves with public desires may want to think more about this group.

Parties' degree of responsiveness

The third and final aspect of representation speaks to the idea of responsiveness. Within idealised models of democratic representation, the notion of responsiveness is a recurring principle that explains the degree of interaction between representatives and those they represent. Indeed, Dahl (1971, p. 1) argued that 'continuing responsiveness of the government to the preferences of its citizens [is] a key characteristic of democracy', whilst Spoon and Klüver (2014, p. 48) asserted that it is 'crucial for political representation that political parties are responsive to voter demands' (see also Eulau and Karps, 1977). This idea reflects the normative claim that political parties 'for reasons that range anywhere from self-interest to re-election, organisational discipline, ideological commitment – sympathetically respond to the short-term demands of voters, public opinion and the media' (Bardi et al., 2014a, p. 237).

Responsiveness is, accordingly, widely associated with the legitimacy of the political system and is seen to be correlated with citizens' contentment with the process and outcomes of party politics. And yet this idea has been challenged, with politicians such as Tony Benn (2006) disparaging responsive 'weathercocks who haven't got an opinion, until they've studied the polls, focus groups and spin doctors' in favour of politicians who are signposts that 'point the way they think we should go'. Other questions have been raised by the rise of populism, as it is unclear whether people want parties that listen and respond to their every demand, or favour parties that have more established and stable ideological positions. There are, accordingly, many questions about what citizens desire when it comes to party responsiveness.

When digging into preferences, it is notable that the literature on this topic is more advanced than in the areas discussed above, and many scholars have examined the degree to which parties in government respond to citizen demands (for example see Ezrow et al., 2010; Spoon and Klüver, 2014). For the purposes of this book, perhaps the most interesting work is that by Werner (2016), which examines 'programmatic responsiveness' and 'perceived responsiveness'. This accords with the idea that citizens themselves pay limited attention to parties' programmes and are therefore unlikely to detect subtle shifts in party position. What matters, therefore, is what citizens think about party responsiveness. For this latter metric, Werner examines the extent to which citizens view parties to respond to their desires, first, by directly questioning citizens' views of responsiveness and, second, by exploring the relationship between citizens' perceptions of parties' ideological positions and their own placements (Werner, 2016, pp. 443–4). Using this method, she finds that whilst 'programmatic responsiveness does not seem to affect confidence', levels of perceived responsiveness lead to higher levels of confidence (Werner, 2016, p. 449). In other words, those who believe parties do respond to citizen input have more confidence in the democratic system than those who perceive a lack of responsiveness.

To unpick citizens' preferences within the workshop and Party Survey data, a framework is introduced to distinguish between different types of responsiveness, recognising that parties can respond to citizens' desires to different degrees. Four categories (Table 2.3) capture the possibilities here.

At the first level, parties can be wholly resistive to change. Characteristically 'immutable', these parties are not open to responding to citizen demands and, instead, focus on established messages or elite-derived ideals. At the second level are parties that rarely change

Table 2.3 Degrees of party responsiveness

Attitude towards responsiveness	Description
Immutable	Parties that do not change in response to public demands
Inert	Parties that are in principle open to change in response to public demands but that only rarely change their positions
Receptive	Parties that are in principle open to change in response to public demands and that sometimes change their positions
Adaptive	Parties that change their position in response to public demands to a significant degree

positions, but are known to shift occasionally – these are termed here 'inert'. Third are parties that are more 'receptive' to change and sometimes shift in response to constituent demands. Finally, parties classified as 'adaptive' are those willing to change their position to a significant degree to reflect citizens' demands. The degree of change that constitutes minor as opposed to major change (i.e. the difference between receptive and adaptive) can be contested, but is understood in this book as a willingness to change specific aspects of party policy or message very often as opposed to sometimes.

To assess citizens' desires, the Party Survey asked:

> Now thinking about how political parties should ideally behave, how often would you say that parties *should* change their positions on issues to reflect what people want?[7]

They were also asked to report their current perceptions (see Figure 2.11).[8] In the ideal, answers revealed that, in total, 71% of respondents expressed a desire for parties to change either very often or sometimes, with a preference for receptive (changing sometimes) as opposed to adaptive (changing very often) responsiveness. This was picked up in workshop discussions, where participants expressed a

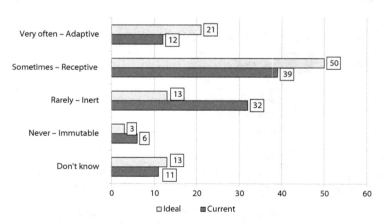

Figure 2.11 Party Survey: perceptions and ideals of party responsiveness

need for parties that were 'responsive to what is going on, rather than just running their own agendas' and that were able to change 'as societies and communities change'. Particularly within workshop 3, but raised by participants in each of the different sessions, there was a desire for parties to be 'open to listening to what people have to say' and 'happy to listen to people', and to show that 'they haven't made their minds up about issues already'.

What is interesting, however, is that limitless change was not desirable. Both the Party Survey and the workshops suggested a preference for receptive rather than adaptive parties. In the Party Survey, 21% of respondents argued that parties should change very often, whilst workshop respondents expressed reservations about shifting position too much in response to public demands. A non-activist argued that 'people are generally like sheep, so people will change their minds, either way', meaning that parties needed to exercise caution in always responding to public demands. This need for caution was explained by activists and non-activists alike with reference to a desire for parties to have clear positions and values. It was argued by a non-activist that parties needed to lead as well as to respond to public opinion, focusing on 'changing social attitudes' as much as responding to external ideas (echoing ideas highlighted above). Others in workshops 2 and 3 similarly argued that 'it is not their job, necessarily, to do what the electorate want' and that some-times 'they need to lead'. Whilst such positions may be expected from activists, the support for these ideas amongst members of the general public suggests that uninhibited responsiveness is not widely desired.

Looking at perceptions of party practice, the Party Survey found that desires were often unrealised. Whilst 50% wanted parties that changed sometimes, 39% felt that they did so (Figure 2.11). Looking at the distribution of responses, most people believed parties change sometimes, but the second most selected response was that parties change rarely (32%). This echoed workshop comments where respondents described parties as currently 'unresponsive both to

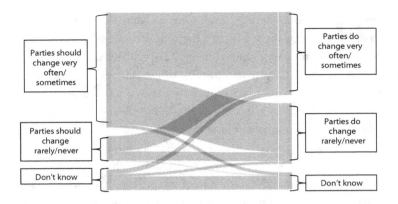

Figure 2.12 Comparing desires and perceptions of party responsiveness

people and people's concerns, but also the issues … so things like climate change, [parties] are very slow to respond'. Looking at the variance between responses (Figure 2.12), a large number of people did see their desires for change very often or sometimes met. And yet 38% of respondents felt that, in practice, parties change rarely or never. This suggests, once again, that a large number of people are not seeing their desires met.

A logistic regression (Appendix 3, Table A.4) was conducted to look at those who wanted to see parties change very often or sometimes but who did not perceive this in practice. Once again, significant predictors included age and trust, with older voters and those with low levels of trust likely to be in this group. Other significant factors in this model included level of education, as those with a degree were less likely to be in this group. There was also a weak gender effect, with women slightly more likely to report unrealised desires. Finally, those saying they supported an 'other' party were also significantly more likely to be in this group. Once again, partisan affiliation and strength of partisanship were not significant, suggesting that this view is held by supporters of different parties.

On this evidence it appears that most people do not desire parties that are immutable signposts that never shift position, but neither do they want adaptive weathercocks that shift blithely in the wind. What appears to be desired are parties that are flexible, adaptive and yet retain certain core ideas. This accords with the earlier finding that almost equal proportions of people feel that parties should stick to their principles *and* follow public opinion.

Conclusion

In returning to the idea of democratic linkage, this chapter has provided insight into what citizens want from parties when it comes to representation. Whilst often pointed to in theories of party decline, our understanding of what citizens view to be ideal, and how they feel parties to measure up to these desires has hitherto been opaque. This chapter has addressed this gap by demonstrating not only the very different ideas that inform citizens' views on representation, but also the many facets of representation that parties need to balance and address. Presenting new data on three aspects of representation, it appears that there is little evidence that citizens are rejecting the principles of partisan representation in favour of an alternative representative model. Whilst attracted to populist and technocratic principles, what emerges from this discussion is a desire for parties to *blend* different representative styles and think about a range of constituencies in determining their position. Indeed, there appears to be support for the idea of parties as 'a body of men [sic] united for promoting by their joint endeavours the national interest, upon some particular principle in which they are all agreed' (Burke, 1998 [1770]), and for parties that are tasked with 'articulating and aggregating otherwise disparate interests, so that electoral majorities [can] be welded together and countries [can] be governed' (Mudge and Chen, 2014, p. 310).

Taking each of the elements considered it turn, it appears that there is little evidence that citizens want parties to prioritise one style of representation. Rather, it appears that partisan, delegate and trustee representation are all seen to have value. Similarly, far from favouring parties that listen primarily to a single group there is a desire for parties that think about a range of voices more than half the time. In addition, there is a wish for parties to listen and respond to public desires, but also to retain certain principles and positions, such that they do not always bend to reflect public demands.

In identifying these desires, this chapter has also shown that, for many citizens, parties are often not currently seen to act in line with ideals. Whilst it is important not to overstate the uniformity in people's responses, and to acknowledge that some people do see their desires realised (or exceeded), there are many areas where a large number of citizens do not see their desires played out in practice. When it comes to representative styles, a large number of people do not see delegate and, to a slightly lesser extent, trustee ideals to be enacted as much as desired, and there are signs that the form of partisan representation is out of kilter with desires. On the source for representation, a large number of respondents similarly feel that parties listen less than desired to the majority (and to a lesser extent special interests and experts), whilst listening more than desired to electors and party members. In addition, many indicate that parties change less than they desire. Interestingly, the people who hold these views are diverse. They are not drawn from one political party and they tend to have diverse demographic traits. Those with low levels of trust in political parties are most consistently likely to feel that their desires are not being realised, but different factors are significant in different models. This demonstrates that whilst public opinion is far from homogenous, there is a large group of citizens whose desires are not being realised. In thinking about whether and how to respond, this suggests that any reaction will not have universal support, but that there is nevertheless an incentive to think about the views of those whose desires are currently not being realised.

Overall, this discussion suggests that citizens often voice complex and even potentially contradictory views and desires. Parties' capacity and willingness to take up and realise these wishes is discussed further in Chapter 6 and in the Conclusion, highlighting the many challenges that parties wishing to respond to this data face.

Chapter 3

Parties, linkage and participation

In this chapter attention turns to a second aspect of linkage, to consider citizens' views of participation.[1] Whilst participation and representation can be connected, they are not, as Lawson (1980, p. 9) argues, equivalent, as each activity can proceed independently of the other. Participating in politics does not automatically guarantee that your ideas and priorities will be taken up and represented. This makes it interesting to explore what is desired from participation in parties and whether these ideals are being realised. This inquiry is particularly important because many parties have made changes in an attempt to boost citizen participation. Reforms include the creation of supporter networks,[2] online communities and expanded procedures for candidate selection (Faucher, 2014; Gauja, 2015; Scarrow, 2014). Whilst widely embraced, we do not know whether these interventions mirror citizens' ideals. This chapter therefore asks, what do citizens desire in regard to participatory opportunities within parties? And are these ideals currently being realised?

Posing these questions, this chapter finds that citizens have clear desires for participation. Exploring perceptions, I find that people want parties to offer a broad range of engagement opportunities via different mediums, and they want their participation to have an effect. There is also evidence that whilst people are attracted to the idea of multi-speed parties (Scarrow, 2014) and voice support for different ways of becoming involved (that vary in intensity and commitment), there remains support for established mechanisms of party engagement. In particular, the idea that certain activities require high levels of affiliation (such as membership) is widely supported. Furthermore, most people are supportive of the idea of members having the right to discuss ideas, make proposals and (to varying degrees) make decisions. This suggests that rather than renouncing established principles of party organisation and conduct, citizens want to see an evolution in the way parties behave; they want to see changes that make it easier for more people to get involved and see the impact of engagement.

In offering this diagnosis it is striking that there are important (and often unrecognised) differences between citizens' stated desires and their own intention to get involved. Echoing theories of 'stealth' democracy (Hibbing and Theiss-Morse, 2002), I find that whilst people find the idea of more participatory opportunities attractive, they have little intention of becoming personally engaged. This suggests that participatory reforms should not be assumed to increase public participation. I also find that parties are not seen to be performing in line with desires.

Cumulatively, what emerges from this chapter is that participation is a compelling idea and citizens want to see numerous opportunities for participation. But more opportunities are in themselves not enough: people also want to be able to understand who has influence in parties and where it is possible to have an impact on how parties work. This requires transparent, accessible party structures – attributes that are discussed in Chapter 5. In addition, drawing on theories of stealth democracy, I show that desires may not impact on citizens' actual behaviour, suggesting that an important distinction between desires and intentions needs to be made.

Parties, citizens and participation

Active participation is often held up as a cornerstone of democracy (Pattie and Johnston, 2013). Whilst participation can be taken to mean many different things (Ekman and Amnå, 2012), it is often argued that a polity that exhibits high levels of voter turnout, party membership or other forms of engagement is operating well, whilst low levels of participation suggest a need for reform. These arguments are, in part, based on the centrality of participation for democratic linkage. For Lawson, participation is key because it allows citizens to 'link themselves to decision makers, that is, by articulating their interests, by helping to recruit nominees, by campaigning, by voting for one candidate rather than another, by maintaining contact with those elected' (Lawson, 1980, p. 8). In a similar manner, Castiglione and Warren (2006, p. 13) have argued that 'it is distinctive of *democratic* representation that persons are represented on the assumption that they actively participate in ... asserting, authorizing, and approving that which is represented on their behalf – through arguing, reflecting, demonstrating, writing, and voting' (original emphasis). Similarly, Deschouwer (2005, p. 85) has argued that:

> democratic representation can function in a meaningful way only if some form of dialogue exists between the political community and the representatives, if there is an exchange of information between them, if the political community knows what the representatives do or want to do, and if the representatives know what the political community expects from them.

These ideas are prevalent in democratic scholarship and demonstrate the significance of participation for communicating desires and holding elites to account, and yet some work has questioned the extent to which active participation is something that citizens themselves desire.

As outlined in Chapter 1, much attention has been directed to indicators of declining participation, with scholars tracing declining turnout, rising distrust and falling levels of party membership (Enyedi, 2014; van Biezen and Poguntke, 2014, p. 206; Whiteley, 2009). For some, these trends suggest that citizens are not satisfied with existing participatory mechanisms. Noting the rise of interest group membership and of e-participation, it has been suggested that people now want to participate in a different way – indicating either that parties are in decline as participatory institutions, or that they require reform that reflects these preferences and ideas (Diamond and Gunther, 2001; Grant, 2008; Lee, 2014). For others, recent trends raise questions about the degree to which people want to participate at all. Indeed, within the highly influential literature on 'stealth democracy', Hibbing and Theiss-Morse (2002, pp. 1–2) argued that:

> The last thing people want is to be more involved in political decision-making: They do not want to make political decisions themselves; they do not want to provide much input to those who are assigned to make these decisions; and they would rather not know all the details of the decision-making process.

Whilst these authors acknowledge that people do still perceive a mechanism for government accountability to be necessary, they also say that 'they just do not want the mechanism to come into play except in unusual circumstances' (Hibbing and Theiss-Morse, 2002, pp. 1–2).

These theories suggest that citizens may want very different things when it comes to participation, and point to different types of response and reform. In order to consider the nature of citizens' desires, this chapter explores four aspects of participation:

- participatory opportunities;
- participatory requirements;
- participatory rights;
- participatory mediums.

These facets of participation overlap, but are discussed separately to disaggregate citizens' views. In tracing citizens' ideas, I argue that people are not rejecting established participatory opportunities but, rather, they want to be able to see more clearly the impact of their participation both in established and in new ways of getting involved.

Participatory opportunities

Recognising the emphasis placed in democratic theory on active participation, and in light of the fluctuating evidence (presented in Chapter 1) on citizens' engagement with parties, it is interesting to begin by considering perceptions of participatory opportunities. Within the Party Survey, participants were presented with a trade-off question that sought to determine whether more opportunities for participation were desired. Specifically, individuals were presented with the following:

> Some people say that there should be more opportunities for ordinary people to get involved in political parties. Others say that there are already enough opportunities to get involved. On the following scale – where 1 means there should be more opportunities for people to be involved and 4 means there are enough opportunities to be involved already – where would you place yourself?[3]

Respondents expressed a preference for more opportunities to get involved in political parties, with 45% of those who answered giving this response. This outweighed the 31% who felt there were enough opportunities, although it should be noted that nearly a quarter of respondents (24%) selected 'Don't know'. These responses may reflect the view, uncovered in the 2014 BSA, that only 28% agree or strongly agree with the statement that 'political parties encourage people to become active in politics'.

On this evidence, it appears that citizens may have unfulfilled desires for participation and accordingly wish for new ways of getting involved. Yet, digging further into citizens' desires for participation, I found evidence that people had little intention of using these opportunities themselves. To gain further insights, the Party Survey included the following item:

> Thinking about your engagement with politics. Have you been, are you, or would you ever get involved with politics in any of the following ways? (Tick all that apply)
>
> Being a party member

Being a registered party supporter (this involves formally signing up to show your support for a party, but is not the same as party membership)

Donating money to a party

Campaigning for a party at election time

Showing your support for a party online (i.e. 'liking' a Facebook post, posting a pro-party status update)

Showing your support for a party offline (i.e. displaying a poster in your window)

Being a member of a political campaigning organisation (such as 38 Degrees, Greenpeace or the Countryside Alliance)

Campaigning through a political campaigning organisation (i.e. by signing a petition or sharing an online campaign promoted by, for example, 38 Degrees, Greenpeace or the Countryside Alliance)

Other (please state)

The response options were:

1. I have done in the past.

2: I do this now.

3. I would consider doing in the future.

4. I've not done this and can't imagine doing so in the future.

Don't know.

The order of presentation for the options was randomised across respondents, and respondents were able to select more than one option.

Looking at Figure 3.1, it is notable that relatively few respondents reported having done these activities either today or in the past – reflecting the findings of other surveys of engagement (Webb, 2013). But perhaps most strikingly, these responses show that few respondents have any intention of participating in the future. On average, 59% of respondents answered that they had not done, and had no interest in doing, any of these activities, a figure that grows to 66% when 'other' is removed. This suggests that, whilst keen to

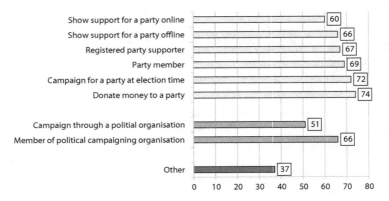

Figure 3.1 Party Survey: percentage of respondents who stated that they had not done and had no intention of doing different activities

see more participatory opportunities within parties, respondents had little personal interest in engaging via the mechanisms outlined. This was particularly the case for party activities such as donating money, campaigning at election times or becoming a member or supporter – types of activity that parties have often sought to promote.

The scale of this disassociation was apparent when combining the above two questions. Filtering the responses, it appeared that many of the people saying they did not currently participate or intend to participate in the future nevertheless called for more opportunities to get involved. Indeed, leaving out 'Don't know' responses from the first question, over half of those who indicated that they had not been involved and could not imagine being so with party activities called for more participatory opportunities – with some activities producing much higher results (Table 3.1). Interestingly, the number of people making this response was lower for non-party activities such as participating in campaigning organisations, suggesting that parties are viewed somewhat differently. Cumulatively, this suggests that whilst the *idea* of participatory opportunities is attractive, the uptake is likely to be less impressive in practice.

Table 3.1 Party Survey: percentage of respondents who felt that there should be opportunities to get involved in parties, but answered that they had not previously done and had no intention of doing different activities

	% of respondents
Party activities	
Show support for a party online	57
Show support for a party offline	65
Party supporter	65
Party member	66
Campaign for party at election time	68
Donate money to a party	72
Non-party activities	
Campaign through a political campaigning organisation	48
Member of political campaigning organisation	62

Unpicking these responses, there are different possible explanations for these trends. For those who argue that there is something 'wrong' with the system that is fuelling disengagement, it might be that the gap between desires for engagement opportunities and intentions can be accounted for by the options presented to respondents in the survey. According to this view, it might be that people want different ways of engaging than the options presented, and this is why they don't indicate a desire to get involved. For example, it could be that people want to participate in focus groups, citizens' assemblies or referenda rather than becoming a party member or donating money. However, when exploring this idea in workshops by asking participants to design preferred opportunities to get involved in their ideal party, limited evidence of a desire for different types of participation was found. Indeed, the most widely called for additional activity in workshops was social activities, with no calls for more participatory engagement ideals.

Alternatively, it could be that whilst *the idea* of participation is attractive, people are not actually interested in engaging with an organisation like a political party. In the workshops, participants offered some evidence for this idea, as many non-activists in workshop 2 made comments such as the following:

> I am just thinking this is the whole reason I'm not involved with a party, because I don't want to be tied to a particular party.

> People don't want to commit to something specifically; they don't want to be labelled as a 'Labour' voter, a 'Conservative voter', a 'Green voter'.

One exchange in the same workshop was as follows:

> I'm not a member of a political party, I think I'd find it incredibly hard to be a member.
> Because then you would have to toe the line on even things that you might find that you don't agree with.

These quotes suggest that whilst some people are attracted to the idea of participation in the abstract, they see engagement with parties as out of kilter with their own individual identities and lives (Duverger, 1954). One possibility is therefore that people may be more willing to engage with other types of political organisation, such as campaign groups. This idea was examined in the Party Survey, which produced mixed indicators. When asked whether 'there are better ways of bringing about change in society than getting involved with political parties', 41% agreed or strongly agreed with this statement, whilst only 11% disagreed (with 32% neither agreeing or disagreeing and 17% answering 'Don't know'). Yet, when asking whether people would consider becoming a member of a political campaigning organisation, the Party Survey found that two-thirds of respondents said they would not, whilst half would not campaign for these types of body. Even those calling for more opportunities for participation were not especially likely to say they would engage in either of these activities (Table 3.1). It therefore appears that engagement with other forms of political organisation is not viewed more positively than engagement with parties, suggesting that the problem (if there is one) does not lie with this type of institution alone.

A different possible explanation is that people experience practical barriers to actually getting involved in parties. The workshops supported this idea, as participants highlighted different barriers related to time and money, making comments such as: 'There are ... more restraints on the time people have available nowadays, what with everything that is going on'. Elsewhere, a discussion in workshop 3 revealed barriers:

> I think we'd all like to get involved in our certain beliefs, but it's the time....
>
> And how easy it is as well, you know, even if you just do something quite small in terms of time, it's still a really valuable way to get involved. If you feel that you have to go to all these tedious policy meetings every week you probably won't go to one.

Another participant in the same workshop noted:

> And if you are a single parent living on a council estate and there is a meeting somewhere and you've got to get there at 7.30 and you've got to get your bike in ... of course they are not going to go, of course you're not going to get involved. Maybe they can't even afford the bus fare to get to the meeting. They are not going to go. How do you reach them?

In line with these views, people may not engage with parties because there is a lack of accessible, easy opportunities to get involved. And yet, looking at the options provided in the Party Survey's presented responses to this question, many are far from high intensity. Whilst it may be expected that campaigning or becoming a member would be too intensive for some people, showing support online requires far less commitment but is only marginally more popular. This suggests that it is not just barriers to participation that are stopping people from getting involved.

One final explanation for these responses relates to the impact of getting involved. Previous public opinion research has found that perceptions of efficacy or the feeling that 'individual political action does have, or can have, an impact upon political process, i.e. that it is worthwhile to perform one's civic duties' (Campbell et al., 1954, p. 187) can have an impact on engagement (Almond and Verba, 1965). Testing this idea, both the Party Survey and workshop data provided significant evidence that people felt that participation did not have an impact.

Adapting a question from the Audit of Political Engagement, the Party Survey asked respondents to what extent they agreed or disagreed that '[w]hen people like me get involved in political parties, we *can* really have an impact on what parties say and do'.[4] A separate question then asked whether they felt they *should* be able to have an impact. The Survey found a big gap between desires and perceived reality (see Figure 3.2). Indeed, whilst 70% agreed or strongly agreed that people like them should be able to have an impact, only 17% felt that they current could have an impact.

Looking at the ways in which people answered these two questions in a Sankey diagram (Figure 3.3), it appears that very few people who felt that they should be able to have an impact believed they would be able to do so. Indeed, many felt parties to be performing below desires. Logistic regression (Table A.5, Appendix 3)

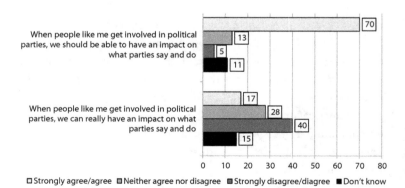

Figure 3.2 Party Survey: perceptions and ideals of efficacy of engagement with parties

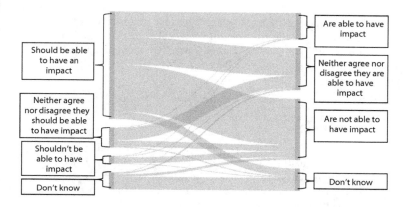

Figure 3.3 Comparing desires and perceptions of citizens' ability to have an impact in parties

showed that people reporting unrealised desires were less likely to be supporters of the Labour Party or Liberal Democratic Party (as compared with supporters of 'no party'), perhaps suggesting that supporters of these parties feel that there are better mechanisms available to them for their participation. And yet it is notable that supporters of 'other' parties (who may be expected to answer similarly) were not statistically more likely to feel this way. It is therefore difficult to draw conclusions about what this result means. What is, however, once again notable is that those with low levels of party trust were significantly more likely to feel that they were not able to have the desired level of impact, echoing the trend in Chapter 2. As with the previous analysis, other demographic and attitudinal traits had limited explanatory power.

The belief that participation did not have an impact was also reflected in workshop discussions. In workshop 2, non-activist members of the general public made comments such as:

> I suppose, again, it comes back to making people believe that they actually have influence, so a lot of people won't turn up to something

because they just don't think it will make any difference, so it is trying to work out, or come up with something that would engage people enough to make them think that they are getting some value out of it. I'm not sure what the answer is.

Party activists also noted the link between participation and perceived impact, with one stating:

I think the reason a lot of people don't get involved is that you don't feel that actually what you're doing is making any difference ... if people did something for charity, it is 'this amount of money is going to do this', you know, they are actually showing the impact of what they have done with their involvement.

Activists and non-activists alike repeated this sentiment, suggesting that people value the *idea* of more involvement with political parties, but feel that in practice it does not have an impact.

In seeking to understand citizens' views of participation, this data shows that many citizens call for more opportunities to get involved. However, in practice, a large number demonstrate little intention of getting involved themselves. This may be because people feel that the impact of engagement is, at present, unsatisfactory. There are also signs, in line with theories of stealth democracy, that people want to know that there are opportunities for being able to get involved that they can utilise if desired. For parties interested in considering how they are currently viewed, it is difficult to disaggregate further insights because specific parties are seen to provide different opportunities for participation. And yet this analysis shows a general desire for more opportunities, identifying a further area in which parties may want to consider citizens' ideals. Equipped with this insight, the remainder of the chapter turns to consider what parties require of people in order for them to participate, the rights people have to participate, as well as the mediums through which such participation can be achieved. Adopting this focus, I argue that there is further evidence of a desire for parties to reimagine the way they currently behave.

Participatory requirements

In traditional conceptions of democratic politics, mass p
is often articulated as the ideal, suggesting that all citizens ̇ ̇ ̇
have the opportunity to engage. However, when thinking about
parties, it appears that these organisations do not treat all citizens
in the same way. Instead, parties often differentiate between groups
by creating participatory requirements such as becoming a party
member or supporter. By engaging in these ways, certain citizens
gain more rights (and responsibilities) than others, but it is not clear
whether citizens support established requirements such as party
membership, or desire less hierarchical organisational structures in
which citizens all have the same opportunities to get involved.

Thinking about these questions, it is useful to look at classic
models of party organisation. Rather than providing equal opportunities for all, parties have traditionally given citizens who choose
to affiliate with their organisation greater participatory opportunities. Capturing this dynamic, in the mid-1950s Duverger offered a
heuristic that distinguishes between electors, supporters, members
and militants (highly engaged members) and shows that parties have
more direct relationships with some types of citizen than others.
Depicting these groups with reference to a series of hierarchical,
concentric circles he describes how:

> The widest [circle] comprises the electors who vote for the candi-
> dates put forward by the parties at local and national levels.... The
> second circle is made up of supporters, a vague term for a vague
> concept corresponding none the less to a reality: the supporter is an
> elector, but more than an elector: he acknowledges that he favours
> the party; he defends it and sometimes he supports it financially;
> he even joins bodies ancillary to the party.... Finally the third, the
> inmost circle, is composed of militants; they consider themselves to
> be members of the party, elements in the party community; they
> see to its organization and its operation; they direct its propaganda
> and its general activities.... In parties that have members, these
> constitute a fourth circle, intermediate between the last two: wider
> than the circle of militants, narrower than the circle of supporters:

membership involves a greater degree of participation that the sympathy of the supporter, but less than militancy. (Duverger, 1954, p. 91)

Duverger's heuristic helps to distinguish the different kinds of interactions that citizens can have with parties, demonstrating that whilst some citizens can associate themselves closely with the organisation and management of parties through party membership and (militant) activism, others can take up a more passive role, whereby they decide only to participate by lending support or voting for a party at election time. This model is, of course, focused on describing how citizens *do* engage and hence does not recognise the potential for citizens to decide not to participate with any particular party, but it is useful in introducing the idea that parties can have different constituencies that they provide with different opportunities for participation. Hence, members may be given a voice in party organisation whilst supporters, electors and the wider citizenry are excluded from having a say.

Since Duverger's model was developed, changes in communication technology have meant that party elites are no longer reliant on members and supporters to communicate with the electorate and wider public (Gibson, 2015; Scarrow, 2014). It is therefore possible for party elites to target and engage different groups in isolation, providing participatory opportunities for members, supporters, electors or the wider public. Recognising these possibilities, parties have begun to open up to provide different ways of getting engaged – creating supporters' networks, running public consultations and allowing people to select electoral candidates – all without requiring people to join the party. These changes have been described by Scarrow (2014, p. 128) as evidence of a 'multi-speed' membership that 'seeks to bolster traditional membership while at the same time creating new affiliation options for supporters who may or may not eventually acquire traditional membership'. Distinguishing between types of affiliation, it appears there are different possible connections between parties and citizens. In this book, four kinds of affiliation are

Table 3.2 Levels of affiliation

Level of affiliation	Descriptor	Indicator
High – full affiliation	Party membership (as either a normal or a cyber member)	Party membership
High – formal partial affiliation	Party supporter (a registered supporter not entitled to the same rights as a full member but affiliated in a formal way)	Registered party supporter
Low – informal partial affiliation	Party contact (individual who has signed up for information from a party or who assists in party activities but does not have a formal affiliation with the party)	Sign up for information
Low – no affiliation but some interest	Party audience (individual receptive to party messages who may, from time to time, give money, donate time, attend party events or engage in other party activities, but who are not formally or informally affiliated to a party)	Engage without having to sign up

identified, ranging from full affiliation characterised by membership to low affiliation (Table 3.2).[5]

Recognising these possibilities, it becomes useful to ask what level of affiliation citizens think is preferable for getting involved in parties. Do citizens still find membership (either as ordinary or cyber members) desirable? Are looser forms of membership such as supporters' networks favourable? Or do people want to get involved in parties and/or show their support for these organisations without the need for a formal affiliation? These possibilities are of interest because across Europe there are examples of parties moving away from Duverger's hierarchical model of engagement, to promote flatter structures in which anyone can engage with minimal, if any, formal affiliation. Parties such as the Pirate Party in Scandinavia and elsewhere (Bolleyer et al., 2015) and Podemos in Spain (Borge and Santamarina Sáez, 2016, p. 109; Lavezzolo and Ramiro, 2017) allow citizens to feed directly into policy formulation and select leaders without having to become formally affiliated in the ways traditionally associated with membership (Gerbaudo, 2019). It is therefore not clear where citizens' preferences for affiliation may lie and whether they favour a move away from established, hierarchical models of party organisation.

To examine preferences, the Party Survey asked about the level of affiliation citizens desired with parties, disaggregating different functions to determine if preferences are consistent or varied across the different tasks that parties can perform. Specifically, respondents were presented with the following:

It is possible for ordinary people to get involved in what political parties do, but it is often necessary for people to sign up to show their support for a party before they can get involved. What is the least that people *should* have to do in order to get involved in each of the following party activities? (Select one for each activity.)

Making party policy

Selecting party leaders, MPs and other representatives

Campaigning to win elections

Campaigning on specific issues (i.e. raising the minimum wage, fracking, etc.)

Political discussion and debate

Respondents were able to select between the following five options for each of the listed activities. The first two options are examples of low affiliation requirements: 'People should be able to get involved without having to sign up to a party in any formal way' and 'People should at least have to sign up for information from a party'. In contrast, 'People should at least have to register as a party supporter' and 'People should have to become a party member' are examples of high requirements. Alternatively, participants could indicate whether they felt that these activities 'should be done by party leaders, not ordinary people', suggesting a desire for party functions to be performed by elites. There was again a 'Don't know' option.

As Figure 3.4, reveals, it appears there is a desire for participatory opportunities that require low levels of affiliation, but that desires

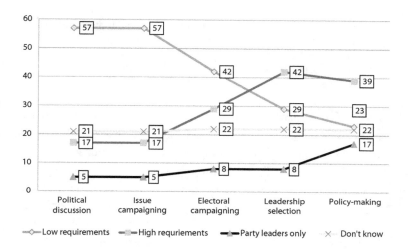

Figure 3.4 Party Survey: ideal levels of affiliation for different party activities

vary by activity. Grouping together responses, for political discussion and issue campaigning 57% of respondents wanted to be able to get involved at most by signing up for information. This reflects a desire, voiced in workshops, for easy engagement, with one participant in workshop 3 noting that people are more likely to engage with parties if 'they are not having to commit themselves, they are not having to sign up to anything'. One-off opportunities that engaged people on their interests were seen to be particularly enticing. However, as activities become more demanding (i.e. election campaigning, leadership selection and policy-making) there is greater support for higher affiliation requirements. Indeed, looking at leadership selection, 42% felt that people should at least have to be a supporter or a member, whilst 39% felt that high requirements were needed for policy-making. These results appear to reflect a belief, expressed in workshop discussions, that those involved in weightier party activities should demonstrate a commitment to a party. One non-activist in workshop 2 reflected:

I want people who are part of the party to decide, to help with the decision, not external people ... because they may not hold the same values ... yeah, great to get expert advice, but ultimately it should be ... people who are part of that group, of that political party ... party members.

This suggests that the idea of collective responsibility impacts on people's views of affiliation and suggests that people believe that citizens need to affiliate in some way in order to gain certain rights. It is not therefore the case that respondents want parties to become flat organisations that require minimal affiliation; rather, there are important preferences for affiliation *across* party activities. Interestingly, this question also showed that there is support for some activities being conducted only by party leaders. This response was not widely selected, but for policy-making 17% of people wanted party leaders in control, indicating that there are some activities for which elite dominance is more acceptable.

Having canvassed these desires, it is important to state that I did not explore citizens' perceptions of the participatory opportunities offered by parties in general. This is because the political parties in Britain have very different structures, making it challenging to speak in general terms about what parties do.[6] Indeed, parties differ in both the types of affiliation they offer citizens (for instance, with some having supporters' networks and others not) and the power that these actors are given (with party members, for example, given power to make policy in the Green Party, but significantly less power in the Conservative Party). As the aim of this book is not to interrogate the practices of specific parties, but rather to trace the form of citizens' desires, these differences are not explored in detail here. What is, however, useful to note is that certain parties do not offer the range of affiliation opportunities that citizens desire, suggesting that there are likely to be areas in which specific parties do not live up to citizens' desires.

Summarising what citizens want, this section suggests that many people feel that different forms of participation and engagement require different forms of affiliation. In addition, there is evidence that people want to see participatory hierarchies retained. Some activities such as policy-making and leadership selection are seen to require higher levels of affiliation, whilst others are seen to require less. This suggests support for Scarrow's (2014) multi-speed membership model, by showing that people want different ways of getting involved. It does not suggest a desire to abandon established principles of party organisation; rather, it appears there is a desire to reimagine established principles, complementing existing forms of engagement with more sporadic means of getting involved. Given parties' recent attempts to implement participatory reforms, these changes may be favourably viewed. And yet there is a need for parties to think through which rights citizens are given and how these relate to the affiliation preferences shown above.

Participatory rights

Building upon the discussion above, attention now turns to the kinds of power people want to be given when engaging with parties, specifically exploring the kind of power people want members to be given. To interrogate citizens' views, this section draws on the literature on party membership, where Scarrow has distinguished between different types of member. Her work describes the potential for party members to exist as fans, adherents, community members or stakeholders. Scarrow herself ties these membership types to certain types of party – describing the existence of personalistic, ideological, elite, cleavage representation, subscriber democracy, political process and political market parties – but these frames can be abstracted to isolate distinctive types of interaction. First, Scarrow (2014, pp. 20–4) describes fans as 'a type of member who are valued for their loyalty, but who are not expected to exercise voice'; adherents are those who 'believe in party doctrine and are willing to help advance its cause'; community members are individuals from a specific group that parties seek to represent; and stakeholders are those with 'clearly defined rights to help determine party goals and to help select party leaders'. These categories reveal the potential for citizens to perform and be assigned different roles, rights and obligations. The first three labels could be said to describe instances in which people are given little substantive control, as fans are expected to be largely passive in determining internal party positions and policies, and adherents and community members have an undefined role in shaping the agenda of their given party. In contrast, stakeholders are attributed a greater and more formal role, being given rights and influence to shape party activities and focus.

Scarrow's framework is useful in highlighting differences in how individuals can be engaged by parties, but it is not focused directly on the types of power individuals possess. Drawing on these ideas, and developing a simple schema with distinct types of activity, seven descriptors are identified. These are not imbued with normative ideas around the *best* form of participation, neither are they seen to be hierarchical; rather, this schema acknowledges the potential for different types of engagement (see Table 3.3).

Teasing apart the distinctions, citizens can be engaged as 'observers', where they are not conveyed any rights, but are passive recipients of information. This describes instances such as press conferences or party meetings where party elites simply convey information. As 'discussants', people are given the opportunity to express an opinion, but not exercise choice. For example, party meetings often provide opportunities for people to express their views but do not provide them with a forum to make proposals or vote on what the party will actually do. The next two categories see citizens given the chance to make decisions, but with different types of input into that process. Whilst 'decision-makers' can cast a vote, they do not have opportunities to discuss their ideas or make proposals. This would therefore describe circumstances such as when a person receives a postal ballot to vote for representatives and completes this at home, alone. In contrast, a 'participant' does have the chance to engage in discussion. This could reflect opportunities such as

Table 3.3 Forms of member participation

Type of activity	Description	Example
Observer	Unable to discuss, make proposals or make decisions	Seeing press releases on policy announcements
Discussant	Able to discuss but not make proposals or decisions	Attending a party meeting
Decision-maker	Unable to discuss or make proposals, but can make decisions	Casting a postal vote
Participant	Unable to make proposals but can discuss and make decisions	Participating in hustings
Proposer	Unable to discuss or make decisions, but can make proposals	Making a submission to a policy consultation
Exponent	Able to discuss and propose ideas, but not make decisions	Attending a policy forum
Stakeholder	Able to discuss, make proposals and make decisions	Attending a conference where attendees suggest and make policy

attending a husting or Q&A session before casting a vote, but would not allow individuals to make their own proposals. As 'proposers', citizens can only make proposals. This describes instances such as making a submission to a policy forum, or making a proposal via a consultation. Such instances are not accompanied by opportunities for discussion, but do allow some input. 'Exponents' are able to discuss and propose ideas. The category covers contexts such as policy forums where people can input in both these ways. Finally, a 'stakeholder' is able to discuss, propose and decide on ideas. This may describe a democratic party conference in which people are able to specify, discuss, define and decide on courses of action.

Recognising these distinctions, and using this schema, the Party Survey examined the powers respondents wanted members to have. Specifically, respondents were presented with the following:

Now thinking about how political parties should ideally behave and what you feel members should be able to do, how important would you say it is for members to be given the following types of power?

Discuss ideas

Propose ideas

Make decisions

Respondents were asked to identify how important each of the above three powers was on a four-point scale.[7]

As Figure 3.5, shows, there was a feeling that each of these powers was important. Indeed, nearly all respondents felt it was very or fairly important to be able to do each thing, suggesting support for party members as stakeholders. And yet there was some evidence of caution about the idea of members being given decision-making power. Within the Party Survey data, it appears that a slightly smaller percentage of respondents felt that it was very important for party members to be able to make decisions (as opposed to proposing and discussing ideas), with 32% giving this response (compared with 55% and 58% for the other responses). This suggests that some people are more cautious about the idea of members being stakeholders or decision-makers and potentially would like to see members as exponents (who can't make decisions). Digging into

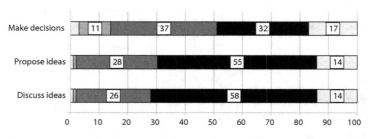

Figure 3.5 Party Survey: preferences for the type of power given to members

these results, logistic regression showed that respondents who held a degree were significantly more likely to answer that discussing and proposing rights were very important aspects of party membership, but were not likely to say the same of decision-making (Appendix 3, Table A.6). This may suggest that more educated respondents are less comfortable with the idea of party members making decisions, perhaps recognising that these individuals tend to be unrepresentative of the population at large. It was also the case that people who did not report themselves to be partisans were statistically more likely to say it was very important for members to have the right to discuss and propose ideas, but were not statistically more likely to say that decision-making power was important. This suggests that those not invested in the party system are cautious about giving members power.

Caution over the rights given to party members was also evident in the workshops, where some participants – especially non-activists – viewed members in negative terms. Often discussing members as different from the general population, these actors were seen to be 'a very narrow group with their own agenda', and were often described as dogmatic and highly partisan, placing them out of line with the public interest. A non-activist questioned the principle of membership:

> Why is somebody who has paid more important than somebody who hasn't? Why because you pay £10 to be a member as opposed to somebody who has just supported? Their input would probably be more important than somebody who just put in £10 to be a member.

This indicates that although there is support for members having some rights, certain citizens (and especially those who are not invested in the party system) are cautious about members having decision-making power. This suggests that parties may be better to focus attention on providing more opportunities to discuss and propose ideas.

Participatory mediums

The final issue considered in this chapter is the mediums through which people want to engage with parties. Traditionally, participation has required physical engagement and has often been a time-consuming activity that requires individuals to attend meetings or conferences to have their voice heard. Focused on interpersonal connections, engagement traditionally revolved around geographically organised party structures in which individuals could come together and get involved. And yet recent changes in political communication have transformed the ways in which people can connect, supplementing traditional face-to-face meetings with digital engagements and remote modes of participation through websites, social media pages, blogs, online electoral databases, phones and email. These possibilities raise questions about how people desire to get involved. Whilst it is often presumed that citizens will embrace online activism, there have been few studies of what citizens actually prefer.

To explore preferences, the Party Survey asked participants whether they would consider getting involved in parties in different ways. This involved creating a matrix that allowed respondents to specify their preference for the site of activity and the medium of engagement. On the first dimension, participants were presented with different sites of activity and could specify preferences for getting involved with a party nationally, locally, with a group within the party that has shared characteristics (such as with other male or female members, or with people from a shared ethnic background), with a group within a party that has shared interests (such as an interest in the environment or small business), or with a party generally (being given the prompt that this would involve activities such as campaigning, policy discussion and candidate selection). On the second dimension, five options were presented, with online and offline mediums of engagement: respondents able to answer that they 'would consider getting involved and would prefer to do so online', 'would consider getting involved and would prefer to do so

Parties, linkage and participation

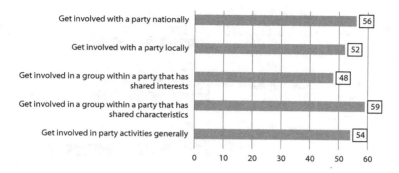

Figure 3.6 Party Survey: percentage of respondents who wouldn't get involved in parties in different ways

offline', 'would consider getting involved and have no preference for how to do so', 'wouldn't consider getting involved in this way' or 'Don't know'. These diverse options were presented to build up a broad picture of the ways in which citizens would like to participate.

When presented with these alternatives a majority of respondents did not want to get involved in any way (Figure 3.6) – echoing earlier findings. The most unpopular activity was getting involved with a group that has shared characteristics (59%), perhaps reflecting the declining appeal of liberation campaigns. Even for getting involved with a group within a party that has shared interests (the most popular option), 48% said they wouldn't get involved in this way.[8]

Of those who *did* want to engage, the largest proportion indicated a preference for getting involved online (Figure 3.7). Indeed, 14% favoured getting involved in parties' activities 'generally' online, with 7% favouring offline. This gap was particularly pronounced when it came to being involved with groups representing shared interests, with 18% favouring online as opposed to 6% offline. It should be noted that around 10% of respondents didn't indicate a preference for online or offline across these activities.

The possibilities afforded by the internet were emphasised by workshop participants who felt they unlocked new opportunities

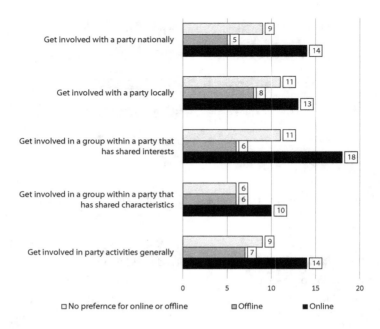

Figure 3.7 Party Survey: preferences for online or offline engagement

for engagement. In contrast to time-consuming and often boring meetings, it was argued that digital tools could be used to engage people in different ways. An activist in workshop 1 argued that parties could 'draft a response, and circulate it by email and see if people approve', or offer opportunities for people to review proposals and indicate their preferences. Another activist similarly argued that 'it's very easy nowadays to get all your members to make a decision on a vote in a week ... you should be able to go to the party and say you've got 24 hours to vote on this'. A non-activist commented:

> I think that online has the potential to engage people better, so, at work for example, we've got this new intranet system and it is based on social media, and we have got this one sort of team of like a half-hour session where anyone can go on and ask any question they've got and get an answer to that, and quite a lot of people are engaging in that and getting involved in it, so it's working really

well, so it is kind of easy for people. You don't have to do anything or go anywhere. You are already sitting … the effort is minimal, so I suppose it is finding ways to make it as easy as possible, but also making it attractive and interesting enough to encourage them getting involved as well.

Online tools were also seen to be useful because they allowed people to engage in small ways, overcoming barriers of time and commitment (Margetts et al., 2015). As one activist noted 're-tweeting or re-posting or supporting things like that, and getting the message out, basically, you might think it is only a little, small thing, but actually if lots of people do that it has a big impact'. Technology was therefore seen to unleash new opportunities for parties that could herald new types of participation, changing not only the activities people were engaged in, but the kind of connection that existed between the individual engaging and the party.

There was, however, also caution around the internet and social media, with many participants suggesting that online opportunities should be a supplement to, rather than a replacement for, existing offline activities. Participants contended that technology 'cuts off a large section of the population' and argued that an online strategy 'would definitely exclude a lot of older people'. There were also concerns about the limits of this medium, with one non-activist arguing that online engagement was 'very impersonal compared to meeting someone locally', and a participant in workshop 3 noting that 'you never decide anything anyway online'. Such comments indicate that whilst new online tools and portals are viewed favourably, they are not seen as a replacement for established mediums. Participants therefore argued that there should be 'lots of different ways of doing it' and that parties need to have 'different avenues for involving people', recognising that 'some people can engage better online, whereas there might be older people in the community who don't do it, so, kind of meet down the pub?'

These findings suggest a desire for parties to reimagine the way they communicate with citizens, using new mediums and engagements that build on (rather than dismiss) established principles. However, progress towards implementing online engagement was seen to be limited. Whilst acknowledging the value of websites and social media, workshop participants argued that parties were not using interactive online tools because 'they don't necessarily want to listen to people's opinions, even though they now can – they don't want to have to know what people are thinking'. Although the Party Survey did not canvass knowledge of parties' online engagement, the workshops revealed that the potential of engaging people online had yet to be realised. People called not just for offline opportunities to be available online, but for 'an open line of communication', with participants receiving feedback on their engagement and being able to see the impact of their decision to get involved. Discussions about medium show that preferences for participation are deeply connected to the questions of power and efficacy outlined above, and that there is a desire for parties to reimagine their practices here.

Conclusion

Looking at citizens' views of participation, this chapter has explored an aspect of linkage that is often conflated with representation, but which raises an array of separate preferences and ideals. Whilst it is often claimed that there is a crisis of participation, and that citizens want more opportunities to get involved, this chapter has found mixed evidence to support this claim. There are signs that citizens have clear desires for participation and want numerous opportunities where they can see the impact of getting involved. And yet it appears that citizens often have little intention of getting involved themselves. This resonates with the theory of stealth democracy and suggests that there is an important distinction to be made between desires for participatory *opportunities* and desires to actually get involved. This distinction can usefully be recognised by parties thinking about responding to citizens' views, as it appears that giving people what they want is unlikely to result in higher levels of participation.

In thinking about the kind of desires citizens would like to see realised, it appears that, once again, there is a desire to build on and reimagine existing organisational structures. Rather than calling for radical change in how parties work and are organised, there appears to be a desire for evolutionary change. Indeed, this chapter has shown that people want to see new ways of getting involved, are supportive of the idea of lower participatory requirements (for some activities) and value new mediums of engagement. The analysis has also shown that many people remain supportive of the idea of membership and feel that members should have the right to act as exponents, with some also supportive of members having decision-making power. What appears to be desired, therefore, is a range of participatory opportunities that allow people to get involved in different ways.

Thinking about many parties' recent efforts to boost participation by creating supporters' networks, online communities and expanded selection procedures (Faucher, 2014; Gauja, 2015; Scarrow, 2014), these findings suggest that people are likely to be open to these ideas. And yet there are some important caveats to this point. This chapter has shown that citizens feel they should be able to see the impact of getting involved, hence it is critical for any new initiative to demonstrate the impact of engagement. Moreover, it appears that people's preferences for affiliation depend on the task, making it important to think through what new initiatives are enabling citizens to do. Furthermore, it is unlikely that these initiatives will boost participation, making it unclear whether they will realise party objectives. Although such initiatives have the potential to deliver positive outcomes, this chapter therefore shows that there are many reasons why they may not be viewed in positive terms.

Looking back to the previous chapter, the desire for parties that provide a range of opportunities to get involved mirrors the desire for an inclusive approach to representation. If people only have to sign up for information about how to get involved, then a wider range of individuals will be able to contribute to parties, creating

a more open and inclusive environment in which a range of different voices can be heard. In thinking through desires for parties, it
therefore appears that citizens want to build on and improve existing
party structures and practices, reimagining existing processes to
reflect modern desires and norms.

Chapter 4

Parties, linkage and governance

In understanding public desires for political parties, scholars have not only focused attention on the connections between citizens and parties, they have also examined the link between parties and the state. In democratic theory, parties are unique organisations because they have the capacity to balance representative *and* governing roles (Bartolini and Mair, 2001, p. 339; Caramani, 2017, p. 60; Mair, 2009, p. 5), allowing people's voices to be translated into governing actions. Studies of vote choice suggest that citizens possess views about the way parties govern. Indeed, Green and Jennings (2012, p. 488) have argued that citizens' views of parties are heavily informed by an 'evaluation of issue competence and government performance' see also Butler and Powell, 2015; Green and Jennings, 2017; Popkin, 1991; Stokes, 1992; Tilley and Hobolt, 2011; Whiteley, 1984). Paired with contentions (outlined in Chapter 1) that parties have evolved into catch-all and cartel organisations that present themselves as 'good governors, administrators and managers of the polity' rather than representative organisations (Mair, 2009, pp. 8–9), it appears that there are grounds to consider how party governance is viewed. For this reason, this chapter explores what citizens want from parties in terms of governance.

In interrogating citizens' desires for party governance, and exploring their perceptions of current practice, I argue that governing performance is a vital dimension of how political parties are seen.

Unpicking what citizens desire, the Party Survey and workshops offer evidence that people want reliable, trustworthy parties that deliver their promises, take advice and act to promote the national interest. At present, however, parties are seen by many to be self-interested, electorally focused, unreliable organisations that focus on short-term demands rather than long-term needs. This suggests, once again, a gap between desires and current practice, and indicates a need for parties to rebalance to emphasise responsible as well as responsive governance.

Parties and governance

In addition to their role as representative and participative organisations that channel citizens' interests into the political system, parties perform a range of administrative, governing functions. They recruit individuals to enact key offices of state, devise and implement policies on virtually all areas of life, and oversee and manage key public services. As Mair (2009, p. 5) has argued, parties organise and give 'coherence to the institutions of government ... [building] policy programs that ... serve the interests of their supporters and of the wider polity'. Through these actions, parties provide political stability, ensuring that key functions of the state continue to be performed regardless of which party is in office.

In the context of linkage theory, parties' governing output is often related to citizens' input and the idea of representation, as Mair describes:

> Parties played two major roles in the development and organization of modern democracies. First, they acted as representatives – articulating interests, aggregating demands, translating collective preferences into distinct policy options, and so on. They linked civil society to the polity and did so from a very strong and well-grounded foundation in society. Parties gave voice to the citizenry. Second, parties governed. They organized and gave coherence to the institutions of government. From their positions in government they sought to build the policy programs that would serve the interests of their

supporters and of the wider polity. The unique contribution parties offered to the development of modern democracy and to the process of legitimizing democracy was that they combined these crucial two roles into one. (Mair, 2009, p. 5)

These dual capacities mean that parties have historically been seen as capable of delivering responsive *and* responsible govern-ance, whereby they balance representative input with governing concerns. As Bardi et al. (2014a, p. 236) argue, it was therefore seen to be 'desirable for the parties in government (and the opposition as well) to be sympathetically *responsive* to their supporters and to public opinion and, at the same time, *responsible* toward the internal and international systemic constraints and compatibilities' (original emphasis). This combination of attributes is seen to be 'almost universally regarded as both desirable and important' (Birch, 1964, p. 13) as, by representing the state to citizens and citizens to the state, parties can govern in a way seen to be legitimate by citizens, but also feasible within the confines of the state. It is on this basis that Keman (2014, p. 310) has argued that '[l]egitimacy is enhanced if and when parties are responsive to the electorate and governments also responsibly deliver policies.... The more this is the case the stronger the democratic performance will be and thus the legitimacy of the system'.

However, theories of party organisation have indicated that the balance of these functions may have changed over time. Ignazi has argued that parties have had to respond to both social and political impetus:

> In order to survive as a complex organization, parties reacted to the changing and more hostile environment (i.e. society) by migrat-ing towards a more plausible environment, which was eventually identified in the state. Parties forsook society and encroached on the state because they were not isomorphic to post-modern society: parties could no longer live in the new societal environment with the shape and features they had inherited from the mass party model. This meant that they could not obtain all the resources they needed from society alone. That reservoir was almost exhausted:

all the spontaneous, free of charge, even enthusiastic, support that members and activists had given to the party had vanished with the emergence of a dominant new mood for neo-liberal, individualistic thinking. (Ignazi, 2014, p. 163)

In line with this idea, Lees-Marshment (2001, p. 27) has argued that parties' dominant goal is now not representation but 'to win long-term electoral success: thus, to win general elections and control of the Government over a long-term period'. This objective is seen to have altered party behaviour in different ways. Some scholars have diagnosed the rise of technocratic tendencies, whereby parties are seen to be 'increasingly becoming just neutral executors of policies' that can be characterised as 'trustees of depoliticised and flexible issue-based positions' (Pastorella, 2016, p. 958). No longer focused on representation and mass participation, parties are seen to be professionalised administrators that differ little from one another and emphasise their governing credentials rather than ideological positions.

For others, however, parties have sought to maintain power by becoming highly responsive. Tracing a growing reliance on opinion polls, message testing and focus groups, scholars have highlighted parties' increased responsiveness to citizen demands (Goetz, 2014, p. 387). Parties are seen to have become hyper-adaptive, especially to the demands of electorally important 'swing' voters, meaning they are often focused on short-term wins, rather than the long-term national interest (Caramani, 2017, p. 58).

Both of these diagnoses are accompanied by recognition that it is increasingly challenging for parties to deliver desirable outcomes. Mair (2009, p. 15), for example, has argued that 'external constraints and legacies have become weightier in recent years', making it harder for parties not only to deliver responsive and responsible governance, but to deliver either of these aims in isolation.

From this work, it appears that citizens may judge parties' governing behaviour in very different ways. There may be a desire for parties that balance responsible and responsive imperatives, that focus on responsible decision-making, or that deliver responsive, short-term politics. At present we have few insights into what it is that citizens desire and how parties are currently seen to perform. In the analysis that follows, I present evidence of a desire for responsible and responsive politics, but show that, at present, parties are seen to act in a short-term, self-interested manner that does not align with this ideal. In presenting this argument, this chapter looks at four aspects of governance. First, it considers the extent to which governing functions are prioritised by citizens, and it then goes on to look in more detail at people's preferences for and perceptions of:

- governing performance;
- governing timeframes;
- governing motivations.

Governing functions

To examine citizens' views of party governance, it is useful to start by looking at the degree to which citizens weigh the importance of parties' representative and governing functions. Whilst often held up in idealised accounts of party democracy as mutually reinforcing ideas, the degree to which citizens themselves focus on parties' governing *and* representative functions is unclear. Party Survey respondents were questioned about their own behaviour when judging parties. The Survey asked:

> We judge how well political parties work in different ways. We can think about how well they represent those who voted for them, and we can think about how well they run the country. If you had to choose, which of the following statements most closely describes how you judge parties?'
>
> 1) I focus mainly on how well parties represent those who voted for them and don't really think about how well they run the country;
>
> 2) I focus mainly on how well parties represent those who voted for them, but do think a little about how well they run the country;

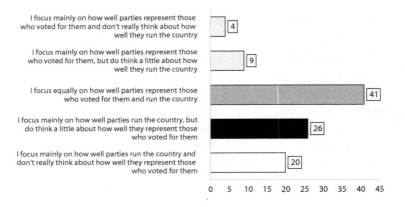

Figure 4.1 Party Survey: distribution of representative or governing judgements of parties

3) I focus equally on how well parties represent those who voted for them and run the country;

4) I focus mainly on how well parties run the country, but do think a little about how well they represent those who voted for them;

5) I focus mainly on how well parties run the country and don't really think about how well they represent those who voted for them.

As Figure 4.1 reveals, when asked in this way, the largest proportion of respondents reveal that they think about both representation and governance, with 41% selecting this option. This supports the idea that citizens uphold the ideals of party democracy (where parties both represent *and* govern) as opposed to viewing parties as purely administrative organisations.

This perspective was explained by a group in the activist workshop, who reflected:

If you got voted in on your manifesto and then you are delivering that, then is that representing the people really?
Yeah.

If you had to choose one though [between representation and governing functions]?

I don't think you can.

You think it is that close?

Yeah, I think there are two sections to it, and the first section is committing to that and that is the representation, and then implementing that is the governance and you can't split it, because either one of those, if you lose either one of those, you are not delivering.

As Figure 4.1 suggests, however, it appears that the distribution of responses is focused more on governing as opposed to representative imperatives, with 46% indicating that they focus (to different degrees) on how parties govern. This finding was mirrored repeatedly in the three workshops. In a 45-minute exercise, participants were asked to prioritise different measures for how parties should be judged. They were given a range of cards that had different statements on them highlighting representative and governing functions. These included statements such as 'I judge parties on whether they put their principles into practice' (representation) and 'I judge parties on whether they produce good outcomes' (governance). Asked to discuss and prioritise these cards, participants indicated that they valued both imperatives, but tended to prioritise governing indicators such as competence, delivering a balanced budget and delivering good outcomes (in all three of the workshops). This response is interesting because, within the workshops, when asked to reflect on whether they prioritised representative or governing judgements, a number of participants said that they didn't 'feel super-comfortable' selecting these options, explaining that it was out of kilter with their desire for accountability and representation (voiced in earlier tasks). Rationalising their preferences, participants argued that governing was vital because otherwise parties would be 'totally incompetent' and wouldn't 'achieve things'.

Extending the above question to consider perceptions of current performance, respondents were asked 'How well do you feel that parties today currently do this?'[1] Respondents were then able to

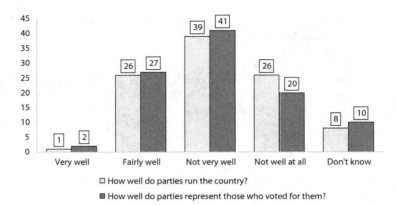

Figure 4.2 Party Survey: aggregated assessments of parties' representative and governing functions

select whether parties both governed and represented 'very well', 'fairly well', 'not very well' or 'not well at all'. Looking at the amalgamated responses (Figure 4.2), respondents suggested that parties are not being seen to perform well on either front, but do slightly worse on governing performance, with 65% answering that parties govern 'not very well' or 'not well at all', compared with 61% who selected these answers for representation.

The dominance of negative perceptions is particularly evident when looking at the percentage of those who answered that parties performed 'very well' as opposed to 'fairly well', 'not very well' or 'not well at all', as just 1% indicated that parties governed very well and just 2% felt the same about representation. The overwhelming majority therefore feel that there is room for improvement in parties' execution of both functions. What is not clear, however, is whether the respondents who said that they focus on governing more than on representation feel that parties are performing better in this function than those who selected a different response. To consider this, answers from the two previous questions are combined in Figure 4.3.[2] In this diagram, the three segments report,

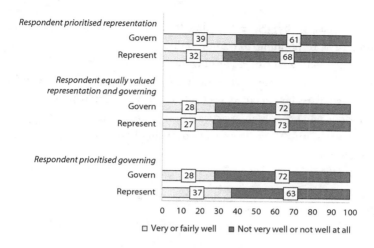

Figure 4.3 Party Survey: perceptions of how well parties represent and govern

respectively top to bottom, the views of those who say they judge parties mainly in accordance with representation, of those who say they judge parties equally on both factors, and those who focus on how parties govern.

It appears that across the three groups of respondents, parties are seen to be performing poorly in both areas. And yet there are some interesting variations. For those who said that they focused mainly on representation, there was a difference in how parties were judged to currently represent and govern, with more people saying that parties did not currently represent well (68%). This suggests that people perceive parties to be underperforming in the areas they focus their judgements on. This trend was also found in responses from those who said they focus on governing. Indeed, the third block of the diagram in Figure 4.3 shows that 72% of respondents felt that parties did not govern well, whilst only 63% felt they didn't represent well. For those who focused equally on representation and governance, parties were seen to perform almost equally poorly in both areas, with 73% feeling that they didn't represent voters well and 72% responding that they didn't run the country well. This suggests that views of governing do depend on its perceived importance but, overall, it is notable that this function is not seen by any group to be executed well. Given this, attention now turns to consider what, precisely, parties are seen to be failing to do, by examining in turn three aspects of governing behaviour: performance, timeframe and motivation.

Party performance

First, in exploring citizens' desires, it is useful to draw on the literature on voter choice. For many years, scholars have argued that voting decisions are informed by perceptions of governing competence and performance, with ideological affinities becoming less significant in explaining which parties citizens support. Often discussing the rise of what is called 'valence politics', scholars have shown that voters judge parties by making 'evaluations of rival parties likely ability to deliver policy outcomes in issue areas characterized by broad consensus' (Clarke et al., 2009, p. 1; see also Finer, 1949; Fiorina, 1981; Himmelweit et al., 1985; Stokes, 1992). Parties' ability to make progress on issues such as economic prosperity, low levels of crime or effective public service has been found to be key to how they are publicly assessed, with voters focusing on '"who can do the job" rather than on "what the job should be"' (Clarke et al., 2009, p. 15). Building on this idea, scholars have shown that voters reward or punish legislators for their record of legislative performance (Butler and Powell, 2014, p. 493) and that 'poor handling of official duties, crises, and problems depress parties' vote shares ... [meaning] that parties are systematically punished at the polls as their valence scores decline' (Clarke et al., 2009, pp. 121, 460). From this perspective, citizens' views of parties appear to be informed by an 'evaluation of issue competence and government performance' (Green and Jennings, 2012, p. 488; see also Green and Jennings, 2017), with direct experiences, evaluations of government performance, and emotional reactions affecting judgements (Clarke et al., 2009, p. 18).

To assess citizens' views of party performance, this section draws on a distinction made by Richard Katz (2014, p. 190) between parties' *service* and their *managerial competence*. This recognises that, as governors, parties can deliver policies and produce outcomes, but they can also provide on-going administration and governance – tasks that differ subtly in form. Whilst the former directs attention to parties' capacity to deliver outcomes such as manifesto promises, legislative commitments or unplanned initiatives, the latter is more technocratic, focusing on parties' caretaker activities in ensuring the smooth running of government and public services. This difference is significant because whilst parties may be viewed to be competent in one area, there is no reason to assume that judgements are uniform. For this reason, further analysis can help to unpick how different aspects of governing behaviour are viewed.

Applying this logic, in the Party Survey respondents were asked about their views of parties both as service organisations that 'deliver promised policies' and 'deliver good policy outcomes', and as managerial bodies that 'manage the day-to-day running of government' and 'deal with crises'. Assuming that all of these outcomes are desirable, attention focused on citizens' views of how parties presently behave. Respondents were therefore asked whether, for each option, they felt that 'parties do this extremely well and no improvements could be made', 'parties mainly do this well, but small improvements could be made', 'parties tend not to do this well and a lot of improvements could be made', or 'parties don't do this at all well and huge improvements could be made'.[3]

The results present interesting variations (Figure 4.4). Although most respondents consistently answered that parties don't perform these functions well, it appears that service activities are viewed more negatively than managerial roles. Indeed, the two indicators of service governance – delivering promised policies and good policy outcomes – showed considerable dissatisfaction, with just over

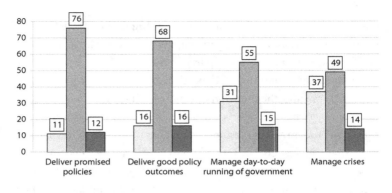

Figure 4.4 Party Survey: perceptions of parties' service and managerial performance

three-quarters of respondents (76%) answering that parties didn't deliver their promises, and over two-thirds (68%) stating that they didn't deliver good policy outcomes. The measures of managerial competence – managing the day-to-day running of government and crises – were viewed less negatively, with closer to half of respondents indicating that parties do not do these things well. Given the expectation that parties would ideally do all of these things well, these results suggest that parties' service roles are more acutely out of kilter with desires.

The workshops produced further evidence that service and managerial functions are viewed differently, and also showed that parties are not currently seen to behave as desired. Within the workshops there was sustained critique of service functions and it was argued that parties are not seen to deliver their promises and good outcomes for the country. Across all three workshops there was a feeling that 'parties don't deliver on their promises' and displayed a 'lack of honesty, delivering on their manifesto'. One non-activist group reported feeling that 'at election time, it's just, we'll do this, we'll do this, we'll do this', 'It's pie in the sky, isn't it?', whilst a participant in workshop 3 commented that parties say 'anything to get into power ... and then renege'. These trends were directly linked to the fact that 'people are totally disillusioned', with one non-activist participant joking: 'I've seen all these promises since the 1960s, and I'm still waiting'.

In comparison, when it came to managerial functions, there was limited discussion of parties' managerial capacities. Although some participants argued that all parties are useless in every way, a short discussion by one group of party activists produced the conclusion that 'more political parties are competent than incompetent'. Whilst these are perhaps unsurprising views given the connections between these participants and parties, non-activists also acknowledged that parties often did their best within the constraints of the current political system. One non-activist reflected:

> Perhaps it's the rules that they are working under that are the problem because no one is actually ... evil ... everybody kind of wants to do the right thing.... I think the rules are a really big problem.

Issues of managerial competence therefore did not appear to define citizens' views.

Breaking down perceptions in this way, it appears that the public do not perceive parties' governing roles homogenously, but rather differentiate between governing activities. Whilst parties are seen to be better at performing administrative tasks and handling crises, they are viewed less positively when it comes to keeping promises. This raises interesting questions about the way parties should behave when performing service tasks, as it is not immediately apparent what a 'good' governing outcome looks like or what kind of promises people want parties to keep. One possibility is that citizens want parties to be more technocratic and less ideological in executing these tasks, and hence see a party focus on specific interests to be preventing their desires from being realised. To test perceptions here, in the Party Survey respondents were asked the following trade-off question:

Some people say it is more important for political parties to govern in the interests of the whole nation, even if this means there is not much difference between parties. Others argue that parties should govern in the interests of specific groups and have different agendas, even if this means they do not focus on the national interest. Using the scale below – where 1 means it is more important for parties to govern in the interests of the whole nation and 4 means it is more important for parties to govern in the interests of specific groups – where would you place yourself?[4]

Respondents indicated a strong desire for parties that focus on the national interest, with 48% strongly in favour of this option (and 25% slightly in favour). In contrast, only 3% strongly favoured a focus on specific groups (with 9% slightly favouring this, and 15% answering 'Don't know'). These views were also apparent in the workshops, where non-activists in particular argued:

Once you're in government, whoever got you there, you need to be making sure that everyone's needs are met.
You need to represent everybody.
Yeah.
Not just the ones who voted for you.

A non-activist also commented that parties 'should represent their whole community, including those who voted against them because they are our representatives', whilst another agreed that 'the national government, they should work in everyone's interests'.

Given the nature of the trade-off presented in the Party Survey, it was not possible to determine whether citizens' support for the national interest meant that they wanted parties to offer identical platforms that addressed a 'neutral' or non-partisan conception of the national good. However, within the workshops there was evidence that people did not support this approach. In calling for the 'national interest' to be promoted, an activist questioned what was meant by this term:

Brexit is the clearest example of how you can't define the national interest. The country has split right down the middle, and the parties have split right down the middle as to which direction is in the

national interest and they are polar opposite directions and it's just a
term you can't define.

The ambiguity surrounding the 'national interest' was widely recognised and after some discussion participants tended to articulate the
problems in defining it. One table of non-activists therefore voiced
initial support before the following exchange:

> Everyone has a different idea of what is in the national interest
> though.
> The national interest isn't what is in the good of the country.
> Like I would say that fracking is good for the country but...
> Who decides what is in the national interest?

Another table in the same workshop similarly reflected that they
could not define the idea of the national interest because 'I think
everybody has got interests that are completely different to anybody
else'. There was therefore recognition that, as one activist noted:

> there will still be underlying ideology that pervades the subjectivi-
> ties of everyone involved in that process, and so the actual specific
> ideologies of different people involved in that are going to end up
> serving, in the practical outcomes, different interests to what people
> in the whole process are conceiving as the national interest.

This conclusion reflects Sarewitz's (2001, p. 84) contention that
'[p]eople have legitimately different interests and perspectives that
they will naturally attempt to protect and promote'. Although some
workshop participants felt that parties should follow 'the utilitarian
principle, the greatest good for the greatest number of people',
most rejected this view and felt that parties needed to define their
own conception of the national interest. After consideration, participants tended to argue that parties should be 'trying to persuade
the whole country that this is the best way, this is for the good of
everybody', highlighting a difference between initial reactions and
more considered responses (Kahneman, 2011; Stoker et al., 2016).
This perspective also reflected the view that there was 'too much
similarity in parties' and indicated the perceived importance of
political choice.

Rather than suggesting a desire for technocratic or administrative conceptions of the national interest, the workshops therefore indicate that people support the idea of parties outlining their own vision of the national interest. Mirroring earlier discussions about the importance of partisan styles of representation, it was argued that 'if everyone is kind of focused on government and being a competent government, that doesn't give you a tribe to sign up to', making it hard for people to become engaged. Importantly, this comment was voiced by a non-activist in workshop 2, suggesting that it is not just partisans and activists who support such ideas. Whilst activists may be expected to call for parties to have a 'fixed or firm ideology' that prevents them becoming, as one activist noted, a 'management consultancy rather than politics', these views are more widely held than may be presumed. Voiced across the different workshop groups, there accordingly appears to be a desire for parties that act to promote 'the *general* interest by expressing distinctive visions on the future of the polity' (White and Ypi, 2010, p. 814, original emphasis), entwining representative agendas with governing skills.

Based on these varied insights, it appears that citizens presently perceive parties to be unreliable governors who fail to deliver on promises or produce good outcomes. However, parties are seen to perform better (if far from perfectly) when it comes to administering state apparatus and dealing with crises. These perceptions matter because they mean that parties are often not seen to focus on the national interest, but instead to be concerned with their own survival and ideas. Whilst this perception may lead some to conclude that there is a desire for parties to adopt more technocratic, administrative approaches to governance, this analysis reveals that people desire parties that do offer different visions of the national interest. This reflects White and Ypi's observation that parties and politics remain essential as long as different political ideals remain (White and Ypi, 2010, p. 813). It also suggests that people would like to see parties reimagine their message, placing greater emphasis on their distinctive conception of the national good.

Short-term responsiveness or long-term responsibility?

In addition to judgements of party performance, governing assessments may also be related to the perceived status of parties as responsive and/or responsible governors. As outlined in the Introduction, parties' democratic capacities are closely tied to their ability to 'respond to the short-term demands of voters, public opinion and the media' and to take into account 'the long-term needs of their people and countries, which have not necessarily been articulated as specific demands … (e.g. intergenerational fairness, sustainability of public expenditures, long-term investments in security, education etc.)' (Bardi et al., 2014a, p. 237). Parties can take up these imperatives simultaneously or in isolation, but it is commonly argued that they should ideally balance these demands (Birch, 1964; Mair, 2009; Flinders and Judge, 2017).

This idea is of interest because recent scholarship has highlighted parties' increasing inability (or unwillingness) to reconcile these roles. The diagnoses of change vary. On the one hand, scholars have argued that parties themselves are increasingly focused on responsive governance. Caramani (2017, p. 59) has contended that, in a mediatised environment, parties are under constant scrutiny, forcing them 'to focus on short-term results, policies, and proposals that can be easily sold in the media market place'. Similarly, Goetz (2014, pp. 385–6) has suggested that the pressures of electoral cycles, and parties' need to secure on-going electoral success, encourages 'short-term time horizons in political decision-taking', a dynamic not conducive to the time-consuming procedures and long-term traits of responsible governance (see also Majone, 1996). Additionally, Enroth (2015) has contended that parties have abandoned responsible government as they have become ever more electorally focused on short-term demands. On the other hand, however, Mair and others have suggested that parties have become focused on responsible administration. Parties are therefore seen to have focused their attention on being 'good governors, administrators and managers of the polity' (Mair, 2009, pp. 8–9). For Pastorella (2016, p. 958), 'governments are increasingly becoming just neutral executors of policies', meaning that parties can be characterised as 'trustees of depoliticised and flexible issue-based positions'. These narratives, whilst often not overtly discussing time, suggest that parties have moved away from short-term responsive governance (focused on citizens' interests and representative agendas), and now focus on the realisation of long-term outcomes and governing ideals. This scholarship therefore depicts parties in different ways, indicating that parties can vary in their degree of responsiveness and responsibility. What is unclear is how citizens would like parties to behave along this distribution, and how they view them to currently act.

To test citizens' views, the significance of time was explored. As outlined in Table 4.1, options were presented that distinguished desires for responsive parties, responsive and responsible parties, or solely responsible parties. Specifically, Party Survey respondents were told 'When parties govern, they can make decisions that focus on citizens' short-term demands (such as a desire for tax cuts) and long-term needs (such as a need to invest in state infrastructure)'. They were then asked:

> Now thinking about how parties *should ideally* behave when they make governing decisions, which of the following statements do you think describes how parties *should* think about these things?

Table 4.1 Possible variations in party responsiveness and responsibility

Type of party	Description
Responsive	Focused primarily on delivering short-term demands, often associated with electoral outcomes
Responsive and responsible	Focused equally on short-term demands and long-term needs
Responsible	Focused primarily on long-term needs, often associated with the national interest

Respondents could then select between the following three options:

Parties should focus more on short-term demands and less on long-term-needs

Parties should focus equally on short-term demands and long-term needs

Parties should focus more on long-term needs and less on short-term demands.

Then, to consider current perceptions, individuals were asked 'Which of the following statements do you think describes how parties *currently* think about these things?', and they were presented with the same three options.

Responses on ideal behaviour suggested a desire for parties to balance long-term needs and short-term demands, with 63% giving this response. The next most favourable option was for parties to focus on long-term needs (32%), with just 4% choosing a short-term focus. This suggests there is support for the idea of parties as responsible and responsive governors, with a secondary preference for responsible parties and limited support for responsive organisations (an interesting finding given growing support for populist narratives and ideas). Turning to data on current perceptions, parties are, however, currently seen to focus more on short-term demands. Indeed, 57% of respondents characterised parties in this way. Only 23% of respondents felt that parties focused equally on long-term needs and short-term demands, whilst just 20% felt they focused on long-term needs. This suggests that people think parties are currently *too* responsive.

Mirroring the analysis in earlier chapters, a Sankey diagram was used to look at the patterns in citizens' responses. Figure 4.5 shows interesting variations in response. Looking at the largest group – those who think parties should focus equally on short-term demands and long-term needs – preferences run in different directions, but the largest group indicate that they see parties currently focusing on short-term demands. Using logistic regression to explore the kind

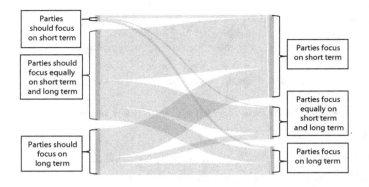

Figure 4.5 Comparing desires and perceptions of governing responsiveness and responsibility

of respondents who wanted an equal focus on long- and short-term goals, but who perceived a short-term focus, it appears that those with a degree were significantly more likely to give this response, as were those who report low levels of trust in parties (Table A.7, Appendix 3).

The idea that parties are not performing as desired was also evident in the workshops. Speaking about current practices, one activist argued: 'when you look at the actual policies they pursue today, there is no long-term thinking … it's all very short-termist'. A non-activist also argued that parties focus on what 'they think people want to hear, not necessarily what they need', delivering quick wins rather than tackling difficult problems. This was seen to occur because, as another non-activist noted, 'by nature they are just looking to boost their popularity for the next election, over what the actual benefit is to the country, or what the right thing is to do. They just want what is best for them.' Parties were often seen to neglect long-term needs because of incentives in the political system, with one participant in workshop 3 arguing that the system 'makes the interests in obtaining and maintaining power override the bigger interest that might require longer-term solutions'. For many, this meant there was a need for electoral reform, with another participant in workshop 3 arguing:

> First-past-the-post results, generally speaking … bring strong majority governments, so parties with that mandate feel that they have to rush through as many policies as they can in four to five years, make whatever changes we think we can, and try and get ourselves elected next year, and present a good enough reason for the electorate to vote for them in the next five years, as well as pursuing their policy objective. Longer-term objectives are like secret, backburner, if we get time we will consider it kind of things, and I don't think that is how programmes in the national interest are made. I mean, in terms of Brexit, how can we trust a government that has half an eye on the next general election to do what is best from the perspective of the next century or two? … I just don't see how it is possible structurally to do that.

In line with this thinking, the parties were seen to be deficient because '[i]t makes tackling the political issues like climate change … impossible because you have to be popular in five years' time to win the next election'. It was also seen to inspire parties to behave in a reactionary way, meaning they weren't, as one activist put it, 'thinking it through' and pursuing the 'best' course of action. At times, this led participants to voice support for technocratic innovations. One non-activist argued that to counter parties' tendency to focus on 'short-term issues [that] are more likely to get votes … there should be independent long-term bodies with people who know what they are doing and are qualified'. This view was, however, in the minority and most others expressed broader desires for parties, as one participant in workshop 3 argued, to get 'rid of the short-term strategies for the long term, and think about the people and the country and not just themselves'. It was contended that parties should recruit 'people who have a bigger picture in their mind … [because they] are more likely to act in a long-term way' – referring to the need for politicians who are able to look beyond electoral self-interest and act in accordance with wider social imperatives. These quotations show activists and non-activists alike to be frustrated with electorally motivated short-term responsiveness, and indicate a desire for responsible governance focused on long-term needs.

These conclusions chime with the finding in Chapter 2 that people want parties that are receptive rather than adaptive. In that earlier discussion, a desire for parties that change sometimes (rather than all of the time) emerged, indicating caution over too much responsiveness. Mirroring this idea, it appears that when it comes to governing, people want parties that balance responsiveness to short-term demands with a focus on the country's long-term needs. Whilst Dahl (1971 p. 1) argued that 'continuing responsiveness of the government to the preferences of its citizens [is] a key characteristic of democracy', it appears that responsibility in the form of long-term thinking is also desired. This conclusion is important because, at present, parties are often not seen to be acting in this way. This suggests an incentive to reimagine the balance of parties' attention, downplaying electoral responsiveness and focusing more on responsible governing in order to rebalance these ideas in line with desires. And yet, as participants themselves acknowledged, the dynamics of the political system may make such behaviours unattractive to those seeking power.

Party motivations

In addition to the above, governing motivation is a further possible influence on citizens' governing desires. Whilst there is less literature exploring this idea, there are some indicators that it may matter why parties are seen to behave as they do. Within existing survey data, for example, in 2010 the BES found that 59% of respondents agreed or strongly agreed that 'political parties are more interested in winning elections than in governing afterwards'. In the same survey, it was found that 85% agreed or strongly agreed that 'there is often a big difference between what a party promises it will do and what it actually does when it wins an election'. These findings echo the tenor of the Party Survey and workshop discussions, which reveal a strong dislike for partisan, electorally self-interested behaviour. They also reflect Martin's (2014, pp. 10–11) assertion that citizens' 'general satisfaction with democracy may be accounted for by citizens viewing parties as electoral organizations negatively while viewing parties as instruments for producing policy outcomes more positively'. Public perceptions may therefore be affected by judgements of parties' motivations and objectives, making it valuable to examine preferences here.

To explore this idea in more detail, it is useful to think about alternative drives for parties' governing activity, and here three ideal types of party are considered: an ideological party, an electoral party and a technocratic party (Table 4.2). Whilst in reality parties combine the motivations that underpin these ideal types, they nevertheless help to show the different imperatives that can be seen to guide parties' governing actions.

In the *ideological party*, attention is focused upon clearly stated principles and ideas. These organisations have an outlook that reflects a specific agenda and/or representative interest, and this informs their policies and actions in government. This leads them to take decisions that advance their ideals and preferred means, even when such decisions may prove detrimental to their own electoral fortunes. In determining what the best course of action is, an ideological party therefore refers to its own vision and ideas, using these reference points as a way to decide between options and justify behaviour to

Table 4.2 Idealised party motivations

Type of party	Description
Ideological party	Focused upon clearly stated principles and ideas
Electoral party	Focused upon winning elections and maximising electoral outcomes
Technocratic party	Focused upon securing the 'best' governing outcomes informed by expert advice

the public. In the *electoral party*, attention focuses on winning elections and maximising electoral outcomes. When making decisions, this type of party acts in accordance with strategic calculations designed to maximise its electoral appeal amongst a target population. Such parties adapt their ideas and positions to reflect perceived preferences, using measures of public opinion such as opinion polling and focus groups to identify public demands. This can lead parties to adopt different positions over time (which can be contradictory) as they seek to accommodate and reflect public desires. Finally, in the *technocratic party* attention is focused instead on securing the 'best' governing outcomes informed by expert advice. Unlike the ideological party, which has a defined view of the best outcomes and preferred means by which to achieve those ends, the technocratic party adopts a more pragmatic and flexible approach. This means that such parties can be expected to take a range of (again, potentially contradictory) positions over time that are viewed to deliver the best outcome at any given moment. At one instance, such a party can therefore justify its actions on the basis of a desire to maximise economic growth, whilst at another it may stress the need to protect minority groups. What is key for technocratic parties' legitimacy is that the public share or, at least accept, their view of what is in the public interest. Parties in this tradition therefore often badge themselves as offering pragmatic, expert-informed and solution-focused governance rather than an ideology or electoral agenda.

Each of these ideal types is underpinned by a different governing motivation, leading to alternative approaches to governance and (it can be expected) different outcomes. In reality, parties combine these motivations, measuring ideological objectives against electoral appeal and adopting pragmatic approaches to identify governing solutions. For the purposes of this analysis, however, it is useful to consider citizens' desires against these simplified models, comparing these with current perceptions of how parties behave. For this reason, respondents were presented with the following (to produce a ranking of 1–3):

When parties govern, they can make decisions by thinking about different things. Now thinking about how parties should ideally behave when they govern, please rank the following phrases to show what you think parties *should* think about the most, where 1 is what parties *should* think about the most and 3 is what parties *should* think about the least.

> Whether a decision fits with the party's principles and objectives
>
> Whether a decision will gain the party votes in an election
>
> Whether a decision is supported by evidence and independent advice

This was accompanied by a further question asking about how parties *do* behave.[5]

The results indicated a clear preference for evidence and independent advice, with 73% of respondents ranking this option highest as an ideal. In contrast (and unsurprisingly) only 10% ranked as ideal parties acting in accordance with what will gain the party votes in an election first, whilst 17% did the same for acting in accordance with party principles and objectives. This echoes the finding, discussed in Chapter 2, that experts have public appeal and are seen to be a positive influence on parties (for more, see Dommett and Pearce, 2019; Dommett and Temple, 2019). In contrast, 64% of respondents indicated that parties are currently motivated by a desire to win votes. The next most highly ranked response (21%) was that parties act in accordance with evidence and independent advice, whilst 16% of respondents felt that parties are primarily motivated by principles and objectives.

Looking at the patterns in responses using a Sankey diagram, it is interesting to note the differences in rankings (Figure 4.6). Whilst almost three-quarters of respondents ranked evidence and independent advice first in the ideal, in reality, most of these respondents felt that it was actually ranked third as a motivation for parties. This trend was reversed in the similar Sankey diagram (not shown) for whether a decision will gain the party votes in an election, where most respondents felt that the motivation to gain votes should be

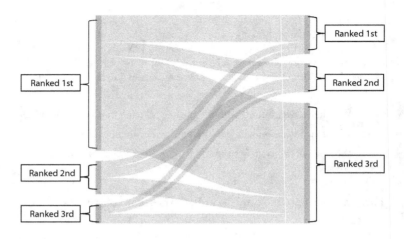

Figure 4.6 Comparing desires and perceptions in the ranking (1–3) of whether a decision should be or actually is motivated by evidence and independent advice

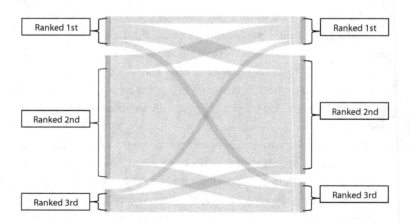

Figure 4.7 Comparing desires and perceptions in the ranking (1–3) of whether a decision should be or actually is motivated by party principles and objectives

ranked third but was actually ranked first. Interestingly, the Sankey diagram for party principles shows that most respondents are content with party principles and objectives, which is ranked second for both questions (Figure 4.7).

The belief that parties focus primarily on gaining votes was widely voiced in the workshops. For example, a participant in workshop 3 argued that 'even a party as democratic as the Green Party is still … I won't use the word triangulating … but is still picking and choosing what [they] say' – showing the resonance of these ideas. Sometimes this behaviour was seen to drive parties to behave counter to their principles, with another participant in workshop 3 arguing:

> Parties are thinking too much, 'Well, people aren't going to vote for this, so we actually won't admit that we want to get rid of Trident', but they don't know … if people were actually given an opportunity to vote for that….

In the place of such electoral motivations, it appears many people want parties to act in a less electoral manner and focus more on evidence and independent advice.

Conclusion

This chapter has engaged with the idea that a third component of democratic linkage – parties' governing behaviour – informs citizens' views and desires. I have argued that citizens have clear desires in relation to governance but that perceptions of current parties do not mirror these ideals. Looking at the relative importance of governing judgements, I have shown that most people profess to focus equally on governance and representation, but that the weight of the distribution emphasises parties' governing traits. Building on this finding, I have shown that people do not currently see parties to be delivering the policy pledges or good outcomes that they desire, but do see them to be performing marginally better as administrators.

In addition, I have shown that there is a desire for parties that promote the national interest. Although often depicted as a neutral idea, workshop discussion showed that citizens recognise the highly contested nature of the national interest and acknowledge the need for parties to outline their own principled agenda for change. Digging deeper into citizens' preferences, I also showed that citizens dislike short-term politics and desire a balance between long-term needs and short-term demands. Furthermore, I have presented data that reveals a desire for party actions to be motived by evidence and independent advice as opposed to electoral considerations.

In thinking about the responses parties may wish to make to this data, it appears that there is a concerted dislike of instrumental, election-focused practice and a desire for parties to focus on long-term imperatives and national goals. However, given parties' need to secure electoral victory and the incentive in a majoritarian system to focus on promoting the demands of small groups of voters, this response may prove unattractive to parties, and be difficult to realise without wider systemic change. When it comes to realising citizens' governing preferences, it therefore appears that there is no simple solution.

Cumulatively, this chapter has shown that when it comes to governing, citizens do not want parties to focus solely on elections or to make promises that they cannot keep. Instead, they want parties that deliver their promises, think about long- and short-term imperatives, listen to experts and promote a principled vision of the national good. Returning to the idea of the reimagined party, this suggests that citizens' preferences resonate with established ideas of party democracy. Indeed, it appears that people want parties to deliver responsive and responsible governance but also to provide choice. At present, however, parties are not delivering on these ideas, suggesting an incentive to rethink how these functions are performed.

Chapter 5

Party conduct

The last three chapters have shown that citizens have multifaceted desires for representation, participation and governance. When asking 'what do people want from political parties?', an analysis of democratic linkage shows that people have many desires that are often not realised. Before turning to consider the implications of these ideas, in this chapter I engage with a second possible influence on citizens' views of parties, exploring the idea of political conduct.

Speaking to a number of findings discussed so far, this chapter explores the idea that people have specific desires for how they would like parties to behave. Identifying seven principles, I argue that there is a wish for parties that are transparent, communicative, reliable, principled, inclusive and accessible, and that act with integrity. However, when looking at how parties are currently viewed, it appears that these ideas are not seen to characterise current party conduct. Once again, there appear to be significant differences between citizens' desires and perceptions of parties. In identifying these seven principles, I argue that citizens' ideals are not incompatible with the party system but suggest a desire for parties to rethink how they engage. These ideas accordingly present a guide for the reimagination of party conduct.

In structuring this analysis, this chapter takes a different form from the previous three. Initially, the research for this book was designed to focus solely on the explanatory power of democratic linkage, and hence the Party Survey was designed to tease apart different aspects of these ideas. However, within the deliberative workshops conducted after the Survey was fielded, it became evident that perceptions of party conduct were a significant drive of public ideas. Reflecting this finding, this additional strand of analysis was introduced, inspiring a reappraisal of the Party Survey data. This inductive approach to forming the argument in this book means that this chapter is not structured to test theories already evident in the literature through survey data. Rather, this chapter explores available data about public views of political conduct, before moving to map citizens' perceptions and desires.

The literature on party conduct

The idea that political conduct or behaviour affects how politics is viewed is not new, and yet within scholarship on public attitudes towards politics it is an idea that has gained less traction than demo-cratic linkage. Whilst scholars have focused on citizens' evaluations of political performance, and have traced views of political outcomes (Easton, 1965; Miller, 1974), less attention has been paid to the idea that political behaviour influences how parties are viewed. This lack appears strange, as the work of Max Weber famously directed attention to the different ways in which political actors can approach politics – distinguishing between those for whom politics is 'a man's [sic] avocation or his vocation' (quoted in Keane and Merlo, 2010, p. 186). Such ideas suggest that those conducting politics may be driven by different motives – motives that the public may approve of to different degrees.

Some scholarship has directed attention to the significance of conduct for judgements of politicians. Citrin (1974), for example, looked at how scandal can affect public views, inspiring a wealth of scholarship that has explored political ethics and the incentives to promote good conduct (Allen and Birch, 2011; Atkinson and Mancuso, 1985; Bowler and Karp, 2004; Hall, 2018). This work has mirrored the tendency in many countries to introduce codes of conduct and regulation designed to guide the way politicians behave. In the UK, the Code of Conduct for Members of Parliament specifies four duties designed to preserve the integrity of Parliament (House of Commons, 2018, p. 3): (1) abide by the declaration of allegiance to the Crown; (2) uphold the law; (3) 'act in the interests of the nation as a whole … and a special duty to their constituents'; and (4) 'act on all occasions in accordance with the public trust placed in them', where this is taken to mean that 'they should always behave with probity and integrity, including in their use of public resources' (Hall, 2018, p. 397). These developments are of interest within this chapter because a number of scholars have argued that political conduct is pivotal to how political actors are viewed.

Often associated with literature seeking to explain political dis-affection, it has been argued that politicians' conduct is an important influence on citizens' ideas. Jennings et al. (2016, p. 894) have claimed that '[t]he most intense points of citizen disillusionment with the political class resides in perceptions of its flawed character, in particular its fixation with headlines and protection of its own interests and those of the already rich and powerful'. Rather than being critical of political institutions and processes, they argue that it is the 'attributes of … protagonists' that explains citizens' discontent (Jennings et al., 2016, p. 894).

Developing this theme, Allen and Birch have also explored the way that politicians' conduct is viewed. In *Ethics and Integrity in British Politics*, these authors have shown that the public in Britain have expectations for political conduct and yet are 'generally unimpressed with the moral fibre of those who govern and represent them' (Allen and Birch, 2015, p. 118). Pointing to the significance of events such as the UK parliamentary expenses scandal of 2009 (Pattie and Johnson, 2012), they show that political conduct is often viewed in negative terms. Indeed, in relation to that scandal they elsewhere reported the YouGov survey finding that 86% of respondents said there was 'a widespread problem involving a large number of MPs claiming money to which they are not entitled' (Allen and Birch, 2011, p. 61–2). Similar negative views of politicians have been found elsewhere, with McAllister (2000, p. 24) showing that, in 1996, 78% of respondents to an Australian survey agreed or strongly agreed that '[m]ost federal politicians/MPs will tell lies if they feel the truth will hurt them politically'. These trends are seen to matter because, as Allen and Birch (2011, p. 62) have argued, 'citizens clearly value standards of conduct in public life', but there is currently 'a pronounced gap between citizens' aspirations as to how their politicians should behave and their perceptions of how politicians actually behave' (Allen and Birch, 2015, p. 7). When it comes to a range of different behavioural attributes, they show – using qualitative and quantitative data – that 'most Britons perceive their politicians to be unethical and dishonest, if not outright crooked, even though the overwhelming majority of politicians go through their careers without having been implicated in, let alone having been found to have engaged in, misconduct' (Allen and Birch, 2015, p. 128). For some academics, therefore, politicians' failure to live up to these ideals is a driver of political discontent. Indeed, Webb (2002, p. 455) has argued that there is a strong 'likelihood that popular distrust of parties stems in part from the widespread perception that they are self-interested, unduly privileged and inclined to corruption'.

For the most part, studies of political conduct have focused on politicians and political leaders, but there is some evidence that these ideas are pertinent for parties. Martin, for example, has argued that 'evaluations of parties and their leaders affect the level of confidence citizens have in the political parties more generally' (Martin, 2014, p. 9). Elsewhere, there is survey data that suggests that the public have negative views of party conduct. A battery of questions asked in the 2014 BES found that large proportions of respondents tended to agree or strongly agree that parties are more interested in winning elections than governing (75%) and spend too much time bickering with each other (84%). It also found that people think there is a big difference between what parties promise before elections and do in office (59%).[1] Such views have led scholars to describe how parties are viewed as 'quarrelsome and costly machinery composed of *prime donne* and parasites, social climbers and rent-seekers' (Ignazi, 2014, p. 160).

This review of this body of work suggests that citizens' views of parties may be conditioned by judgements of party conduct. What is not clear, however, is how prominent views of party conduct are in shaping evaluations of parties, or whether the public have clear desires in this realm. For this reason, this chapter explores how party conduct features in citizens' views of parties. I find evidence that conduct is a prominent component of how parties are viewed and that negative views characterise citizens' views. The chapter next turns to ask how party conduct features in citizens' views of parties, before it considers the type of conduct that citizens would like to see. Finally, it presents seven principles that characterise these desires.

How does party conduct feature in citizens' views of parties?

In thinking through the resonance of political conduct for our understanding of public perceptions of parties, it is useful to begin by presenting the results of an initial activity conducted at the start of the three deliberative workshops. Asked to begin by writing down three words that they associated with political parties on separate sheets, participants across the three workshops produced 196 words or short phrases. Given the minimal contextual information that participants were given at this point about the study, this exercise offers a glimpse of the prevailing norms that surround parties and allows an assessment of the degree to which party conduct features in citizens' views of parties. Using NVivo software, all 196 words were searched for recurrent ideas. The top 10 words and phrases are shown in Table 5.1. This list is striking in two key ways. First, it suggests – as discussed in Chapter 1 – that parties are viewed in highly negative terms. Indeed, when asked to indicate whether their words were mostly negative, positive or neutral, participants in each

Table 5.1 Top 10 words[a] used by participants in all of the deliberative workshops to describe parties

	Words and phrases	Word count
1.	Divided	10
2.	Unrepresentative	9
3.	Undemocratic	7
4.	Corrupt	6
5.	Self-interested	6
6.	Not listening	4
7.	Tribal	4
8.	Self-serving	4
9.	Dishonest	3
10.	London	3

[a] The counts include highly similar terms (variants and synonyms) to those listed.

workshop overwhelmingly concluded that their ideas were negative. Only a small proportion of words and phrases such as 'organised', 'full of possibility' or 'takes action' were neutral or positive – prompting one participant to ask 'Have any of us said anything positive?!' The uniformity of this outcome is interesting because of the different compositions of each workshop. As one party activist reflected, 'It'll be interesting if this is the tone [negative] on every table because this is a workshop of members who are actually involved in parties'. The fact that every table in every workshop produced such negative accounts of parties reveals the extent to which parties are viewed in poor terms.

Second, the actual words and phrases themselves suggest that ideas associated with party conduct are highly pertinent for how parties are viewed. Whilst the second most prominent term – unrepresentative – is connected with the ideas discussed in Chapter 2, the other key terms are often connected to party conduct: divided, undemocratic, corrupt, self-interested, not listening, tribal and self-serving evoke ideas about how parties behave. Viewed against

Table 5.2 Top 10 words used by participants in each of the deliberative workshops to describe parties

	Party activists		Non-activists		Mixed group	
1.	Unrepresentative	4	Divided	5	Undemocratic	4
2.	Corrupt	3	London-centric	3	Male	3
3.	Divided	3	Not listening	3	Unrepresentative	3
4.	Tribal	3	Short-termist/ short-sighted	3	Self-interested	2
5.	Self-serving	2	Self-interested	2	Short-termist	2
6.	Self-interested	2	Argumentative	2	White	2
7.	Undemocratic	2	Ideologically driven	2	Party allegiance	1
8.	Unfair/unjust	2	Insular	2	Arrogant	1
9.	Unresponsive	2	Out of touch	2	Bubble	1
10.	Anti-democratic	1	Aloof	1	Chauvinism	1

literature on political conduct, this suggests that many individuals' perceptions of parties are coloured by factors other than the form of democratic linkage. What is interesting, however, are the continuities and differences in description that emerged across the different workshops. Taking the terms produced in each workshop in turn, three lists were produced that showed the top 10 words cited by activists, non-activists and the group composed of both these groups. The results, shown in Table 5.2, suggest that whilst many of the same terms were evoked, there were some interesting differences.

The list produced by activists demonstrates that even amongst those most invested in the party system, there was a belief that parties were unrepresentative, corrupt, divided, tribal and self-serving, with significant emphasis placed on behavioural traits. In contrast, non-activists made numerous references to party division, to the London-centric focus of parties, to a lack of listening and a short-term focus. The mixed group tended to focus more on demographic traits, but also cited the tendency for parties to be male and white as well as echoing the aforementioned aspects of party conduct. Thus, there were interesting similarities (with many overlaps) and differences in the responses.

Further evidence for the significance of party conduct was found in Party Survey data, where respondents were asked how satisfied they were with political parties. The precise question wording was: 'Thinking about parties in general, how satisfied or dissatisfied are you with the way that political parties work in the UK?' Possible responses were: very satisfied, fairly satisfied, fairly dissatisfied, very dissatisfied, don't know. The results showed that 69% were fairly or very dissatisfied with parties, whilst 21% were very or fairly satisfied. Of relevance for this chapter, respondents were then asked an open-text follow-up question:

> You indicated that you [are very satisfied; are fairly satisfied; are fairly dissatisfied; are very dissatisfied; 'don't know'] with the way that political parties work in the UK. Why do you say that?

Separating out the responses of those who were satisfied, the answers stating dissatisfaction were coded using NVivo to discern recurring analytical themes. What emerged was a similar concern with party conduct. Looking at the top three types of explanation for dissatisfaction, analysis revealed concerns around party trustworthiness, an overly electoral focus, and a belief that parties acted in line with partisan rather than public interests. Whilst there are some connections here to citizens' views on representation and governance, these themes suggest that people are concerned about the way parties conduct themselves. To gain a deeper understanding of respondents' views, it is useful to present a more detailed overview of these answers. This is complemented with additional material from workshop discussions.

Party trustworthiness

By far the most prominent type of explanation for dissatisfaction concerned parties' trustworthiness. Many Party Survey respondents pointed to the idea of parties as untrustworthy in comments such as:

'They are not always truthful', 'They only reform or apologise when they are caught', 'They never do what they say they will', 'They all promise things but nothing happens. The country remains the same, nothing improves' and 'They promise lots to win the vote and then do not stick to the promises when in government. They bicker amongst each other, do not support the leader of the party and MPs put their own ambition above most other things.'

Others felt that the people parties are composed of are a 'Bunch of liars' who 'won't give a real answer'. With references to the expenses scandal and broken promises, comments stated that parties and politicians could not be trusted. For some, these ideas were connected to corruption, as they stated, for example, that there are 'Too many stories of incompetent and/or inappropriate actions' or 'They're all, like, corrupted'. These findings echo earlier studies that have shown a pervading belief that 'the British political system … [is] wracked by corruption and misconduct' (Allen and Birch, 2015, p. 207). These explanations suggest that many respondents view parties as being too focused on their own objectives and interests.

This theme was also echoed in workshop discussions, where many participants referenced parties' dishonesty. A non-activist argued 'they're all fake', whilst a participant in workshop 3 stated 'You can't believe what they're saying'. It was also argued that parties could not be trusted because 'you cannot rely on individuals to behave like decent human beings … people take advantage, don't they?' This line of thinking was often connected, as above, to ideas of corruption, with one non-activist arguing that 'They are all greedy; that is part of human nature'.

Electoral focus

In addition, a second prominent theme emerged connected to parties' electoralism. Coded as a separate set of ideas, a high proportion of respondents described parties as being too focused on their own electoral goals. Open-text comments were made in the Party

Survey such as 'Their main aim in life is to win elections at all costs', with respondents arguing that 'Political parties say they will do this and that but it's only so they will get elected'. It was also argued that they become 'infect[ed] with the overarching desire to be re-elected', but some respondents also felt that parties 'only seem to be interested in electors approaching an election'. These comments reflected findings elsewhere within the Party Survey, where 74% of respondents agreed that 'parties are more interested in winning elections than in governing afterwards', a belief that has been shown to have 'a significant negative effect on people's perceptions' (Garland and Brett, 2014, pp. 28–30).

This idea also emerged prominently in the deliberative workshops when participants were asked to explain their ideas about parties. In discussing the words they chose in the exercise outlined above, one non-activist argued that parties 'only look as far as the next election and how they can possibly win that one', whilst another noted that they are focused on 'self-perpetuation rather than [acting for] the people'. A participant in workshop 3 also argued that parties were more interested in 'tactical electoral consideration, in order to maintain their current state of power', and even the activists reported feeling that party elites were preoccupied by elections and campaigning as opposed to listening to and implementing members' views. This focus on electoralism was seen to lead parties to neglect the national interest. A non-activist argued that parties 'don't necessarily have the public interest at heart when they are trying to get into power' and another observed that 'by nature they are just looking to boost their popularity for the next election, over what the actual benefit is to the country, or what the right thing is to do'.

Partisan rather than public interests

Finally, Party Survey open-text data also identified a belief that politicians pushed dogmatic partisan agendas and ignored people's desires. Comments revealed that people thought that parties 'hold up progress by constantly being obstructive, automatically taking the opposite view just because of party political reasons'. It was also argued that 'Political parties appear to be more interested in point scoring over rivals, not improving the lot of the masses' and 'all put party before country'. One participant summed up the dissatisfaction by stating 'In one word: tribalism'. This diagnosis was widely offered, and many open-text responses suggested that parties were 'far too entrenched in their dogma'.

These different diagnoses of partisan conduct were again echoed in workshop discussions. For many participants, party politics was 'dogmatic', uncompromising and 'too tribalistic'. Even within the workshop of party activists, one participant argued: 'the party system is fundamentally anti-democratic because it demands loyalty'. In another workshop, non-activists argued: 'the party comes first, even if their electorate in their constituency ask for something … they follow what the party says'. Particularly prominent in the workshops was a dislike of the party whip. This system – whereby parties discipline their MPs to vote in line with party positions – was seen to be emblematic of the problems with parties. Rather than allowing parties and the politicians that constitute them to listen to the people and take up thoughtful, principled positions, an organisational focus on discipline and control was seen to pervade. One activist argued that once an election has happened, 'democracy stops', because apparently faceless and undemocratic party elites decide how individual representatives vote. Participant after participant – in workshops composed of party activists and non-activists – made comments such as: 'whoever you elect to be your MP they will have to toe the party line, and will only be allowed to follow their conscience occasionally, having the whips and stuff'. Such interjections suggest that a strong link exists between perceptions of partisan conduct and undesirable party behaviour. Indeed, one participant in workshop 3 argued that party representatives are:

> functionaries of a brand. They are selling their brand of the political party rather than … actually doing the job of taking their constituents'

questions that they hear in email correspondence or constituency office hours; they are constrained from taking that to Westminster because the system that exists there is so heavily dominated by government timetable, votes under whip, and it just gets lost.

The party whip was therefore closely tied to representation, with participants arguing: 'it's very hard to be principled because you have to toe the party line'.

Connected to these comments, there was also evidence of a dislike of partisan debate. Throughout the three workshops – and even, as Table 5.2 attests, amongst party activists – there was sustained dissatisfaction with the point-scoring, tribal mentality that electoral competition engendered. It was repeatedly argued that parties 'spend too much time having a go at each other' and that 'It all seems to be about point-scoring rather than necessarily having proper discussions with other parties over what is the best thing to happen'. Many participants reported being alienated by such behaviour, with one activist having even 'switched off from so much of the political discussion because I don't like the nature of it anymore'. Although not calling for uniformity in political views, the workshops showed people – and especially non-activists – to see 'tribalistic bickering' as counter-productive. One participant in workshop 3 argued: 'I know they have different opinions, but sometimes it feels just like having arguments for argument's sake'. A non-activist in workshop 2 similarly asserted: 'it feels like the fact that the parties all hate each other stops things from happening'" Different aspects of parties' partisan behaviour therefore produced negative views of party conduct.

Summary

Whilst the above three explanations are distinct, there is clear overlap between these ideas; moreover, they are adhered to by activists and non-activists alike. It appears that parties are seen to exhibit untrustworthy behaviour, be electorally focused and dogmatically partisan, impeding their ability to act in the interests of those they serve. Reviewing data from the Party Survey and workshops, it appears that views on party conduct are a prominent influence on how these organisations are viewed. Indeed, both open-text responses and workshop discussions showed the resonance of this idea. Whilst some alternative influences on citizens' views were apparent – such as a perceived failure of the first-past-the-post electoral system, problems with the system of party finance, and a lack of choice between parties – these explanations were infrequently referenced when compared with discussions of party conduct, suggesting the pertinence of this idea. For this reason, it appears that certain undesirable behaviours and attributes colour how parties are viewed. What is as yet unclear is whether citizens have desires for how these organisations should ideally behave, and so the chapter now turns to consider the type of conduct that citizens would like to see, before it goes on to present seven principles that characterise these desires.

What type of desires do citizens have for party conduct and ethos?

In beginning to isolate whether citizens possess a vision for party conduct, it is once again useful to draw on a further exercise conducted at the outset of the three deliberative workshops. Having voiced their immediate views of parties today in the first exercise (described above), participants were asked to write down three words or short phrases that described their ideal political party. Whilst many participants took longer to identify an appropriate word than in the first task, 215 words were identified. The top 10 most common responses are listed in Table 5.3. This list shows a strong public concern with *how* parties behave. A desire for parties that are honest, transparent, democratic, accountable, that listen, are open, diverse and inclusive suggests a desire for a certain type of behaviour. These wishes are accompanied by calls for parties that are representative (mirroring the findings above and those in Chapter 2) and that are local – reflecting work that has shown local representatives to be

Table 5.3 Top 10 words[a] used by participants in all of the deliberative workshops to describe ideal parties

	All respondents		Party activists		Non-activists		Mixed group	
1.	Honest	17	Democratic	8	Accountable	5	Representative	8
2.	Transparency	14	Inclusive	4	Honest	5	Honest	7
3.	Representative	13	Representative	3	Transparent	5	Transparent	6
4.	Democratic	10	Transparent	2	Listen	3	Listen	4
5.	Accountable	9	Accessible	2	In touch	3	Open	3
6.	Listen	9	Accountable	2	Represent	2	Diverse	3
7.	Local	6	Collaborative	2	Expert	2	Integrity	3
8.	Open	5	Listen	2	Fair	2	Accountable	2
9.	Diverse	5	Local	2	Follows through on manifesto promises	2	Clear policies	2
10.	Inclusive	5	Progressive	2	Local	2	Democratic	2

[a] The counts include highly similar terms (variants and synonyms) to those listed.

viewed more favourably than national figures (Fenno, 1978). Again, there were variations across the workshops in the terms evoked, but there was a prominent emphasis in all on conduct.

Looking at these lists, many desires mirror the drivers of dissatisfaction identified above. Calls for honest parties speak to concerns about trustworthiness; a desire for listening mirrors the belief that parties are self-interested, electorally focused organisations; and a wish for diversity reflects a dislike of career politicians. And yet these terms also suggest a desire for other attributes – such as transparency and democracy – that were less prominent in the discussion above. To gain greater insight into citizens' desires, transcripts from the deliberative workshops were coded to identify citizens' wishes in relation to party conduct. Using successive exercises, participants were asked to discuss how they would ideally like to see policies formed, how they would like parties to provide opportunities for participation, and how they would like to see parties governed. These discussions offer a wealth of data on how party activities are viewed and how people would like to see parties conduct themselves. To gather data, participants were led through tasks in which they needed to generate their own ideas, prioritise different options and mediate different demands (many of which have been discussed in previous chapters). Specifically, the workshops contained activities designed to test the resilience of citizens' ideas, with participants asked, for example, to reflect on how their priorities for policy formulation would change when faced with a need for urgent policy formulation or a political crisis. Using such techniques, the workshops allowed the principles and priorities citizens most valued to be identified, offering additional insight into public desires.

Seven principles for party conduct

In this section, I identify seven principles that capture the ideals citizens desire from parties, arguing that there is a wish for parties that are transparent, communicative, reliable, principled, inclusive, accessible, and that act with integrity. To provide a more detailed overview, I argue that citizens want parties to have the following characteristics:

- Transparent – people want to understand what parties do, how decisions are made and what influence they can have. This is crucial for citizens' understanding, but also for enabling accountability.
- Communicative – people want to know what is happening and why, and they want to know when something has gone wrong. They want parties to explain and take responsibility when something does not work out as planned.
- Reliable – people want to see parties that outline an agenda and stick to it, enacting their manifesto promises and sticking to pledges. This means that when they do need to change, there has to be a clear explanation for why change is necessary.
- Principled – people want to see parties that have principles. This does not mean that parties should be highly partisan or dogmatic; rather, they should have a clear idea of what they want to achieve.
- Inclusive – people want parties to include a range of different voices and ideas.
- Accessible – people want a range of ways to engage with parties, but want parties to give them a realistic picture of the kind of power that they will receive.
- Integrity – people want parties that act with integrity and that are honest, ethical and dignified.

Each of these ideas is unpicked in the analysis below. It is important to note, however, the differences between each of the three workshops. Whilst these ideas were voiced by all groups, they received different degrees of support amongst activists and non-activists and hence were favoured with varying degrees of intensity in the different workshops. These differences are highlighted in the discussion below.

Transparent

Throughout the previous chapters, and specifically in Chapter 3 (on participation), evidence has emerged that citizens want to understand how parties operate. Whether wanting to comprehend the impact of participation, or to appreciate the influence of different actors on policy and decision-making, there have been indications that people want to know how parties work. Within the list of priorities outlined above (Table 5.3), transparency featured highly in each workshop and, when asked to explain the importance of this idea, participants made comments such as:

> if they are transparent then more people can feel like they understand and are involved. That they can get a grip on it, that it doesn't feel like this thing that they are totally disconnected from.

Information was therefore seen to be key, but transparency was desired for different reasons. Some suggested that transparency was vital for representation. Indeed, one non-activist argued that parties should 'provide open and transparent information for people; let them tell you what they want and just be a channel to make that happen'. Other comments suggested that participants wanted transparency to enable them to judge the motivations behind party governance. It was argued by activists and non-activists alike that there was a need to be able to identify 'vested interests', in line with a desire to 'know the real reasons they are doing things … why they don't seem to be behaving in the way I think they should be'. This transparency was seen to overcome the tendency, voiced by one activist, for citizens to think 'how do they come to decisions? Sometimes politicians speak and parties say things and you think, where has that come from?'

The desire for transparency was often connected to trust, with a belief that a lack of information and an inability to access information promoted public distrust. One non-activist argued that transparency was important because 'In terms of trust, people feel like if third parties are involved, things would be seen to be different and it would change things'. Transparency and the availability of information were also seen to be an important metric against which citizens judged party governance, with another non-activist arguing that they 'judge parties on how transparent they are, because whatever they are doing you want to know about it, really' and another responding 'I suppose that comes into competence as well, because you need to see that they are doing it right'. Elsewhere, another non-activist similarly argued: 'I'd like to see what they say, what they do, that they're accountable. Then you can measure somehow what they've achieved and how they've achieved it.' Transparency was therefore seen to be essential to accountability, allowing citizens to scrutinise party activities and hold representatives to account.

Transparency accordingly enhanced favourable attributes when it came to representation, participation and governance, with activists and non-activists alike arguing that it could have a positive effect on how parties are viewed. There was a wide-ranging desire to understand more about how parties work, in order to be able to scrutinise their activities and identify how to get involved. Indeed, one non-activist noted, to wide agreement, that 'the most important thing is that you provide open and transparent information for people', suggesting this is a strong influence on citizens' ideas.

Communicative

Closely connected to the idea of transparency, and emerging in discussions of all three aspects of democratic linkage, participants also desired communicative interactions with parties. Although not directly cited in the lists of words above, workshop discussion revealed a desire for more frequent, proactive communication between parties and citizens, especially outside of election periods. This was often a reaction to the belief that parties failed to listen, explain their actions or communicate their successes.

Non-activists were particularly likely to argue that 'there need to be channels to let your MP know your demands on an on-going basis ... there are just no channels really', and that parties have 'got to communicate'. At a basic level, there was frustration about a lack of on-going engagement, with one non-activist noting: 'If I contact someone, I want them to get back in touch ... just something to say I acknowledge, I will get back in touch with you ... not just ignoring'. This desire was often connected to a feeling that politicians did not do what was commonplace in other realms. One non-activist noted:

> I worked in customer service. Customers demand a response and expect it with a certain timeframe. If you don't respond in a certain timeframe, they whinge and whinge and whinge and it ends up costing you more time. But our MPs and councillors don't seem to do that; they just ignore you.

Whilst voiced primarily by non-activists, the desire for more on-going communication was also acknowledged by activists, with one reflecting that 'some MPs are quite engaged and responsive to their constituents, but not all'. There was therefore widespread recognition that parties needed to do more to engage citizens, but activists were notably more aware of the challenges of executing this desire.

Many participants linked a desire for on-going communication and engagement to the issue of accountability and transparency. In open-text survey answers as well as in each of the three workshops, a raft of comments along these lines were made, including '[there] isn't really accountability as they are not held to what they say', 'there is a lack of scrutiny' and 'there is no formal accountability for what they don't do, and there is no formal accountability for what they do differently to what they say they are going to do and I think there should be'. In calling for more communication, one participant in workshop 3 contended that more proactive communication from parties would make it easier to check whether parties were 'acting on your behalf, because they may not be acting according to what a lot of people think'. A desire for communication was therefore seen to promote transparency and to allow people to hold parties to account.

Participants were often quite specific about the kind of communication they desired. Reflecting on current dynamics, a non-activist argued that they'd 'like to know the real reasons they are doing things … why they don't seem to be behaving in the way I think they should be', whilst another reflected 'I want to see what they think'. Further comments revealed a wish for two-way on-going communication and transparency, with a participant in workshop 3 expressing a desire for parties to talk to citizens 'about all their own deliberations', to offer more insight into how decisions are made.

Interestingly, developing insights about parties' mediating role, there was recognition that parties would have to explain and communicate how different perspectives influenced eventual decisions. One participant in workshop 3 commented:

> We're not able to say directly to the politicians, 'this is what we want and please' … because there then has to be dialogue with other people who say they want the other thing and we are not speaking to those people.

Communication therefore required parties to 'be honest with people as well. It might be bad news, but at least people will know what to expect.' Interactions with citizens were accordingly not seen to be about acting as a simple transmission belt (listening to and passing on views) but acting to mediate and shape public demands. This meant both communicating 'news about the good stuff that parties do', but also informing citizens about when things did not quite go to plan.

From these comments it became clear, as one non-activist observed, that 'Communication has come out as quite important'. Participants, and especially those not involved in parties, frequently called for parties to provide more information and engage people in on-going dialogue designed to improve understanding and facilitate engagement. Rather than treating citizens as 'consumers of politics' who are not 'active participants in the political process' (Garland and Brett, 2014, pp. 28–30), many people wanted parties to engage citizens in open, honest and inclusive dialogue.

Reliable

In addition to more transparency and communication, workshop discussion suggested a further desire, connected to reliability. When thinking about party representation and governance in particular, citizens often voiced disparaging views of parties as electorally motivated, instrumental actors. Indeed, as Party Survey data has shown, parties are seen to change position more often than desired and to be motivated by short-term as opposed to long-term imperatives. Echoing these ideas, within discussion a desire emerged for parties that are more reliable and consistent, with many participants (and especially non-activists) calling for a move away from electoral game-playing and short-termist decision-making towards more reliable political agendas and actions.

In identifying this desire, workshop activities demonstrated a clear frustration with current governing behaviour. As discussed above, citizens often feel that parties are dishonest and unreliable and will 'promise anything' at election time. In workshops 2 and 3, there was particular frustration at parties' tendency to renege on manifesto promises, leading to calls for binding promises and more reliable behaviour. A discussion in workshop 3 ran as follows:

> [I think parties should be] following through with promises, or following promises in your manifesto.
> Well, no, to be honest … manifestos are just like travel catalogues … what happens is you go on your holiday and it rains for the week.
> I don't think manifestos are designed to be followed as they are generally unworkable, financially.
> They would be more realistic if they had to follow through, whereas at the moment it is just like a wish list.

The desire for binding manifesto promises was routinely voiced by non-activists. Indeed, another group called for 'realistic targets':

> They need to do more short-term targets so that you can judge them.
> Well, deliverable, achievable.
> Yeah, SMART targets.

For 5, 10 years perhaps.
There have got to be more markers along the way.

Yet it was evident that many activists were cautious about this idea and were likely to highlight the need for parties to have flexibility. In the activist workshop the challenge of implementing manifesto promises was explicitly discussed:

> But what about if one of your manifesto promises is rubbish, though, or what about if the circumstances change and therefore … ?
> But if people voted you in on that manifesto…
> But say, for example, when the financial crisis, say something happens which is an unpredictable event which affects, which you can't do anything about and therefore you have to take certain steps which mean you can't deliver on all of your manifesto promises…
> Yeah, but it doesn't say all…
> But that is kind of, like, you were judging them against that. I don't think I would kick out a party just because they didn't deliver a manifesto policy.
> Yeah, that's true; they have got to be flexible along the way.
> What about if they delivered something that wasn't in the manifesto but was actually quite good? Would I go, 'No I didn't want that!'?

This suggests a split in approach, with different degrees of support for binding promises. What was common, however, was the idea that parties needed to be more reliable. A participant in workshop 3 argued: '[y]ou need to believe they are representing what they are supposed to be representing and saying what they're doing'. This echoes a finding of the Audit of Political Engagement: in 2018, 32% of its survey respondents said that judgements about whether a 'party can be trusted to keep its promises' were important when deciding on who to vote for (Hansard Society, 2018, p. 23). Although there is no consensus about how reliability can be achieved, it appears that there is a common desire for more reliable conduct. In part this idea overlaps with the idea of communication discussed above, as it is important for citizens to understand what parties do and why parties need to change position. These desires therefore appear closely interlinked.

Principled

The fourth trait distilled from workshop discussions is again connected most to preferences for representation and governance. As evident in previous chapters, far from rejecting partisan agendas, citizens show support for partisan representation, with 66% of respondents answering that parties should think about their principles and objectives when developing policy positions. And yet there are signs that people favour a certain kind of partisan behaviour, with a dislike of partisan, dogmatic and tribalistic politics and a desire for more principled parties.

In the place of dogmatic agendas, focused, as one participant put it, on 'brainwashing people', workshop discussions revealed a desire for parties that share their 'point of view' in the hope of winning appeal. As discussed in Chapter 2, citizens do not want signposts that rigidly point in one direction and are unyielding in the promotion of certain ideas, but want parties to offer reliable, principled agendas that are then used to interpret and mediate between citizen desires. Interestingly, these desires were found in each of the workshops, with even the most engaged activists lamenting the overly dogmatic ways in which parties currently work.

Support for principles was particularly evident in discussions of representation and governance, where it was argued that parties need to mediate between diverse demands in accordance with principles. A non-activist reflected:

> I think if the leadership is really clear about its core principles and values, then it helps to guide decisions, even if that decision has to be made in a way, if you are really clear that we are not going to start a war ... that is against our principles, period, then it helps to guide your debates ... but if you are kind of, like, like a lot of politicians do, like sitting on the fence, just trying to say, what is going to get them most popularity at the time dependent on where emotions seems to be going then it can go either which way.

This suggests that people do not want parties that simply listen to and relay citizen demands but, rather, want organisations that mediate between demands in accordance with certain principles and ideas. This idea was voiced in all three workshops, in comments that called for parties to be 'clear about their principles and values'. The particular importance of this approach was underlined in discussion of how parties should make policy in times of crisis. Asked to design a policy-making process, participants sketched highly inclusive, lengthy consultation processes. When asked how they would make policy in a crisis (over a short space of time) most groups recognised that it was not possible to gather views, and called for parties to take 'cues from the philosophical basis' of the party. This suggests that citizens do not want parties to be empty vessels, but recognise the importance of ideological foundations for party activities.

These ideas were also reflected in discussions of governance, where it was argued that as well as listening to people, parties 'need to lead' and to offer principled statements where they say 'we are going to [do] this because ... and this will benefit X, Y and Z'. Intersecting with previous calls for reliability and communication, it appeared there was a desire for parties that made it clear that 'this is a red line, this is what we're standing for'. Many recognised that, in being principled, parties needed to be 'open to the fact that people may not want to vote for you', but they were often cautious about parties becoming dogmatic. Indeed, when asked how they would react if a policy a party had developed was deeply unpopular amongst the public, many participants argued that that party should 'go back and re-consult, find out what the problem is'. One participant responded, 'if it isn't against the core values of your party then maybe you would back-track'.

Principles therefore appear to be essential to parties, suggesting that rather than being wholly responsive to citizen whims, there is a desire for parties that offer a vision. And yet a delicate balance is required here, as citizens also reject the idea of rigid and dogmatic parties, suggesting that this desire may be challenging to fulfil.

Inclusive

Throughout the data collected, evidence also emerged that citizens would like to see a shift in the communities that parties engage. Whilst historically many parties have been aligned to specific sets of interests, there was evidence that citizens would like parties to display a more inclusive approach. Indeed, amongst activists, 'inclusive' was the word mentioned second most often (see Table 5.3).

In workshop discussions, this desire emerged forcefully in tasks related to representation, but was also apparent in debate around participation and, to a lesser extent, governance. Indeed, data in Chapter 2 shows that when it comes to representation, respondents want parties to listen to a range of different voices, with one non-activist voicing a desire for parties to not be 'so sort of bound up with one set of ideas that you are not open to variation or different sets of ideas'. Looking further into this idea, workshop discussion showed a strong desire for parties to engage a wider community of actors with different perspectives, and to have 'proper discussions with other parties over what is the best thing to happen'. Whilst wanting parties to have principled agendas, there was also a desire, particularly from non-activists, for parties to listen and take on alternative views. Participants in workshop 3 had the following discussion:

> ... if you're not speaking to people with different interests to you, then you are not going to be forming the strongest argument to take forward in your party to then take forward and argue in Parliament.
> People don't have to agree on the things, they can agree to disagree, so it is being diverse.
> And it is disagreement that drives policy forward as well.
> Yeah.
> It drives debate, it drives recognition of different points of view.
> Yeah, it helps refine.
> It's incredibly important. I think if you are just reaching out to the same kind of person time and time again, you're in a party that is going nowhere.

This desire was particularly evident in an exercise focused on policy-making where participants were asked to discuss who should ideally inform the policy-making process. The groups participants wanted to see included were diverse (see Table 2.2). Indeed, it was argued in workshop 3 that, for policy-making:

> I think I'd want to try and get people from a wide range of different areas of life, with different interests and if you want to make good policy, then we need those experts from a wide range of different points of view, so, yeah, I think we've got to go for people with different interests.
>
> Well, you've got to, you've got to have people who disagree and not have the same opinion. Otherwise, it's just a one-way road, isn't it?
>
> Everyone with the same interests and the same points of view.
>
> It's no good.

Activists also called for inclusivity, with different tables in workshop 1 voicing support for the idea of including experts, the general public and charities alongside party actors (such as policy forums, party representatives and leaders). Whilst activists tended to focus on including those already engaged in parties more meaningfully, there was also a willingness to listen to a wider range of voices.

And yet, as suggested above, when asked about policy-making in times of crisis, many participants were willing to re-evaluate this inclusive approach. Participants were presented with the following scenario: 'It's close to the election and your manifesto needs to be printed. There is a crisis which none of your policies currently are able to address. How will you develop policy with only one week to go?' Only a small number of groups maintained that their initial, highly inclusive policy-making processes should apply; the majority instead argued that in such circumstances party leaders and experts should make policy, albeit with reference to party principles. One activist justified this decision by saying 'if there is only a week, because there is insufficient time to liaise, so it becomes the party leader'. But, interestingly, non-activists also voiced the same ideas, making comments such as:

> I think this is when the leadership, not the leader, the leadership of the party becomes more important.
> So they are going to have to pull in what they need and do it quick.
> And that is presumably that is how they got to that position, because they are good at doing those things.

These comments suggest that people are willing to compromise on inclusivity in certain circumstances, but believe that the idea of being inclusive and open is an important objective that parties should pursue.

Accessible

The sixth principle identified diagnoses a desire for parties to be accessible. Mirroring the finding of Chapter 3, it appears that citizens want to understand how they can get involved. Within workshop discussions, evidence emerged of a wish not only for more participatory opportunities, but also for a more proactive approach from parties in terms of engagement.

As discussed above, parties are often seen to be remote organisations, uninterested in citizens' views. In early workshop activities, non-activists frequently voiced the belief that parties didn't listen and needed to be 'visible more often, because you just don't see them till election time'. There was, accordingly, a desire for parties to be visible and to have 'a presence in the constituency', and 'not one that is just open on a Wednesday morning for two hours'. Although to some degree reflecting a desire for local representatives (as opposed to London-based actors), these comments also showed a wish for parties to be proactively courting engagement. A non-activist called for 'your local representative being accessible to you; it's you not having to go and find them where they are'. A participant in workshop 3 voiced a desire for parties and particularly party representatives to be 'proactively introducing themselves to every constituent'. When asked to reflect on party functions and what these organisations should be doing, many participants stressed the idea of accessibility, with people in workshop 3 asserting that parties should be 'being creative with drop-in sessions' and 'making themselves accessible'. In particular, there was a perceived need for parties to be reaching out to those who do not currently engage, as indicated by participants in workshop 3:

> [There is a need to compel parties] to ensure that they get out to the hard-to reach people and talk to them as well.
> It's door to door, isn't it?
> It is a little bit more than that … I am thinking about the hard-to-reach estates … the disabled.

These desires were voiced most forcefully by non-activists, but activists were also open to these ideas. Indeed, the idea of accessibility featured in the top 10 words cited by activists in workshop 1. Workshop discussion saw them noting the importance of being 'open to lobbying and influence, but … also transparent – that what it does is visible, that it has that culture of engaging in that way'. There was also a willingness for parties to engage and get more people involved, although activists were cautious about the practical implications of this for parties. Accessibility was not, therefore, valued only by non-activists but was seen to have wider appeal.

Elsewhere, workshop discussion showed that desires for accessibility were particularly tied to representation. In order to represent people effectively, there was a perceived need for parties to be in contact with a range of views, and to not be guided by the party whip. Mirroring calls for inclusivity, a range of perspectives were valued, but it was acknowledged that, at present, many people were unwilling or unable to engage. In an ideal world, therefore, many citizens – and especially non-activists – saw proactive parties as key to securing inclusive political debate. One mechanism for achieving such accessibility was seen to be social media, with a number of groups arguing that:

You can access lots of people on that.

Absolutely, because not everyone is going to go to a social event because of work commitments and so on, but they can always join a group on their break or whatever.

So it is not geographically based, is it? So you can get people from all over.

Activists and non-activists alike were therefore keen to explore ways of getting people involved, especially thinking about new channels that could ensure that people were engaged in a way that is, as one activist put it, 'meaningful … [and feels] as though it is actually building up to something which is a decision point or about informing choices and alternatives'. Dovetailing with the importance of efficacy raised in Chapter 3, there accordingly appeared to be a desire for accessible parties, in which people can have an impact, and, importantly, be aware of that impact.

Integrity

A final desire for party conduct falls under the heading of integrity. Apparent in participants' current views of parties, there was a prevailing belief that parties and their representatives are untrustworthy, duplicitous, corrupt and self-interested individuals. Reflecting these beliefs, activists and non-activists alike were quick to articulate the need for parties to display more integrity in each facet of democratic linkage.

Tracing participants' desires, authenticity and honesty recurred as key ideas associated with integrity. One table discussed the idea of politicians being role models:

I know nobody is perfect, they are only human, but I think that maybe what is missing … is being a good role model, being an ethical person, by what we would all judge to be, like, you know, not cheating on your tax expenses.

Yeah.

… So you want integrity?

I am just wondering how we can term this.

So a leader that is ethical.

> What I am trying to say is … a good political [party] should be a
> good role model.

In particular, participants in workshops 2 and 3 indicated that
'honest is the fundamental thing, because you need to believe your
politicians'. It was therefore argued that '[i]f they were a bit more
honest we can believe and trust them', with others contending that
they desired 'honesty and integrity because even if it is something
bad, if they are honest about it then they are not being deceptive at
all'. There were, accordingly, routine calls for parties to be 'honest
with their agenda'. This idea also connected to communication,
with a non-activist arguing that parties needed 'honesty to face
unpleasant facts sometimes, and to tell the electorate whatever that
might mean'. A participant in workshop 3 similarly stated, 'even if it
is something bad, if they are honest about it then they are not being
deceptive at all'. Interestingly, these kinds of comment were not
routinely voiced in workshop 1, with only a few activists describing
parties as dishonest. This is perhaps unsurprising, given that these
actors are invested in the political system, but it does suggest that
there may be different views here.

What was particularly notable from workshop discussions was
the degree to which ideas about integrity and favourable conduct
informed wider desires for democratic linkage. Asked to think
about the kind of reform (if any) parties needed, one participant
in workshop 2 argued that 'all these things [representation, participation and governance] are great, but if you haven't got that
perception of being honest and representing people then I don't
think it matters how you try and engage'. Another non-activist reflected this idea:

> It comes down to the kind of fundamental kind of principles that
> we talked about first, that unless you are open, honest, trustworthy
> then however you engage with people, it is not going to make any
> difference unless you change the fundamental principles of how you
> operate.

Such comments suggest that integrity is an important benchmark against which parties are viewed, and also that there are concrete desires for certain types of behaviour to characterise how parties work.

Conclusion

This chapter has looked beyond theories of democratic linkage to explore the relevance of party conduct for citizens' perceptions and desires. Reviewing workshop and Party Survey data, I have argued that citizens pay attention to party conduct, and have relatively consistent perceptions and desires. By examining prevailing views, I have shown that party conduct is currently seen in negative terms, with concerns about integrity, an electoral focus and dogmatic partisan behaviour. Perhaps most notably, these negative views are held by activists and non-activists alike, revealing a wide-ranging desire for change.

In terms of desires, this chapter has identified seven principles that capture citizens' desires. Many of these ideas overlap and intersect, offering a vision of how people would like parties to conduct themselves. Although supported by activists and non-activists to different degrees, these ideas were not opposed by any single group; rather, they were seen to be important or feasible to different extents. Characterising citizens' desires, I have argued that there is a wish for parties that are transparent, communicative, reliable, principled, inclusive, accessible, and that act with integrity.

In thinking about the kind of reforms these findings suggest may have appeal, it is likely that initiatives designed to recruit representatives from a wider range of backgrounds or to spread more information about party actions and rationales are likely to have appeal. It also appears that initiatives such as codes of behavioural conduct are wanted. There are, accordingly, a number of different reforms that appear to align with these desires, suggesting that this is a fruitful area in which to pursue change.

In outlining these principles, this chapter has shown that people desire a shift in the way parties conduct themselves. As with previous chapters, this does not signal a radical change in the way politics is done, neither does it suggest a nostalgia for the politics of the past. Instead, these findings indicate a desire for parties to update their practices in line with modern ideas and norms. In calling for a more inclusive, less dogmatic and more reliable politics, citizens indicate a desire for party conduct to be reimagined.

The next chapter turns to review the findings thus far in this study, asking whether citizens' desires are coherent and what traits define this reimagined ideal.

Chapter 6

What do citizens want and can this be realised?

As outlined so far in the book, people's desires for parties are complex and multifaceted. Having interrogated how citizens' view democratic linkage, and explored their ambitions for party conduct, it appears that people possess a range of desires. Moreover, previous chapters have shown that, for many respondents, parties are not living up to their wishes, resulting in gaps between perceptions and ideals. For parties seeking to understand how they are viewed, and potentially considering how they might respond to these cumulative findings, this poses a dilemma, as it is not clear what form of response parties should make or how any reaction is likely to be received.

In this chapter, I revisit the findings reported in the previous chapters to highlight areas of possible response. Reviewing data collectively, I challenge the idea that parties are seen in uniformly negative terms and that citizens want parties to change in every respect. Rather, I argue that it is possible to identify different kinds of ideal that are supported to different degrees. Reviewing first quantitative and then qualitative insights, I argue that it is possible to highlight a small number of areas in which a large number of citizens would like to see parties change. Identifying these ideas, I do not prescribe specific reforms or initiatives that address particular data points, but instead distil the principles that underpin citizens' unrealised desires. This approach leads me to consider the *kind* of change that people desire. I identify an interest in parties that are open and inclusive, responsive and responsible, and that offer principled leadership. By comparing these ideals with established principles of party democracy, I argue that people's wishes do not amount to a rejection of partisan politics, but rather suggest a desire for the ethos of party politics to be reimagined.

In this chapter, therefore, I indicate a direction for possible response and identify a set of reimagined party ideals. However, in doing so, I argue that it is important to recognise certain challenges that may frustrate any attempt to change. Discussing issues of universality and reliability, I show why reimagined ideals may not be greeted favourably, and why efforts to change are not guaranteed to produce desired results. Highlighting these dynamics, I reflect on the challenges parties face in producing favourable views.

What do citizens want from parties?

In reviewing the last four chapters it appears that citizens have a range of unrealised demands, suggesting there are many possible areas in which parties may wish to consider change. And yet what has also begun to emerge is evidence that citizens' perceptions are not uniformly negative, and that there are, indeed, interesting variations in the way people answer questions about their ideals and views. In turning to think about this data cumulatively, I argue that it is important to recognise and contemplate these differences in order to identify areas where parties may want to prioritise any response.

In outlining this objective it is important to acknowledge the challenge of drawing insights from the different forms of data presented throughout this book. Whilst quantitative and qualitative methods have allowed a rich picture of citizens' preferences to be developed, they also produce different kinds of insight, which can make it difficult to draw neat conclusions about citizens' desires. In considering, for example, the extent to which citizens support a certain ideal, quantitative data can be easily explored to determine the precise extent of support, and yet qualitative workshop data is less amenable to such simple quantification and analysis. In thinking about the form of change that citizens want to see, and the areas where there is most consensus around the need for change, I therefore adopt a two-stranded approach, looking first at quantitative survey insights, before turning to integrate and explore the qualitative workshop findings. To aid this analysis, it is useful to begin by reviewing the findings presented in previous chapters, offering a simplified overview of the data gathered thus far.

First, looking at findings on representation, Chapter 2 revealed that:

- Most respondents favour delegate (72%) and trustee (72%) representation and, to a slightly lesser extent, partisan representation (66%). However, in practice, parties are seen to realise these desires to different degrees, with 61% feeling that parties act in line with partisan desires, and under half feeling this way about trustee (42%) and delegate (36%) behaviour.
- Over half of respondents think that special interests (50%) and the majority (65%) should be thought about more than half the time in party policy-making, but in practice the only group seen by over half of respondents to be listened to is electors (51%). Special interests, experts and the majority are seen to be listened to less than desired (with large gaps regarding the majority and experts). In contrast, party members and electors are seen to be listened to more than desired.
- Half of respondents want to see parties respond 'sometimes' to citizens' demands, and yet only 39% believe them to do so. A similar gap is evident in the ideals and perceptions of those who want parties to change 'very often', but fewer respondents selected this option (21% ideal, 12% current).

Chapter 3, on participation, went on to to present the following key findings:

- Whilst 45% of respondents say that want more opportunities to participate, on average two-thirds (between 51% and 74%, depending on activity) voice no intention of actually engaging.

- Whilst 70% of respondents think participation should have an impact, only 17% report feeling that they can have an impact.
- There is support for different forms of affiliation for different party activities, with 57% favouring low requirements for discussion and 39% favouring high requirements for policy-making.
- Over half of respondents think it is very important for members to have the power to discuss (58%) or propose (55%) ideas, with 32% thinking it is important to be able to make decisions.
- Respondents want opportunities for participation online and offline, with workshops showing a desire for different mediums to be used simultaneously by parties.

Chapter 4, on governance, revealed that:

- People want parties to deliver promised policies and good policy outcomes, but 76% do not see parties to do well on delivering promises and 68% don't see them to deliver good policy outcomes.
- People want parties to manage the day-to-day running of government and crises, but 55% do not see parties to manage day-to-day running well and 49% do not see them to manage crises well (the single largest group in each case).
- Most respondents (63%) want parties to focus equally on short-term demands and long-term needs, but people don't perceive this to happen in practice, with attention instead seen to be focused on short-term demands (57%).
- Nearly three-quarters of respondents (73%) think that it is most important (out of three possible options) for parties to make decisions supported by evidence and independent advice. However, in practice only 21% see parties to make decisions in this way, whilst 64% see them to make decisions by primarily thinking about electoral motivations.

Finally, Chapter 5, on party conduct demonstrated that:

- People want parties to be transparent, providing more information about structures and decision-making. However, parties are currently seen to lack transparency and to provide limited insight into how decisions are made.
- People want parties to be communicative, engaging people in two-way communication and explaining outcomes. However, parties are currently seen to communicate only at election time, and to offer limited feedback or outreach.
- People want parties to be reliable by presenting and enacting consistent positions. However, parties are currently seen to break promises and to be untrustworthy.
- People want parties to be principled, offering distinctive visions of the national interest. However, parties are currently seen to be opportunistic and self-interested.
- People want parties to be inclusive by incorporating a range of different voices and ideas. However, parties are currently seen to be closed and dogmatically partisan, shutting out alternative voices.
- People want parties to be accessible, providing a range of different ways for people to get involved. However, parties are currently seen to be accessible to only a few.
- People want parties to act with integrity, being honest and trustworthy. However, parties are currently seen to be dishonest, untrustworthy and corrupt.

Looking at the findings in this simplified way, it appears that people often outline desires that they do not perceive to be realised. Whether thinking about the style of representation, impact of participation, governing focus or party behaviour, there are many areas in which citizens articulate an ideal that is not reflected in reality. This suggests that people want parties to change, and to change not only in how they link to citizens but also in how they behave. This presents a daunting prospect for parties, which appear to need to react simultaneously to a range of different demands. And yet, as the data summarised above suggests, there are differences in responses that suggest more or fewer people hold the same view. This makes it important to consider these findings in more detail, exploring the extent to which parties are seen to be out of kilter with desires, and the degree to which people have a unified conception of party practices and ideals. In thinking about these points, I first consider quantitative insights from the Party Survey findings.

Analysis in previous chapters has shown there to be many underlying patterns in people's survey responses. As the Sankey diagrams have shown, people do not answer the same questions in entirely the same way, but often display very different configurations of views. Whilst some people may hold ideals that they do not see to be realised, others may have their desires exceeded, and others may be content. Although unrealised desires are likely to be of most interest to those wanting to identify a direction for party change, it is important to recognise that there are instances in which most respondents do not exhibit such views. For many questions, respondents indicated that current practices aligned with their ideals – a point conveyed by the presence of a horizontal line on Sankey diagrams between two equivalent statements. Figure 2.3 provides an example of this: when answering a question on representative style, the single largest group of respondents answered that parties should think about partisan representation and in practice did so. Throughout the data gathered in this book there are, however, interesting variations in the number of people answering questions in different ways. Figures 2.4 and 2.5, for example, which report data on trustee and delegate styles, show that many people felt that parties acted in line with their desires, but in these cases the number selecting this option was lower than for the partisan case and, in the delegate question, was not the most popular answer. What these diagrams therefore reveal, and what the headline figures often mask, is that change is not always desired, and that varying numbers of people are content with how parties work.

Noting this, it becomes interesting to consider how many people report that their ideals have been met and how many feel that they have not. Large numbers of respondents report that their ideals are met in regard to representative style (Figures 2.3–2.5) and responsiveness (Figure 2.11), but far fewer people report the same about representative source (specifically in regard to the majority) (Figures 2.9 and 2.10) or participatory impact (Figure 3.3). This indicates that these are areas where more people (and often the majority of respondents) are not having their desires met. For parties interested in reacting to this data, this suggests that there are certain issues (i.e. representative source and participatory impact) for which there is a larger incentive to react to citizens' views.

Building on this point, the data summarised above also indicates that there are differences in people's understanding of ideal and actual party behaviour. Far from thinking that the same practices are ideal or evident, different respondents think about parties in different ways and there can, accordingly, be different degrees of consensus about the way that parties are viewed. These differences are, once again, evident in the Sankey diagrams. Whilst in some cases almost equal numbers of people selected different options (suggesting a lack of consensus about what is happening or should be done), in others people coalesced around one response (suggesting more unified views). Focusing on ideals, evidence of consensus could be seen in the question on governing motivation, where almost all respondents ranked evidence and independent advice first as an ideal (with very few people selecting other rankings) (Figure 4.6). A similar example was evident in the question on responsiveness and responsibility in governing (Figure 4.5), which showed that most people believe parties should act equally in line with short-term and long-term imperatives. Looking at the data in this way, it appears that parties may want to prioritise responsiveness, participatory opportunities and impact, governing focus and governing motivations, as here there was a high degree of consensus around ideals. However, they may wish to deprioritise representative source (except in the case of the majority) and representative style (except in the case of delegate representation), where a single ideal was not widely favoured.

Thinking about the quantitative data as a whole, it therefore appears there are important variations in the survey questions that suggest different degrees of demand for change, and different degrees of consensus for the kind of change required. Given the likelihood that parties will want to respond most urgently to views that are widely held and agreed on (as opposed to being contested), it appears that when both of these traits are evident there will be a greater incentive to pursue change.

Thinking about this point in regard to the data summarised above, it appears that, on representativeness, parties are not incentivised to act on partisan representation, but have a slight incentive to promote more delegate forms of representation (as fewer people are satisfied, and the single largest group of people favour an alternative form of behaviour). On representative source, there is an incentive to promote majority views, as few people feel that parties act in line with their desires and there is consensus around this ideal. On responsiveness, there is a compelling case for change, as very few people feel that their desires are met, and there is strong support for parties to change 'sometimes'. When it comes to participation, where less quantitative data on ideals and perceptions was collected, there is some evidence to support reform. There appears to be a high level of consensus around the need for participatory opportunities, for citizens to understand their impact, and for multi-speed engagement opportunities. However, it should also be noted that few people actually intend to use more participatory opportunities, a finding that may deprioritise this form of change for those interested in driving increased engagement. Finally, on governance, the last area in which quantitative data was presented (Chapter 4), it appears that there is an incentive to focus on improving managerial (over service) governing functions, with the largest proportions of respondents viewing parties to perform these functions well. There is also considerable support for parties to focus more on balancing short-term demands and long-term needs, as few respondents feel their demands are met, and there is a high degree of consensus around ideal behaviour. Finally, there is also compelling evidence for parties to prioritise incorporating expert voices into their governing motivations, as few people had their ideal ranking met and there was, again, clear consensus around the demand for change. Looking at the data in this way, it appears that citizens' responses are not uniform, and that there are different desires that parties are likely to be more or less attracted to pursuing.

And yet, as acknowledged above, this analysis reviews only part of the data presented in previous chapters – a wealth of qualitative material and insights have also been provided that can help refine this understanding. In turning to integrate the insights of the qualitative data, I focus upon the data presented in Chapter 5, where a wealth of information around citizens' ideals for party behaviour was reviewed. Focusing on this data, it is possible, as above, to consider the extent to which participants were calling for change, and the degree to which there was consensus around the form that change should take.

In considering the first question, around demand for change, the analysis presented in Chapter 5 demonstrated a concerted interest in reform. Gathering data on activist and non-activist perceptions of party practices, it appeared that parties were almost uniformly viewed in negative terms, with even those invested in these organisations calling for change. The form of this change was expansive and, as summarised above, highlighted a need to shift seven aspects of party behaviour that were viewed negatively. On this evidence, it appears that there is a demand for behavioural change. And yet, as above, when looking in more detail at this data, it is possible to identify variations in the extent of support for certain shifts.

Revisiting the qualitative material, it is important to restate that, far from being uniformly supported, there are differences in the extent to which different types of participant (activist or not) favour these ideas. Reviewing the comments made by actors within different workshops, it appears that activists and non-activists alike voice considerable support for the idea that parties should be transparent, principled, inclusive and accessible. However, less universal support is found in regard to the other principles. Indeed, support for parties being communicative and acting with integrity was primarily emphasised by non-activists, with only limited support from activists on these themes and often different reasons for such support. Non-activists tended to call for on-going proactive communication from parties, whilst activists raised concerns about the feasibility of executing such ideas. Similarly, non-activists highlighted the need for more honesty and integrity, whilst activists did not tend to place much prominence on these themes (although, it is notable that activists in workshop 3 did not contradict these ideas when raised by non-activists). In the final case, that of reliability, support for this idea was almost uniformly voiced by non-activists, who repeatedly called for binding manifesto promises and metrics by which parties could be held to account. But these demands were not made by activists and, indeed, within workshop 3 (the mixed workshop), many activists raised concerns about such ideas. When it comes to reliability, therefore, there are signs of less extensive support for this idea.

These insights are likely to be of interest to parties because they suggest that any attempt to enact these ideals will appeal to different groups. Attempting to become more reliable may attract support from non-activists, but it may do little to address the ideals of activists or those previously engaged with the party. Whilst specific parties are likely to pay differing degrees of attention to the views of activists, depending on their significance to the party organisation as a whole, it is likely that they will be attracted to those views that are most widely held. In line with this supposition, it appears that parties are most incentivised to take action to become more transparent, principled, inclusive and accessible. There is a weaker incentive to focus on being communicative and acting with integrity, as there is less consensus amongst different actors about what this means (and more reticence from activists about the practical implications of such an approach). However, if parties are interested in reaching out to those not engaged in the party, there does appear to be a wide degree of agreement amongst non-activists about what is desired here, with more proactive communication and on-going engagement widely called for. A similar conclusion may also be drawn in relation to reliability, but it is notable that, in this case, the idea is actively contested by activists, suggesting that it may not be greeted in positive terms by this group. When looking at this data in more detail, it therefore appears that there are certain areas in which there is consensus around the desirability and form of change.

In pooling insights from these two forms of data, it appears that there are widely held, unrealised desires for parties that promote majority views, change sometimes (but not very often), provide more participatory opportunities and demonstrate impact, improve their managerial (over service) governing functions, balance short-term demands and long-term needs, and incorporate expert voices into their governing motivations. There is also an incentive for parties to be more transparent, principled, inclusive and accessible. What is particularly notable is that, far from being confined to one area of party activity, these desires span different aspects of party linkage and behaviour, suggesting a need for change not in one area but in a range of different spaces. Indeed, many of these ideas interlink and overlap, with calls for more transparent and inclusive attributes dovetailing with desires for parties to integrate majority views and demonstrate the impact of engagement. In noting these tendencies, I argue that it is useful to develop these findings by thinking not about the specific policy responses or actions that parties may want to take in relation to specific data points, but rather about the principles that appear common to these different ideals.

This approach is necessary because the data gathered in this book was not collected in a way that tested specific policy ideas. In discussing the concepts of representation, participation, governance and conduct, I explored often abstract principles that can be advanced in very different ways. This makes it challenging to prescribe specific policy responses, as it is not clear that people will view certain initiatives as likely to advance favoured ideas. For instance, a call for open primaries may not be seen as making parties more accessible, and a larger online web presence may not be deemed to promote transparency. This makes it difficult to use this data to prescribe specific policy responses, as the relationship between ideals and policy interventions has not been directly explored.

For these reasons, I re-examined the widely held, unrealised ideals identified above to explore whether there are certain recurring themes and ideas that connect these desires. Through an iterative, reductive coding process, I identified three clusters of ideas: a desire for 'open and inclusive parties', 'responsive and responsible parties' and parties that offer 'principled leadership'. Each theme is summarised below. By discussing these findings I hope to make two points. First, I show that, far from amounting to isolated demands, these widely reported unrealised desires coalesce around certain themes and highlight a wish for an alternative party ethos that spans all aspects of democratic linkage and party behaviour. In essence, I argue that citizens want to see a reimagination of political parties. Second, and building on this point, I use this approach to consider the extent to which these desires represent a departure from traditional conceptions of party democracy. In the context of support for more populist and even technocratic forms of government, I examine the extent to which citizens desire a different form of democratic politics.

Open and inclusive parties

In beginning to consider the kind of parties that many citizens desire but do not perceive, it is useful to note a clear and recurring interest within the data in openness and inclusivity. Apparent in exercises and survey questions, both the Party Survey and the workshop discussions showed activists and non-activists' desires for parties to listen to a range of representative constituencies. In particular, there was a wish for parties to listen more to majority views – with unrealised ideals around delegate representation and the majority as a representative source. These ideas were not just confined to discussions of representation, but also appeared in reflections on participation and party conduct. Chapter 3 showed a desire for parties to make it easier for people to get involved, and to see the impact of that participation. Chapter 5 showed that both activists and non-activists support the idea of parties acting in a transparent and inclusive way, with non-activists also interested in communicative, accessible parties. These desires span different aspects of linkage and conduct and highlight an important way in which parties need to change. It therefore appears that many citizens are likely to be attached to initiatives designed to integrate different voices and that make it easier to understand the influence different individuals have.

What is interesting in drawing this conclusion is that, when looking back to the Introduction and the principles seen to define parties' institutional status, these desires do not suggest a radical shift away from the core principles of party democracy. As outlined in the Introduction, parties emerged as the key mechanism through which citizens could channel their ideas into the political system. Traditionally, these organisations have been seen to enable representation by facilitating participation, integrating and aggregating different views, managing conflict and expressing citizens' demands (Sartori, 2005). The above desires suggest on-going support for these ideas, indicating that people want parties to aggregate different perspectives and mediate between these demands. And yet, unlike in previous conceptions of parties as 'mass party' organisations that tended to aggregate the opinions of certain sections of society (Duverger, 1954), this data suggests that many people want parties to integrate a wider variety of views and ideas. There is a desire for parties to look beyond party supporters, by engaging experts and those with alternative views. There are also calls to make it easier for people of all persuasions to participate in (certain) party activities, by adopting multi-speed party structures. It therefore appears that there is a desire to reconcile established principles with more pluralist, inclusive ideas.

Responsive and responsible parties

Looking at the other widely held, unrealised ideals distilled above, it also appears that there is support for the idea of parties being responsive and responsible. Indeed, many respondents simultaneously reported unrealised desires for parties to be more responsive to citizens *and* made demands for parties to act in the long-term interests of the nation. These findings emerged most prominently in chapters on representation and governance, where the Party Survey directly asked about citizens' views. In regard to representation, there were some signs that people favoured responsiveness, with calls for parties to listen to the majority and significant qualitative data demonstrating a desire for parties to listen to the people more. And yet further analysis suggested that people were not demanding entirely responsive or populist governance, but also recognised the need for responsibility. When asked about representative responsiveness, participants indicated a desire for parties to be receptive to change (changing 'sometimes') rather than being entirely adaptive (changing 'very often'). There was also support for trustee representation alongside delegate representation and Chapter 4 additionally showed a wish for parties to focus equally on short-term demands and long-term needs. There were also indicators that many citizens had unrealised desires for the role of experts in decision-making, with qualitative analysis showing the perceived importance of these actors in helping to identify desirable long-term goals. Far from calling for responsiveness *or* responsibility, this data therefore indicates the perceived value of both ideas. From this evidence, therefore, it appears that many people are likely to be attracted to parties that are simultaneously open, inclusive and responsive to people's demands, but that also pay regard to and explain the influence of longer-term factors. It also indicates a desire for parties to redistribute the weight of their attention, focusing less on electoral responsiveness (Caramani, 2017; Goetz, 2014; Lees-Marshment, 2001), and more on longer-term needs and interests.

In thinking about the principles of party democracy, it is interesting to note that these ideas do not contradict established principles, but actually reflect an established tension that parties negotiate. As outlined in the Introduction, parties are seen to be responsive and responsible organisations that navigate the demands of both citizens and that state. Indeed, parties are seen to be distinctive from other organisations because they perform these dual roles. As Keman (2014) has argued, this can make it hard for parties to secure legitimacy, as it is necessary for them to deliver publicly acceptable outcomes, and yet there is established precedent for parties to act contrary to public demands. Parties have therefore traditionally been seen to need to manage the balance between responsiveness and responsibility, suggesting that these desires, whilst challenging to satisfy, are not impossible to realise.

Principled leadership

Reviewing the other findings, a third cluster of widely held, unrealised ideals emerged that related to the idea of party principles and leadership. Whilst perhaps appearing to be in tension with calls for majority representation and a role for experts, there was evidence that many citizens believe that parties need to offer principled agendas and leadership. These indicators were diverse and emerged when discussing different aspects of party activity and conduct. In Chapter 2, for example, explicit support for partisan representation and constituencies was shown. Although there are some questions about the degree to which the equivalence between ideals and perceptions reflects slightly different understandings of the term 'partisan representation', it appears that most citizens support the idea of parties being motivated by partisan drives. There was also majority support for the idea of parties listening to special interests more than half the time, and a wish for parties to demonstrate leadership when deciding when to respond to public demands, and when not. In addition, as discussed in Chapter 4, participants voiced strong support for parties acting in the national interest but, in doing so, they recognised that the national interest was not neutral, but was defined by distinctive partisan ideas. As such, participants acknowledged that principles were important for parties' ability to outline alternative visions of the national good. Support for principles and leadership was also stressed in Chapter 5, where activists and non-activists alike called for parties to outline their principles and explain difficult decisions when acting as governors. Cumulatively, these findings suggest that, far from calling for populist government that focuses solely on enacting the will of the people, many people have unrealised ideals for parties that outline and enact their principles and offer strong leadership. This does not suggest that people want parties that are dogmatic; instead, people want parties that are willing to reconsider positions and ready to explain why a decision has been made. It accordingly appears that many people want to see parties reimagined as actors that offer a different form of principled leadership, one that is less dogmatic and closed.

In thinking about the implications of these ideas for our understanding of democratic preferences, it once again appears that there is alignment between citizens' unrealised desires and established principles of party democracy. As argued by White and Ypi (2010, p. 814), it is widely agreed that parties should promote 'the *general* interest by expressing distinctive visions on the future of the polity' (original emphasis). Indeed, the provision of political choice through the presentation of different programmes and ideas is seen to be a vital mechanism through which citizens can display their preferences and hold governors to account. Whilst there is support for listening to the majority, this does not mean that citizens desire populist governance or direct democracy; rather, they are calling for more responsive governance within the context of a partisan system.

Summarising reimagined ideals

Having identified the findings likely to be of most interest to parties and having re-examined the data pertaining to these findings in more detail, it appears that there are certain common values and ideas that unite citizens' desires. Far from calling for isolated shifts that are confined to one area of linkage or party conduct, there is a desire for wide-ranging, cultural change. These findings are significant because many previous attempts to diagnose the 'problem' with parties have focused on one aspect of party behaviour – most commonly an element of democratic linkage – and yet these findings indicate that people's desires are multifaceted. This conclusion was supported by a question posed at the end of the workshops. To bring the four hours of discussion to a close, participants were asked about the relative importance of reforming policy-making processes, participatory opportunities or party governance. Faced with this question, participants could not confine their response to a single idea or to one of these areas; rather, their comments suggested a desire for more expansive change. A non-activist participant in workshop 2 asserted the importance of good governance, but explained this comment by saying that delivering 'good outcomes and competence depends on both representing what people want as well as carrying that out in a competent manner'. Another indicated the entwined nature of their ideas by responding that 'all these things are great [representation, participation and governance], but if you haven't got that perception of being honest and representing people then I don't think it matters how you try and engage'. These indicative comments suggest that a focus on specific data points as the inspiration for isolated reforms or initiatives is not sufficient to capture the kind of change that many respondents want to see. Rather, this data shows a desire for a change in party ethos, reimagining the way that parties operate.

In thinking about these principles and ideals, it is particularly notable that, rather than suggesting the rejection of partisan politics and the principles of party democracy, they instead represent an extension or reinterpretation of established principles. This indicates that it is not party politics per se that is seen to be problematic but, rather, the way in which established functions and ideas are currently being discharged. This is likely to be reassuring for those invested in political parties, as it suggests that, far from being re-dundant or dying institutions, these bodies continue to be seen as valuable by citizens.

Enacting reimagined party ideals: the challenges parties face

In identifying these unrealised ideals, this chapter has attempted to spotlight principles by which those interested in responding to these findings can react. And yet, in offering these conclusions, it is impor-tant to note two caveats about this public opinion data that affect how any response that parties do make will be viewed. These relate to the idea of universality and reliability, and highlight the fact that, first, these ideals are derived from the responses of a certain group of respondents (i.e. those with unrealised desires) and, second, they focus on abstract views of parties in general as opposed to judge-ments of how specific parties behave.

The first aspect of public opinion that needs to be recognised is the heterogeneity of public views. Throughout the analysis offered in this book, I have sought to show the diversity of opinions held by the public. As discussed above, the Sankey diagrams have been particu-larly illustrative in demonstrating the diversity of people's views. In isolating instances where there is a high degree of consensus around an unrealised ideal, the above analysis does not explore the views of those who expressed views different from those of most others. Recognising this focus is important: not all citizens hold the same views, and there will, accordingly, be a number of citizens who do not support reimagined ideals. Parties interested in responding to this data have to recognise that any reaction designed in response to these principles is likely to be seen positively by some citizens (who indicate unrealised desires) but negatively (or at best indifferently) by those who do not hold such views.

One point that is likely to reassure parties interested in responding to these ideals is that the types of people who voice unrealised desires are relatively diverse. Indeed, returning to the logistic regressions conducted in previous chapters, it appears that few consistent variables predicted the tendency to indicate unrealised desires. Across the different models, it variously appeared that, at different points, age, gender, educational level, voting behaviour and knowledge about how parties work helped predict how a question was answered. However, the only consistently present factor in most of the models was trust, with people who reported low levels of trust in parties more likely to say that parties are not behaving in line with desires. Importantly, it did not appear that the party a respondent supports or level of partisanship made significant differences in how people answered questions, with only a few instances where these variables were likely to predict response (see Tables A.2–A.8, Appendix 3). These insights are important, as they suggest that those who are not seeing their desires realised are relatively heterogeneous. It is not, therefore, only supporters of one party or non-voters who have unrealised desires. For parties that are conscious about the audience they are trying to reach, this should provide some reassurance, as they are not reacting to the views of a single group whose desires and ideals they may not share.[1] Rather, this data reflects views held by a cross-section of society.

The second aspect of this public opinion data that parties may want to contemplate is the extent to which the findings can be seen as a reliable guide for how parties will actually be judged. As suggested in the Introduction, citizens' views can often be unpredictable, and previous research has shown that people answer questions differently when asked about abstract or specific propositions. This raises questions about the extent to which this data on unrealised desires provides a reliable guide to the evaluations citizens make in practice.

In thinking about this point, it is useful to acknowledge that there is significant evidence that partisan filters affect how particular parties are viewed (Bartels, 2002; Jerit and Barabas, 2012; Mayne and Hakhverdian, 2017). This point was particularly evident in workshop discussions and the open-text Party Survey comments that revealed that parties are viewed in different ways. In the workshops, one activist commented '[i]t's difficult, because it depends on which party. If I think of that party I'll give that answer, if I think of that party I give that answer', whilst others noted that negative words applied 'differently to Conservative and Labour'. In part this reflects the belief that some parties are more or less aligned with citizens' desires – as evident in the assertion that 'some parties have better structures within them to try and find what matters to people, so that those beliefs can be represented'. However, in other instances, partisan judgements were made despite little knowledge of differences in how parties worked. Instead, it appeared that pre-existing judgements and preferences coloured citizens' views. This suggests that partisan preferences are a powerful lens through which parties' activities are judged, and that even when parties exhibit the traits citizens profess to favour, they may not be viewed in positive terms.

This insight has important implications when considering parties' capacity to address citizens' unrealised desires. It makes it unlikely, for example, that reforms to make the Conservative Party more open and inclusive will be judged in the same way by Conservative and Labour Party supporters (with the former more positive and the latter more sceptical). Similarly, supporters of the UK Independence Party (UKIP) and the Green Party are likely to have different views about the extent to which UKIP offers principled leadership. Far from operating on a level playing field, it therefore appears that parties have to contend with different prejudices and ideas, which makes it almost impossible for parties to be seen to realise all citizens' desires. In the Conclusion, I return to this point, to consider the extent to which specific parties are seen to align with stated desires. Yet here it is useful to note that parties looking to promote the reimagined ideal identified above should not expect to elicit uniformly positive views, as variations in public opinion will continue to play an important role in shaping how parties are viewed.

Conclusion

Looking back over the data gathered in the previous four chapters, a formidable series of desires can be observed. It appears that people have multifaceted wishes for parties, and value different things when it comes to representation, participation, governance and party conduct. Moreover, it appears that for many people these high ideals are not fulfilled. In seeking to draw conclusions from this data, in this chapter I have argued that it is possible to discern a range of insights. Looking at both quantitative and qualitative findings, I have shown, at the most basic level, that citizens' views are not uniformly negative and that there are many areas in which parties are acting in line with majority desires. There are also seen to be important variations in the degree to which citizens agree about the form of ideal party practices. Taking these points together, it appears that there are certain areas where there is a greater incentive to pursue change, namely, where large numbers of respondents and/or activists and non-activists report the same unrealised desire.

In highlighting the specific data points that parties may want to consider reacting to, within this chapter I have not sought to prescribe specific policy responses, but instead have identified the common principles that underpin unrealised desires. Adopting this approach, I have identified a desire for parties that are open and inclusive, that balance responsive and responsible imperatives, and that offer principled leadership. This approach helps to highlight the desire for change not just in one area of party linkage or conduct, but across the breadth of party behaviour. It also reveals that, far from calling for a departure from established principles of party democracy, many citizens instead appear to desire an evolution in the way parties behave. These principles therefore signal the form of adaptation and change that many citizens would like to see – providing guidelines for parties seeking to reimagine their practices in line with unrealised desires. In planning any response it is, however, vital for parties to recognise that change will not be viewed in uniformly favourable terms. The heterogeneous nature of public opinion and the influence of partisan filters mean that any reaction will be judged in different ways by different people. There is, accordingly, no quick or easy solution for parties interested in changing how they are viewed. Equipped with these insights, the next chapter turns to consider how parties may wish to respond.

Conclusion

This book set out to explore what citizens want from political parties. Recognising the generally negative terms in which parties are described, and noting many parties' interest in improving how they are viewed, I was keen to explore what, precisely, citizens want from parties and how they see parties to measure up against these ideals. Examining three different facets of democratic linkage and looking at citizens' views of party conduct, I have offered a range of nuanced insights into how parties are viewed that will be of interest to politicians and other party actors. Viewed collectively, these findings have shown that people's views of parties are not uniformly negative and that their desires are multifaceted. Although it is not possible to talk in singular terms about what 'the public' thinks about parties, I have argued that many people have unrealised ideals that demonstrate a desire for parties to be more open and inclusive, responsive and responsible, and to offer principled leadership. I argue that these principles capture the kind of reform that many people would like to see. Moreover, they offer a vision for party reimagination that does not suggest a radical departure from established principles of party democracy but, rather, a desire to bring old ideas into line with modern ideas and norms.

In this final chapter, I reprise the idea of the reimagined party and, building on this foundation, consider how parties may wish to respond. This involves thinking about this data in a slightly different way. Whilst up until this point I have discussed views of parties in general, in this chapter I present new data, which explores views of specific British parties. Testing the resonance of the reimagined ideas outlined in Chapter 6, I consider the extent to which different parties are seen to exhibit these ideas, and explore the way that partisan preferences affect how parties are viewed. This allows me to consider the incentive for different parties to react to the insights presented in this book.

In considering parties' different fortunes, I then argue that it is important to interrogate the nature of any response parties may wish to make. Whilst the book has so far made an implicit assumption that parties will want to reform in line with these insights, in this chapter I argue that there are different ways in which parties may wish to react. Whilst many parties may wish to pursue *reform* that attempts to mirror citizens' ideals, I also highlight the potential for parties to *re-educate* public views to show how they already exemplify many of the traits that citizens value. There may also be a wish to *recalibrate* citizens' views by challenging the ideals and benchmarks that citizens outline. Discussing these alternatives, I consider the influence an understanding of public perceptions may exert on contemporary politics. This involves, finally, considering the implications and limitations of this analysis to reflect on what this book tells us about the relationship between parties and citizens.

The reimagined response

The idea of the reimagined party provides a useful way of aggregating the insights provided in this book. Whilst it is possible for parties to draw valuable conclusions from the different data points presented in Chapters 2–5, cumulatively this data provides a different kind of insight for parties, highlighting unrealised ideals and common principles. Although not voiced by all respondents, throughout the book I have shown that a consistently large proportion of participants voice a desire for parties to behave differently. Although this finding may appear to suggest that citizens want it all, the data actually shows that citizens' desires are not insatiable, and that people have nuanced views about where parties are acting more or less in line with ideals.

In thinking about the nature of citizens' unrealised ideals, the last chapter demonstrated how synergies across different data points reveal a wish for parties that are open and inclusive, that are responsive and responsible, and that offer principled leadership. These desires appear to be a reaction against closed, electorally focused, dogmatic parties and suggest instead a wish for parties that include a diverse range of voices, that focus equally on long- and short-term goals, and that outline principles that guide but do not rigidly determine party views. There is, therefore, a preference for pluralist parties that are communicative, transparent and informed by values (as opposed to rigid ideologies). Statistical analysis has shown that a wide variety of people report this view, indicating that this type of reform is likely to appeal to a range of different individuals.

In identifying the principles that unite unrealised desires for representation, participation, governance and conduct, over successive chapters I have sought to move away from the tendency to specify particular policy responses or reform initiatives. Reflecting on certain challenges with this data and acknowledging the expansive range of desires identified, I argue that it is important not to reduce these findings to an endorsement of an isolated initiative or a quick fix. Rather than being confined to a single aspect of party activity, citizens' unrealised desires reflect multiple features of party organisation, suggesting that reforms aimed at just one area of party activity – such as participatory opportunities – are unlikely to satisfy unrealised desires. As such, parties interested in responding to public views need to think expansively about the form of change that may be required and the extent to which their current practices align with these ideals. A response that aims simply to add new functions or procedures to existing infrastructure is unlikely to address the unrealised desires identified, as what appears to be desired is a rethinking and updating of established principles of party democracy.

It is important to recognise that there is no single template for such reforms; rather, parties will need to interpret and promote these ideas in different ways. Reflecting pre-existing views and distinctive organisational practices, a range of reactions can be expected. In making this point, the analogy of reimagination as it occurs in the car industry is particularly valuable, as suggested in the Introduction. In the car industry, designers can think of many different ways in which they can incorporate desired features and traits into a new design; similarly, parties can react to these findings differently, resulting in distinctive interpretations of these reimagined ideals.

In reaching this conclusion, this book echoes a long-standing tradition of observing and prescribing organisational adaptation and change. Far from being static organisations that thrive or decline, parties continually evolve. These changes are often induced by external factors, with parties adapting to the cultural and organisational norms of any given time. The principles for party reimagination outlined in this book provide a new drive for change. By offering hitherto unavailable insights into what it is that citizens want from parties, I have attempted to stimulate debate about how parties may want to change. In taking this approach, one particularly striking feature of these findings is that, far from rejecting the principles of party democracy, citizens' desires are entirely compatible with the tenets of the party system. Indeed, whilst certain elements of populist and technocratic democracy are seen to have appeal, direct democracy and expert input are seen as a supplement to (rather than a replacement for) customary party norms. These findings therefore suggest that people want to see established principles of party democracy updated to reflect modern ideas and norms, suggesting that party democracy is here to stay.

Theorising party response

As outlined in the Introduction, public perceptions are an important component of politics, and political institutions and parties are often highly concerned with the way they are viewed. In electoral systems where parties need to court public appeal, and where awareness of public disengagement and disaffection is high (Hansard Society, 2019), there are many incentives for parties to attempt to respond to citizens' desires. For this reason, parties are likely to be interested in data on how they are viewed. And yet two questions need to be answered before parties are able to determine how they wish to respond. First, how do specific parties measure up against these reimagined principles? Second, what kind of response can parties make? Considering both these questions, I argue that different parties may wish to respond in very different ways.

General and specific perceptions

As outlined in the Introduction, this book has analysed attitudes towards parties at a regime level, asking about views of parties in general. This approach was adopted to explore whether certain ideas were associated with all parties rather than with specific organisations. As discussed in Chapter 6, there have, however, been indications that respondents think about specific parties differently. This outcome is perhaps unsurprising, as parties in Britain have different organisational structures and processes, and partisan pref-erences are an acknowledged influence on how parties are viewed. Given these points, it is interesting to consider whether certain parties are more closely aligned to reimagined ideals. For this reason, I fielded a small number of additional questions, in Party Survey 2. This survey asked more specific questions about *particular* parties, allowing me to generate additional insight into citizens' views of certain parties as opposed to parties in general. Administered once again by YouGov, it should be noted that the sample of respondents (1,692) was not the same as those who completed the earlier Party Survey, and the context was different – with this survey fielded on 8–9 April 2019 (as opposed to 17–21 November 2017). However, there was a high degree of alignment between the two sample groups – the preliminary survey questions showed the respondents had common demographic and attitudinal traits, and similar levels of party support (Table A.1, Appendix 1).

To test whether the respondents in this new sample (Party Survey 2) viewed the three reimagined principles favourably, the first survey item was:

> Thinking about the following ideas, how important, if at all, would you say it is that parties
>
> > behave in an open and inclusive way;
> >
> > respond to public demands;
> >
> > make responsible decisions;
> >
> > offer principled leadership.

In order to avoid conflation between the ideas of responsiveness and responsibility, the 'responsive and responsible' principle was split in two in the above question. Respondents were then asked to score these ideas from 0, 'not at all important', to 5, 'very important'. Collapsing the response categories to distinguish between those who felt that the ideas were not at all or not very important (options 1 and 2), that they were fairly or very important (options 4 and 5), or who suggested they were neither important nor unimportant (option 3), Figure 7.1 shows high levels of agreement with these ideas, suggesting that the reimagined ideals resonate with this new group of respondents.

Having verified support for these principles, respondents were then asked about the extent to which the Conservative Party, Labour Party and UKIP promoted these ideas. These three parties were selected because Labour and the Conservatives are established mainstream parties, and indeed 49% of survey respondents indicated that they supported one of these two. Support for a number of smaller parties could have been explored, but UKIP was chosen for analysis because it has received much recent attention for its anti-establishment rhetoric and agenda-setting powers (Abedi and

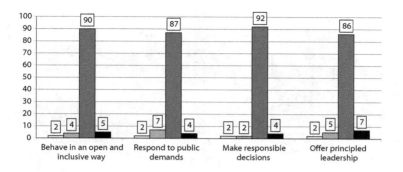

Figure 7.1 Party Survey 2: perceived importance of reimagined principles

Lundberg, 2009; Dennisson and Goodwin, 2015). There are, accordingly, reasons to believe that this party may be seen to be more aligned with reimagined ideals, as it has been claimed to be more responsive to public demands than mainstream parties, and to offer principled leadership.

Looking at the mean scores attributed to each party (Figure 7.2), no single party (of the three presented in Survey 2) is seen to entirely exemplify these ideas, with respondents tending to rank parties just below the mid-point of the scale. However, it is interesting that UKIP scored more highly than the Conservative and Labour Party when rated on 'responding to public demands', perhaps suggesting that UKIP is more aligned to reimagined ideals here. What is most striking, however, is that there is minimal variation between the two mainstream parties and the more marginal party. On this measure, all three parties could fruitfully consider these ideas, but it may be that UKIP would want to focus less on responsiveness and more on the other three ideals.

Developing these findings further, I looked at the extent to which supporters of specific parties are more likely to judge their own party more favourably. As discussed in Chapter 6, partisan filters can be

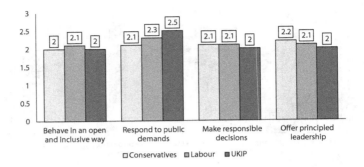

Figure 7.2 Party Survey 2: mean scores on the degree to which parties live up to reimagined ideals

an important influence on party judgements, so it would be expected that respondents are likely to score their own party more favourably, and give a lower score to opposing parties. To assess this, respondents were presented with the following:

> Political parties can be described in different ways. Thinking about the different political parties in the UK, to what extent do you think the [Conservative Party/Labour Party/UKIP] can be described in the following ways?

They were then presented with the same four categories as above and asked to score each party on a scale of 1–5, where 1 = not at all and 5 = completely (there was also a 'Don't know' option).

Looking at Table 7.1, which shows the mean scores for each party, broken down according to the party support of the respondents, it appears that, as expected, party supporters are likely to describe their chosen party in more favourable terms. Looking at the highlighted segments of Table 7.1, it appears that Conservative supporters judge their party more favourably than other parties (giving their party a mean ranking of 2.8 across the four indicators, whilst scoring Labour as 1.7 and UKIP as 2.2). The same phenomenon is also evident for Labour and UKIP, but is particularly striking

Table 7.1 Party Survey 2: mean scores of reimagined party principles by different partisan support groups

Party supporters	Conservative Party				Labour Party				UKIP			
	Open and inclusive	Respond to public demands	Responsible decisions	Offer principled leadership	Open and inclusive	Respond to public demands	Responsible decisions	Offer principled leadership	Open and inclusive	Respond to public demands	Responsible decisions	Offer principled leadership
Conservative	2.83	2.79	2.99	3.03	1.67	2.02	1.65	1.47	2.24	2.79	2.26	2.25
Cumulative mean	2.8				1.7				2.2			
Labour	1.73	1.89	1.75	1.83	3.09	3.14	3.19	3.20	1.60	2.22	1.61	1.62
Cumulative mean	1.7				3.0				1.6			
UKIP	1.63	1.61	1.63	1.74	1.43	1.45	1.41	1.28	3.83	4.16	3.75	3.83
Cumulative mean	1.6				1.4				3.8			
'Other' party supporters	1.76	1.92	1.85	1.96	2.27	2.43	2.28	2.25	1.60	2.27	1.56	1.70
Cumulative mean	1.8				2.3				1.6			
Supporters of no party	1.75	1.85	1.85	1.91	1.73	1.85	1.64	1.73	1.91	2.38	1.83	1.95
Cumulative mean	1.8				1.7				1.9			
Don't know	2.16	2.20	1.85	2.25	2.28	2.32	2.26	2.24	1.97	2.38	2.04	1.92
Cumulative mean	2.2				2.3				2.0			
All supporters	2.06	2.13	2.15	2.22	2.16	2.32	2.15	2.11	2.00	2.53	2.00	2.02
Cumulative mean	2.1				2.2				2.1			

in the UKIP case. UKIP supporters score their party far higher on these measures (3.8) than other party supporters, whilst scoring Labour and the Conservatives low (1.4 for Labour and 1.6 for the Conservatives). It is also interesting to note that those who indicated that they were supporters of no party tended to score each party roughly equally – with a mean score for the Conservatives of 1.8, for Labour of 1.7 and for UKIP of 1.9 across these reimagined ideals. This suggests that there is significant potential for each party to improve how they are viewed by unaligned voters.

Conducting logistic regression to look at the predictive significance of these scores, it appears that supporters of each party are significantly more likely to say their favoured party is enacting a given principle. So, for example, Labour supporters are significantly more likely to say that the Labour Party is 'open and inclusive' than to say that other parties are (Table A.8, Appendix 3). Whilst there are a few exceptions to this rule (see Table A8 for more detail), it is striking how prominently partisanship affects responses here.

Taking these findings as a whole, it appears that, whilst specific parties are seen to advance these principles to broadly the same degree, party supporters judge their favoured party more kindly. Thinking back to the last chapter, this means that attempts by parties to enact reimagined ideals are likely to be greeted differently by respondents with different partisan views. It should not, therefore, be expected that parties will be able to achieve uniformly positive views. Rather, partisan preferences mediate the extent to which different parties are seen to exhibit favourable practices.

Avenues for possible response

Having considered the difference between parties in general and specific parties, attention now turns to the kind of response parties may wish to make to these findings. Much attention has been given to parties' recent reforms of their organisational structure (Faucher, 2014; Gauja, 2015; Scarrow, 2014), reflecting the idea that parties may want to make 'attempts to improve the stature that they are held in among the broader public' (Martin, 2014, p. 15). And yet there is no guarantee that parties genuinely believe there to be 'real dysfunctions of political parties' (Poguntke and Scarrow, 1996, p. 258), or that they might accept the value of the data gathered here. Factors such as the capricious nature of public sentiments, the influence of the media and the seemingly inexhaustible nature of public demands (Hatier, 2012; Flinders, 2009, p. 343; Kimball and Patterson, 1997; Naurin, 2011; Stoker, 2006) may incentivise parties to react in different ways. In this section, I outline three possible responses, arguing that in addition to reforming, parties may reject citizens' perceptions and hence seek to re-educate citizens' ideas, or they may wish to recalibrate citizens' desires. These possible responses reflect Poguntke and Scarrow's (1996, p. 258) contention that the study of political parties is often focused on 'the interplay of elite arguments and mass sentiments'. It should not be presumed that parties will want to enact the principles I have identified, as they may wish to adopt an alternative response – or, indeed, make no response at all. With this in mind, three possible responses are considered in more detail.

Reform

The first course of action considered here is party reform. In recent years, many parties in the UK and around the world have enacted organisational reforms. Whilst a number of different imperatives can drive these shifts, it is common for reforms to be introduced as a reaction to negative public attitudes and engagement practices. Gauja has highlighted how politicians and official government documents have explained their decision to introduce reforms (in her specific case, primaries) by citing their ability to help parties 're-engage with the voters' and make 'parties more democratic, [by] consulting and getting more people involved in politics' (Gauja, 2012, pp. 654–5; see also Gauja, 2017). This rationale has led different political parties to pursue reforms to organisational structure and process by, for example, creating a category of registered supporters, experimenting with open primaries, creating online discussion forums, open policy consultations, and much besides. There are also examples of parties attempting to change their ethos and behaviour, such as when, on assuming the leadership of the Labour Party in 2015, Jeremy Corbyn introduced a new (and short-lived) approach to Prime Minister's Questions whereby he crowd-sourced questions from the public (Pickard, 2015).

Thinking about the precise changes that parties may want to consider, in the previous chapter I avoided outlining specific initiatives or reforms. In part this reflects a desire to think more expansively about the kind of changes citizens would like to see, but it also reflects the fact that initiatives can be implemented and enacted in different ways. It is not therefore automatically the case that an open primary will create a more open and inclusive party culture, or that a pledge to crowd-source parliamentary questions will result in more responsive practice. Parties need to consider that any reaction to reimagined ideals will not be about identifying the correct mechanism, but rather about rethinking party ethos.

Nevertheless, it is useful to identify a range of options available to parties interested in reform. To list just a few recent initiatives, parties have demonstrated the potential to do the following:

- create networks of registered supporters;
- open up leadership or representative selection processes;
- conduct public consultations;
- develop codes of conduct;
- create online discussion forums;
- facilitate grassroots activism and campaigning;
- empower local policy-making;
- bypass the media by using social media to communicate with voters;
- allow members to determine party priorities;

- publish party records online;
- create expert panels;
- open up meetings to the public;
- crowd-source policy ideas or parliamentary questions.

In addition to these established ideas, it is also possible to identify new styles of reform. For example, workshop discussion demonstrated a desire for binding manifesto promises and online interactive communication. The options for reform open to parties are therefore plentiful, but it should by no means be assumed that they will automatically advance the reimagined ideas I have identified.

To illustrate this point, it is useful to consider the idea of a registered supporters scheme. This reform allows members of the public to register their support for a party, often in exchange for a small fee, and, in return, they secure the right to vote in that party's leadership elections. The Labour Party introduced this reform in 2010 (Audickas et al., 2018, p. 14) and the Liberal Democrats have recently consulted on the idea. This reform has the potential to align with the desire for more open and inclusive parties, as it can provide more opportunities for participation and lower the barrier to engagement. These capacities appear to underline the Liberal Democrats' interest in this idea, as they have outlined how a scheme for supporters could 'open up our systems of membership and leadership to much wider participation than we currently enjoy. More accessible, and more responsive, we can become a new movement which will defend, reinvigorate and embody liberal democracy' (Liberal Democrats, 2018, p. 4). On this assessment, this kind of initiative appears well placed to advance the reimagined ideals outlined above. And yet, establishing a network of supporters will not automatically make a party seem more open and inclusive. For example, when the Labour Party used this scheme in its 2016 leadership election, a large number of people were excluded from joining because they had a history of supporting other parties (Schofield, 2016). In such circumstances, the reimagined ideals do not appear to be exemplified.

In evaluating the likely compatibility of specific reforms with these reimagined principles, it should also be noted that unrealised desires are multifaceted. It is therefore not only a desire for open and inclusive parties that is outlined, but also a wish for responsive and responsible parties and principled leadership. If considering an initiative such as a supporters scheme, it is therefore important for parties to think broadly about these different objectives and the extent to which they are promoted by a reform. In the case of a supporters scheme, it is vital to consider whether in addition to promoting an open and inclusive image, it establishes communication between supporters and party elites, to demonstrate responsiveness (or explain non-responsiveness). In essence, it is important to acknowledge the breadth of citizen demands and to think about how any response advances these. In doing so, there is also a need for parties to think about managing citizens' expectations of what specific reforms are able to achieve. Gerbaudo's work on digital parties emphasises this point, noting that an 'evident mismatch' between idealistic discourse and practice are 'bound to produce disillusion in party members and sympathisers' (Gerbaudo, 2019, p. 19). From this perspective, parties need to think not only about which reforms advance reimagined ideals, but also what citizens understand the purpose and likely outcomes of any change to be. This indicates that, to reform in line with unrealised ideals, parties need to pay considerable attention to the way they design initiatives, thinking not only about the processes or functions that can be added to a party, but more broadly about the ethos that reforms seek to create.

Re-educating citizens

Whilst the idea of responding to citizens' demands and giving people what they want is attractive, it is likely that many parties will not recognise citizens' perceptions of current practices, and hence may wish to contest these views. A party may not accept that it is actually out of kilter with desires and may hence seek to inform people that it already aligns with their ideals. This possibility is supported by evidence that citizens are not always well informed about party practices. Indeed, far from possessing full information, citizens often have a poor understanding of how parties work, or indeed politics as a whole. In this research, many professed to know 'not very much' or 'nothing at all' about how parties worked, with 55% of Party Survey respondents and 33% of workshop participants selecting either of these responses. This suggests that many citizens do not have a detailed (if any) understanding of party activities and structures, and that, accordingly, many of the views expressed are uninformed.

The reasons for junctures between citizens' views and party practices can reflect, as Allen and Birch have highlighted, the way in which '[c]itizens' exposure to politicians is largely mediated', with the media being 'major players in the sense of framing and shaping much of the information about politicians that reaches the public' (Allen and Birch, 2015, p. 54). This mediation of information means that parties are often reliant on external actors to spread awareness of their practices in a context where journalists and news outlets are often incentivised to cover events in a short and sometimes superficial way (Vliegenthart et al., 2011). It is therefore not unsurprising that the information citizens receive does not provide a full picture of party activities, and that gaps can emerge between how a citizen perceives a party and what parties actually do.

Take, for example, the desire for parties to be inclusive and responsible governors that listen to expert advice. It may be that a party already incorporates expert views and independent advice into its policy-making and decision-making processes, but is not perceived to do so. This is a situation that the Labour Party seemed to face in 2015, for example. In that year, Labour convened an expert panel to advise on its economic policy, with shadow chancellor John McDonnell announcing how the panel would allow Labour to:

> draw on the unchallengeable expertise of some of the world's leading economic thinkers ... for their specialist knowledge. I give you this

undertaking that every policy we propose and every economic instrument we consider for use will be rigorously tested to its extreme before we introduce it in government.

Despite having such processes, in the present research workshop participants showed little awareness of parties' current attempts to engage expertise.

In thinking about how to respond to this situation, one option parties may wish to take is to re-educate citizens about the degree to which they *already* align with public desires. As parties are often reliant on established media outlets to disseminate information about how they are organised and behave, this can, however, be challenging. The rise of digital media and the provision of new, online channels of communication are often seen to offer a way forward for political parties. Indeed, it has been argued that '[n]ew ICTs offer political actors direct contact with citizens and thereby an advantage over existing media' (Römmele, 2003, p. 9). Developments such as social media and online forums appear to provide 'enhanced opportunities for direct communication and interaction between political actors and citizens' (Lilleker et al., 2015, p. 747–8). A key appeal of these channels is that parties are 'able to control the content and "dosage" of political information that they emit via the Internet ... [allowing them to] offer unfiltered information to the public and also to more specific target groups' (Römmele, 2003, p. 9). Given citizens' desire for greater openness, these alternative mediums provide one way in which parties could promote these desires. And yet it is important not to see digital media as a panacea, as these platforms have a range of disadvantages and limitations that parties need to recognise.

In understanding more about what citizens want, parties may want to respond by re-educating citizens about the extent to which their desires are already enacted. This suggests that reform is not the only option and that the information provided in this book can be valuable in different ways.

Recalibrating citizens' desires

A third option for how parties may wish to respond relates to the nature of the desires that citizens express. Whilst it is often presumed that parties will want to (or be incentivised to) respond to citizens' desires, there are many instances in which parties can also lead or challenge public ideas. This approach reflects the view of parties not as 'preference accommodators' but rather as 'preference shapers', terms used by Hay to capture instances in which parties or political leaders (such as the Conservatives under Margaret Thatcher and the Republicans under Ronald Regan) 'are able to shape the preferences of the electorate' (Hay, 2002, p. 167). From this perspective, it is possible that parties may not wish to accept citizens' stated desires and reform themselves to exemplify these ideas, or promote the ways in which desires are already enacted; rather, parties may want to lead public opinion in a different direction.

The potential for parties to lead public debate and offer new conceptions of desirable practice is an established feature of politics. Indeed, parties such as the Green Party have promoted previously marginal issues such as climate change and environmentalism, helping to make these ideas more mainstream (Carter, 2018, p. 143). It may therefore be that, rather than accepting the idea that parties should be open and inclusive, for example, parties may wish to promote an alternative ideal of parties as elite-led organisations that offer decisive leadership and policies made with little consultation or transparency. Such tendencies would mirror strategies taken up by UKIP under the leadership of Nigel Farage, where few attempts were made to promote inclusivity and instead the leader's personal integrity and authenticity were emphasised. Such examples suggest that parties may not wish to understand or respond to the public's current perceptions and desires, but may want to promote their own ideals. This approach can be particularly attractive if parties are seeking to offer an anti-establishment message that differentiates their organisation and activity from the status quo.

In addition, parties may also wish to challenge or reshape certain perceptions. It is possible, for example, to highlight contradictions and tensions in citizens' desires that raise questions about the compatibility of these goals. Alternatively, parties may wish to challenge the extent to which these ideals can ever be realised. In reviewing and responding to these desires, it may be that parties wish to recalibrate public ideals and redefine the ideals parties should promote. This can be done in many different ways, but by reviewing the data collected in this book parties can appreciate where their vision deviates from reimagined ideals and whether there are certain principles that they want to contest. A desire to meet and accommodate public demands should therefore not be presumed.

Contributions and limitations

In interrogating public perceptions of political parties and asking what it is that citizens want, this book has generated a range of new insights. Not only has new empirical data been gathered on how the public view parties, attention has also been paid to how parties may wish to respond. In reflecting on this endeavour it is, finally, useful to turn to consider the contributions and limitations of this work, reflecting on what this book reveals about the relationship between parties and citizens.

Contributions

Thinking first about the contributions of this analysis, as outlined in the Introduction, in this book I set out to advance two ideas. I wanted, first, to offer empirical insight into how parties are viewed and, second, to unpack the implications of citizens' views for parties. Over the preceding chapters I have presented a wealth of new data on public perceptions of parties. Whilst much data has previously been gathered on public attitudes towards politics (Clarke et al., 2016; Hay, 2007; Stoker, 2006) and politicians (Birch and Allen, 2015), far less has focused exclusively on parties. Moreover, the data that has been provided has often tended to come in the form of survey data.

In offering survey *and* deliberative workshop data that explores public perceptions of parties, this book provides new insight into how parties are seen. Moving beyond established proxies for assessing public views, such as party membership figures and levels of partisan affiliation, I have provided data on citizens' views of representation, participation, governance and conduct. Adopting this approach, I have explored public perceptions of parties and have shown that whilst many citizens do indeed have negative views, there are also areas in which parties are seen to be performing well. This provides an important corrective to existing debates, which have tended to be dominated by claims of illegitimacy and decline. In addition to studying perceptions, I have also explored citizens' ideals. This focus provides unprecedented insight into an aspect of public opinion that has hitherto been largely unexplored. Adopting this dual approach, I have been able to demonstrate the complex patterns of desires and perceptions that colour how parties are viewed, showing that citizens can have their ideals met, exceeded or missed when it comes to different aspects of party activity. In spotlighting these varied patterns in public opinion, this book has offered a wealth of insights into how parties are viewed and, by specifically focusing on unrealised desires, has identified a set of ideals that can inspire party response.

In offering this analysis, one particularly distinctive aspect of this study has been the use of mixed methods. Unlike the many studies that utilise cross-country survey analysis to test public opinion about politics in general (and, occasionally, parties in particular), preceding chapters have presented different types of data, blending survey analysis with discussions in deliberative workshops to gain additional insight into how parties are viewed. This approach has proved to be particularly valuable in gaining new understanding of public views. By combining quantitative and qualitative data, I have been able to test and explore the resilience of different views. This has allowed the contingency of people's ideas to be explored, the degree to which answers change to be traced and the extent to which certain desires recur to be ascertained. It has also provided unexpected insights and explanations. When viewed alone, survey data can be interpreted in many different ways, but the workshop discussions helped to provide valuable insights into the way parties are viewed. Whilst having costs in terms of scope and resources, this approach proved invaluable in identifying recurring principles for reimagination, and is a method that would be fruitful for future studies of this type.

In addition to generating new empirical data, I also set out to unpack the implications of citizens' views for parties. Offering the idea of the reimagined party, I have attempted to show that, whilst public opinion is diverse (and all people cannot be satisfied), there are patterns in response that can usefully guide parties' reaction. Focusing in this book on respondents' unrealised desires, I have identified a wish for parties that promote a specific ethos: one that is open and inclusive, responsive and responsible, and that offers principled leadership. Importantly, these ideas do not signal the rejection of established principles of party democracy but, rather, suggest a desire for parties to adapt to reflect modern ideas and norms. In offering the notion of reimagination, I have attempted to highlight the continually evolving nature of public desires. Building on a tradition that recognises on-going processes of party adaptation and change, this intervention suggests a new way of thinking about public desires, one which recognises that they are not static (and cannot be equated only with practices in the past) but change in line with modern ideas. In this way, the idea of reimagination offers a powerful new conceptual tool with which to think about public desires and party practices, recognising that these will change and evolve over time.

In offering this diagnosis, I have not sought to provide a specific prescription for party reform, but have argued that parties can respond in different ways. Identifying different possible reforms and initiatives, I have attempted to show how parties may wish to react, but have also acknowledged that they may want to adopt an alternative course of action. Whilst much attention is often devoted to the idea of reform, it is possible that parties may want to re-educate or recalibrate citizens' desires, or not to react at all. What this book enables is an informed choice about what parties want to do, and recognition that parties will need to perpetually revisit public demands to trace how they evolve. Whilst in the past parties have relied upon public opinion surveys, private polling and focus groups to determine public perceptions, this book provides data that they can consider in deciding if and how to respond. What I hope has emerged from this analysis is that whilst parties can react in different ways, there is no guarantee that any action will result in positive views. Whilst there are reasons to believe that reform may lead to more positive views of parties' current practices amongst some people, it is also clear that the public are a hard master to satisfy, and that any single response is unlikely to receive universal approval. Recognising this, parties can, however, use this data to make a more educated choice about how they respond.

Cumulatively, these findings suggest that a subtler debate is required, one that recognises the complexity of public opinion, the value of using different research methods and the varied practical insights that such data can provide. In this book, I have focused my analysis on Britain, presenting rich insight into public views in this context. What remains unclear, however, is the degree to which these principles and ideals are shared elsewhere. Scholarship on political parties has a strong tradition of international comparative analysis, and there is a clear case for extending this kind of study. The mixed-methods approach could easily be exported to study citizens' desires for parties in other countries, and it would be interesting to examine the extent to which reimagined ideals are supported elsewhere. Looking around the globe, it is clear that Britain is by no means alone in exhibiting contradictory signals about public views of parties. In countries such as France, Italy and Spain, there is sustained evidence of public dissatisfaction with parties, but also signs of support for new or revitalised party forms (Gerbaudo, 2019).

By extending this form of analysis to other countries, it would be possible to test the resilience of these ideas and the extent to which different contextual dynamics (such as alternative electoral systems) affect citizens' ideals. The potential to improve our understanding of public attitudes to parties is therefore significant, suggesting the value of further inquiry.

In addition, it is also possible to draw lessons from this study for other organisations. Parties are not alone in facing negative public views, but a range of institutions, from civil society bodies to parliaments and state institutions, have been shown to face negative views. Adopting this methodology it is possible to examine public perceptions in a different way, moving beyond survey measures to build up a multifaceted account of citizens' views and ideals.

Limitations

In terms of limitations, in this book I have explored views of parties in general and have looked at views within the British context. These two parameters enabled the form of detailed, mixed-methods analysis offered in this text, but it means that minimal insight has been provided into public views of specific parties. Further inquiry, looking at how specific parties are viewed, would therefore be valuable to extend the insights offered here. For each party, it would be insightful to know which types of practice are seen to promote reimagined ideals, and whether different reform initiatives are able to induce more favourable views. Such inquiries, in addition to the form of international comparison outlined above, would provide greater understanding of the scope and feasibility of reimagined ideals, providing valuable insights for parties considering a response.

A second limitation is that, in offering this analysis, I focused attention specifically on political parties and as such have not looked at views on the wider political system. Within the data, and in particular within workshop discussions, there were indications that disliked party traits and attributes were a product of wider political dynamics that parties themselves could not control. It was therefore argued by one activist that negative views were in part 'about a system ... personally I think we've got political parties we deserve with the systems that we've got'. In other workshops, participants commented that concerns were a result of 'a wider problem with how politics works' and reflected 'the rules that they are working under'. These comments suggest that parties may be unable to realise citizens' desires through their own institutional reforms, and may need to pursue wider systemic change, such as voting reform. As Gidengil et al. (2002, p. 75) have argued 'we should not rush to infer that the problem lies with the parties themselves. It is possible that political parties are simply serving as a lightning rod for frustration with the political process at large.' For this reason, there is a need to extend this analysis to determine the extent to which public views of parties reflect wider systemic concerns.

Finally, it is important to note that across the Party Survey large numbers of people selected the option 'Don't know' when answering questions. This response is interesting because within the workshops it was not the case that people struggled to articulate a view. Many workshop participants certainly had forthcoming opinions, despite being given minimal time to reflect, and were able to articulate complex and thoughtful ideas. With this in mind, it is important to recognise that much is obscured by the presence of 'Don't know' answers. If individuals responding 'Don't know' had been forced to choose another response, it is uncertain whether they would have revealed unrealised desires. This suggests that further investigation into the drives of 'Don't know' responses would be interesting, and that it may be informative to rerun these questions, removing the 'Don't know' option in order to force people to choose a response.

Conclusion

This book offers an important new way to think about public attitudes towards parties. It demonstrates that rather than parties being uniformly despised, most citizens have nuanced views. Far from rejecting these organisations and calling for radical democratic change, it appears that most people remain supportive of political parties, but that many see them to be out of kilter with ideals. For this reason, I argue that citizens want to see parties reimagined; they want parties to expansively rethink existing functions and procedures in line with new norms and ideals, bringing them in line with modern desires. Specifically, I have argued that many citizens want parties that are more open and inclusive, responsive and responsible, and that offer principled leadership. This suggests the importance of a change in party ethos. Whilst scholars have contended that public attitudes reflect the demise of certain favoured democratic functions (and specifically organisational forms of the mass-party era), this analysis suggests that the character of party activity is equally significant for citizens' views. It is not, therefore, the case that parties simply need to represent in a certain way, or to offer more opportunities for participation. Instead, the findings presented in this book indicate that a wider-ranging shift is desired, one that will induce a change in how parties present themselves and act day-to-day.

Reaching this conclusion, it is notable that these ideas are entirely compatible with existing principles of party democracy and do not suggest a desire for a radical shift towards alternative democratic ideals. It appears that most people have not rejected party politics, even if it is often described in negative terms, but want to see these organisations reimagined in line with modern ideas and norms.

In reflecting on how parties may want to react to these insights, I have argued that it should not be presumed that parties will want to pursue reform. Rather, unpicking possible responses to this data, I have suggested that parties may wish to reform themselves in line with public desires, re-educate citizens about ways in which their practices already mirror public desires, or recalibrate citizens' preferences to promote other ideals. Alternatively, parties may wish to make no response at all. In interrogating public opinion, this book has offered insights for parties interested in considering how they are viewed, showing that there is no simple solution to meeting citizens' desires.

Thinking finally about the relationship between parties and citizens, this book has argued that public perceptions are an important component of politics, and that political parties and politicians are likely to be interested in citizens' views. And yet politics is not simply a case of giving people what they profess to want. As this analysis has shown, people's desires and opinions are often far from fixed, and their responses to reforms designed to promote ideals will not always be favourable. This suggests that whilst parties are likely to be interested in public perceptions, there is unlikely to be a simple relationship between public demands and party actions. The interplay between parties and citizens is not straightforward, but greater levels of understanding are likely to help parties and citizens alike to comprehend and meet the challenge of democratic governance.

Appendix 1

Characteristics of the study samples

Table A.1 Attitudinal and demographic information for participants in the Party Survey, deliberative workshops and Party Survey 2

	Party Survey	Work-shops	Party Survey 2
Age			
Mean	48.6	52.1	48.9
Standard deviation	16.8	14.0	17.1
Min.	19	17	18
Max.	87	79	94
Gender			
% male	48.4	44.1	43.4
% female	51.6	55.9	56.6
Average age male	48.7	53.5	48.5
Average age female	48.6	54.7	48.3
Educational level (%)			
Higher	42.4	75.0	43.5
A-level	22.4	13.2	24.2
GCSEs	20.0	5.9	20.4
Apprenticeship/professional	3.9	1.5	3.8
No formal education	6.7	0.0	4.8
Prefer not to say	4.7	4.4	3.3
Previous voting behaviour (%)			
Voted in 2017? – Yes, voted	83.7	Not asked	78.0
Voted in 2017? – No, did not vote	16.1	Not asked	21.0
Don't know	0.2	Not asked	1.6

	Party Survey	Work-shops	Party Survey 2
Political knowledge (%)			
How politics in general works			
A great deal	4.3	15.2	11.0
A fair amount	40.0	72.7	47.2
Not very much	37.2	12.1	30.6
Nothing at all	7.5	0.0	5.7
Can't place on scale/Don't know	11.4	0.0	5.4
How political parties work			
A great deal	3.3	7.6	8.9
A fair amount	29.7	57.6	38.4
Not very much	44.8	33.3	39.5
Nothing at all	10.6	0.0	7.6
Can't place on scale/Don't know	11.6	1.5	5.6
What parties need to do to make laws			
A great deal	5.5	18.18	10.1
A fair amount	31.0	53.0	37.2
Not very much	37.8	28.8	38.1
Nothing at all	12.0	0.0	8.6
Can't place on scale/Don't know	13.8	0.0	6.0
Partisanship strength (%)			
Very strong	9.9	20.6	12.2
Fairly strong	33.1	35.3	34.3
Not very strong	31.2	14.7	21.8
Don't know	2.7	7.4	2.1
No partisan affiliation	23.2	22.1	29.7
Party support (%)			
Conservative	26.6	1.5	26.2
Labour	25.3	36.8	22.8
Liberal Democrats	5.5	4.4	7.7
UKIP	3.9	1.5	2.5
Green	3.1	29.4	0.5
Other	3.6	4.4	2.6
None	22.3	22.06	19.2
Don't know	9.7	0.0	9.0

	Party Survey	*Work-shops*	*Party Survey 2*
Trust: No trust (0) – Complete trust (7)			
Politicians			
Mean	2.0	2.7	2.1
Standard deviation	1.6	1.2	1.7
% Don't know	4.7	n/a	4.1
Civil service			
Mean	3.5	3.6	Not asked
Standard deviation	1.8	1.4	Not asked
% Don't know	10.3	n/a	Not asked
Local MP			
Mean	3.0	2.8	2.8
Standard deviation	2.0	1.8	2.2
% Don't know	12.2	n/a	11.7
Political parties			
Mean	2.1	2.5	2.1
Standard deviation	1.6	1.4	1.7
% Don't know	5.3	n/a	4.7
Parliament			
Mean	2.4	2.6	Not asked
Standard deviation	1.8	1.5	Not asked
% Don't know	6.5	n/a	Not asked
Satisfaction with political parties (%)			
Very satisfied	0.6	0.0	Not asked
Fairly satisfied	19.9	13.6	Not asked
Fairly dissatisfied	43.0	31.8	Not asked
Very dissatisfied	25.9	54.6	Not asked
Don't know	11.0	n/a	Not asked
Satisfaction with democracy (%)			
Very satisfied	4.1	1.5	Not asked
Fairly satisfied	36.9	18.2	Not asked
Fairly dissatisfied	29.9	30.3	Not asked
Very dissatisfied	16.6	50.0	Not asked
Don't know	12.5	n/a	Not asked

	Party Survey	Work-shops	Party Survey 2
Working status (%)			
Full time	39.3	27.3	Not asked
Part time	12.0	33.3	Not asked
Student	1.8	3.0	Not asked
Retired	25.7	27.3	Not asked
Unemployed	4.2	1.5	Not asked
Not working	8.9	3.0	Not asked
Other	3.8	4.6	Not asked
Political interest (%)			
Very interested	10.9	56.1	Not asked
Fairly interested	39.6	39.4	Not asked
Not very interested	26.6	4.6	Not asked
Not at all interested	18.7	0.0	Not asked
Don't know	4.1	n/a	Not asked

Recruitment methodology for the deliberative workshops

Sampling frame (general population)

The populations for this component of the study consisted of adults who were at least 18 years old and living within a five-mile radius of the city of Sheffield. A simple random sample of 1,200 potential respondents was drawn from the Post Address File (PAF) from a licensed Royal Mail provider located in South Yorkshire. The PAF contains valid UK postal names and addresses with a coverage rate of approximately 95% of all households. From the PAF, 918 unique UK postcodes were selected, which included the following postal areas: S1, S2, S3, S4, S5, S6, S9, S10, S35, S60, S61.

Recruitment mailers were delivered by Royal Mail to 1,200 addresses on 19 December 2017. Respondents were instructed to visit a web link to learn more about the project and to register their interest as a potential participant. The website was visited 82 times; 40 respondents started the recruitment survey between 21 December 2017 to 8 January 2018; and 33 respondents completed the questionnaire. The response rate for completed surveys is therefore 2.75% (33/1,200), although this is a conservative estimate because it is unknown how many mailers failed to reach their intended destination.

Recruitment of party activists

Party organisers (or key members) from the local Conservative, Labour, Liberal Democrat and Green Parties in Sheffield were asked to post/send information about the project for recruitment purposes. It is unknown exactly how many members each of these organisations has; thus, calculating response rates is not possible. In total, 111 respondents expressed an interest in the project, and 79 individuals completed the full questionnaire.

Workshop availability and attendance

In total, 112 people responded to the recruitment postcard or request from a local party website, social media page and so on. Below are the numbers of respondents who (1) indicated they were available to attend a particular workshop; (2) were assigned to a workshop; and (3) confirmed their participation (once assigned):

- *Non-party activists*, Saturday 20 January 2018, from 1 to 5 p.m.:
  72 available, 28 assigned, 22 confirmed respondents.
- *Party activists*, Saturday 27 January 2018, from 1 to 5 p.m.:
  68 available, 31 assigned, 22 confirmed
- *Activists and non-activists*, in mixed sample, Thursday 1 February 2018, from 1 to 5 p.m.:
  55 available, 34 assigned, 30 confirmed.

Regression analysis: output tables

The tables on the following pages present the output of the regression modelling of results from the Party Survey and Party Survey 2.

Table A.2 Exploring traits of respondents who are not having their expectations realised for each representation type

	Delegate	Trustee	Partisan
Female	0.26*	0.14	0.51***
	(0.132)	(0.132)	(0.194)
Age	0.02***	0.01***	0.01**
	(0.005)	(0.005)	(0.006)
Degree	-0.04	0.17	-0.32*
	(0.134)	(0.133)	(0.183)
Non-voter in 2017	-0.31	-0.22	0.10
	(0.203)	(0.205)	(0.281)
High party knowledge	-0.02	0.34**	0.26
	(0.140)	(0.141)	(0.190)
Party trust (0–7)	-0.20***	-0.17***	-0.22***
	(0.045)	(0.041)	(0.060)
Partisanship (ref. = No party)			
Conservative	-0.15	-0.26	0.43
	(0.255)	(0.255)	(0.372)
Labour	-0.15	-0.17	0.41
	(0.266)	(0.265)	(0.403)
Liberal Democrats	-0.09	0.51	1.20***
	(0.356)	(0.330)	(0.465)
Other party	-0.01	-0.14	0.82*
	(0.304)	(0.303)	(0.452)
Don't know	-0.13	-0.08	0.29
	(0.256)	(0.266)	(0.358)
Strength of partisanship (ref. = Very)			
Fairly strong	0.09	-0.00	0.36
	(0.236)	(0.241)	(0.326)
Not very strong	-0.01	-0.09	0.47
	(0.245)	(0.248)	(0.361)
Don't know	-0.26	-1.25**	-1.43
	(0.495)	(0.546)	(1.066)
Not asked (no party support)	-0.46	-0.55	0.67
	(0.361)	(0.369)	(0.524)
Pseudo-R^2	0.06	0.07	0.11
n	1,436	1,436	1,436

Standard errors in parentheses, ***p<0.01, **p<0.05, *p<0.1, pseudo-R^2 is McKelvey & Zavoina, in a survey-weighted mode

Table A.3 Exploring traits of respondents who are not having their expectations realised for the degree to which parties should listen to experts or the majority

	Experts	Majority
Female	0.04	0.28**
	(0.129)	(0.132)
Age	0.01***	0.02***
	(0.004)	(0.005)
Degree	0.47***	0.20
	(0.130)	(0.132)
Non-voter in 2017	-0.22	-0.58***
	(0.202)	(0.192)
High party knowledge	0.35**	0.19
	(0.138)	(0.139)
Party trust (0–7)	-0.06	-0.21***
	(0.040)	(0.043)
Partisanship (ref. = No party)		
Conservative	-0.85***	-0.84***
	(0.264)	(0.280)
Labour	-0.19	-0.57*
	(0.272)	(0.292)
Liberal Democrats	0.05	-0.57
	(0.339)	(0.351)
Other party	-0.53*	-0.27
	(0.304)	(0.334)
Don't know	-0.63**	0.04
	(0.267)	(0.266)
Strength of partisanship (ref. = Very)		
Fairly strong	0.35	-0.08
	(0.223)	(0.227)
Not very strong	0.51**	-0.28
	(0.240)	(0.239)
Don't know	0.22	-1.06**
	(0.447)	(0.426)
Not asked (no party support)	-0.30	-1.50***
	(0.359)	(0.365)
Pseudo-R^2	0.08	0.12
n	1,436	1,436

Standard errors in parentheses, ***p<0.01, **p<0.05, *p<0.1, pseudo-R^2 is McKelvey & Zavoina, in a survey-weighted mode

Table A.4 Exploring traits of respondents who think parties should ideally change 'Very often' or 'Sometimes' but who see change 'Rarely' or 'Never'

	Unrealised desires for responsiveness
Female	0.24*
	(0.138)
Age	0.02***
	(0.005)
Degree	-0.35**
	(0.138)
Non-voter in 2017	0.01
	(0.218)
High party knowledge	-0.10
	(0.144)
Party trust (0–7)	-0.24***
	(0.044)
Partisanship (ref. = No party)	
Conservative	0.10
	(0.270)
Labour	0.31
	(0.280)
Liberal Democrats	0.08
	(0.347)
Other party	0.71**
	(0.314)
Don't know	-0.36
	(0.279)
Strength of partisanship (ref. = Very)	
Fairly strong	-0.27
	(0.250)
Not very strong	-0.15
	(0.259)
Don't know	0.39
	(0.485)
Not asked (no party support)	-0.06
	(0.380)
Pseudo-R^2	0.09
n	1,436

Standard errors in parentheses, ***$p<$0.01, **$p<$0.05, *$p<$0.1, pseudo-R^2 is McKelvey & Zavoina, in a survey-weighted mode

Table A.5 Exploring traits of respondents who feel that they should be able to have an impact on what parties say and do, but not perceive an impact

	Unreaslised desires for efficacy
Female	-0.06
	(0.134)
Age	0.00
	(0.005)
Degree	0.28**
	(0.138)
Non-voter in 2017	0.03
	(0.017)
High party knowledge	0.17
	(0.142)
Party trust (0–7)	-0.27***
	(0.043)
Partisanship (ref. = No party)	
Conservative	0.03
	(0.249)
Labour	-0.62**
	(0.262)
Liberal Democrats	-0.64*
	(0.327)
Other party	-0.28
	(0.294)
Don't know	-0.38
	(0.261)
Strength of partisanship (ref. = Very)	
Fairly strong	0.13
	(0.257)
Not very strong	0.39
	(0.260)
Don't know	0.39
	(0.441)
Not asked (no party support)	-0.22
	(0.361)
Constant	-0.47
	(0.467)
Pseudo-R^2	0.08
n	1,438

Standard errors in parentheses, ***$p<$0.01, **$p<$0.05, *$p<$0.1, pseudo-R^2 is McKelvey & Zavoina, in a survey-weighted mode

Table A.6 Exploring traits of respondents who think discussion/proposal/decision is 'Very important' (compared with 'Fairly', 'Not very', 'Not at all' and 'Don't know')

	Discussion	Proposal	Decision
Female	0.16	0.08	0.08
	(0.132)	(0.129)	(0.130)
Age	0.01**	0.01	0.01***
	(0.004)	(0.004)	(0.004)
Degree	0.50***	0.39***	-0.00
	(0.133)	(0.128)	(0.132)
Non-voter in 2017	0.01	-0.19	0.00
	(0.013)	(0.191)	(0.014)
High party knowledge	0.38***	0.48***	0.47***
	(0.143)	(0.138)	(0.137)
Party trust (0–7)	-0.03	-0.02	-0.11***
	(0.043)	(0.041)	(0.041)
Partisanship (ref. = No party)			
Conservative	-0.70**	-0.72***	-0.07
	(0.276)	(0.272)	(0.263)
Labour	-0.29	-0.38	0.37
	(0.291)	(0.284)	(0.267)
Liberal Democrats	0.37	-0.63*	0.00
	(0.401)	(0.348)	(0.332)
Other party	-0.56*	-0.42	0.33
	(0.317)	(0.313)	(0.302)
Don't know	-0.30	-0.58**	-0.24
	(0.248)	(0.249)	(0.271)
Strength of partisanship (ref. = Very)			
Fairly strong	-0.11	-0.13	-0.05
	(0.227)	(0.221)	(0.225)
Not very strong	-0.18	-0.11	-0.12
	(0.246)	(0.234)	(0.238)
Don't know	-0.16	-0.42	-0.04
	(0.428)	(0.425)	(0.445)
Not asked (no party support)	-1.08***	-0.99***	-0.10
	(0.358)	(0.350)	(0.355)
Constant	0.25	0.61	-1.36***
	(0.448)	(0.516)	(0.456)
Pseudo-R^2	0.08	0.20	0.05
n	1,438	1,438	1,438

Standard errors in parentheses, ***p<0.01, **p<0.05, *p<0.1, pseudo-R^2 is McKelvey & Zavoina, in a survey-weighted mode

Table A.7 Exploring traits of respondents who think that parties should ideally balance long-term demands and short-term needs, but who see parties acting in the short term

	Unrealised desires for responsiveness
Female	0.06
	(0.130)
Age	0.00
	(0.004)
Degree	0.28**
	(0.131)
Non-voter in 2017	0.02
	(0.014)
High party knowledge	-0.04
	(0.137)
Party trust (0–7)	-0.07*
	(0.040)
Partisanship (ref. = No party)	
Conservative	-0.15
	(0.253)
Labour	0.00
	(0.262)
Liberal Democrats	0.21
	(0.323)
Other party	-0.26
	(0.297)
Don't know	-0.49*
	(0.258)
Strength of partisanship (ref. = Very)	
Fairly strong	0.18
	(0.242)
Not very strong	0.33
	(0.250)
Don't know	0.76*
	(0.446)
Not asked (no party support)	-0.02
	(0.359)
Constant	-0.79*
	(0.468)
Pseudo-R^2	0.03
n	1,438

Standard errors in parentheses, ***p<0.01, **p<0.05, *p<0.1, pseudo-R^2 is McKelvey & Zavoina, in a survey-weighted mode

Table A.8 Exploring traits of party supporters who think that parties could 'not/not at all' be described as exhibiting reimagined attributes compared with those purporting to support no party

Conservative Party supporters

	Open	Responsive	Responsible	Leadership
Female	-0.09	-0.15	-0.07	-0.23*
	(0.140)	(0.133)	(0.140)	(0.134)
Age	0.01	0.01**	-0.00	-0.00
	(0.004)	(0.004)	(0.004)	(0.004)
Degree	0.32**	0.05	0.29**	0.03
	(0.145)	(0.134)	(0.141)	(0.136)
Non-voter in 2017	-0.54***	-0.34*	-0.59***	-0.54***
	(0.193)	(0.188)	(0.186)	(0.185)
High party knowledge	0.43***	0.35**	0.39***	0.45***
	(0.145)	(0.136)	(0.141)	(0.138)
Party trust (0–7)	-0.55***	-0.45***	-0.53***	-0.48***
	(0.046)	(0.043)	(0.045)	(0.043)
Partisanship (ref. = No party)				
Conservative	-0.99***	-0.86***	-0.85***	-0.69**
	(0.277)	(0.267)	(0.279)	(0.271)
Labour	1.55***	1.02***	1.42***	1.39***
	(0.291)	(0.280)	(0.294)	(0.279)
UKIP	1.20**	1.23**	1.14**	1.20**
	(0.541)	(0.506)	(0.496)	(0.509)
Other party	1.36***	0.76***	1.12***	1.12***
	(0.302)	(0.279)	(0.300)	(0.290)
Don't know	-0.09	-0.35	-0.35	-0.25
	(0.275)	(0.263)	(0.287)	(0.259)
Partisanship (ref. = Very)				
Fairly strong	-0.29	-0.10	-0.24	-0.31
	(0.233)	(0.218)	(0.228)	(0.223)
Not very strong	-0.29	-0.00	-0.40	-0.66***
	(0.247)	(0.238)	(0.252)	(0.242)
Don't know	-0.91*	-0.49	-0.06	-0.51
	(0.489)	(0.473)	(0.496)	(0.459)
Constant	1.48***	1.05**	1.95***	1.94***
	(0.427)	(0.409)	(0.417)	(0.412)
Pseudo-R^2	0.37	0.27	0.34	0.30
n	1,600	1,600	1,600	1,600

Labour Party supporters

	Open	Responsive	Responsible	Leadership
Female	-0.06	-0.14	-0.26*	-0.27*
	(0.138)	(0.131)	(0.144)	(0.142)
Age	0.03***	0.03***	0.03***	0.03***
	(0.005)	(0.004)	(0.005)	(0.005)
Degree	-0.07	-0.24*	0.12	-0.14
	(0.138)	(0.130)	(0.142)	(0.140)
Non-voter in 2017	-0.38*	-0.04	-0.35*	-0.12
	(0.199)	(0.194)	(0.211)	(0.200)
High party knowledge	0.40***	0.31**	0.31**	0.03
	(0.140)	(0.135)	(0.144)	(0.145)
Party trust (0–7)	-0.40***	-0.44***	-0.46***	-0.38***
	(0.043)	(0.041)	(0.046)	(0.043)
Partisanship (ref. = No party)				
Conservative	1.07***	0.79***	0.99***	1.58***
	(0.270)	(0.259)	(0.287)	(0.282)
Labour	-1.35***	-1.00***	-1.84***	-1.36***
	(0.257)	(0.253)	(0.270)	(0.259)
UKIP	1.76***	2.05***	1.95***	2.71***
	(0.574)	(0.539)	(0.566)	(0.596)
Other party	0.07	0.33	-0.13	0.23
	(0.270)	(0.265)	(0.283)	(0.274)
Don't know	-0.70***	-0.38	-0.78***	-0.51*
	(0.267)	(0.275)	(0.278)	(0.271)
Partisanship (ref. = Very)				
Fairly strong	-0.44**	-0.52**	-0.53**	-0.37*
	(0.200)	(0.203)	(0.214)	(0.204)
Not very strong	0.17	-0.39*	0.19	0.14
	(0.239)	(0.222)	(0.245)	(0.241)
Don't know	-0.48	-1.06**	-0.75	-0.58
	(0.538)	(0.467)	(0.457)	(0.461)
Constant	0.39	-0.08	0.45	0.06
	(0.419)	(0.406)	(0.442)	(0.429)
Pseudo-R^2	0.37	0.34	0.45	0.43
n	1,600	1,600	1,600	1,600

UKIP supporters

	Open	Responsive	Responsible	Leadership
Female	-0.44***	-0.14	-0.43***	-0.49***
	(0.123)	(0.120)	(0.123)	(0.122)
Age	-0.01*	0.00	-0.01***	-0.00
	(0.004)	(0.004)	(0.004)	(0.004)
Degree	0.58***	0.27**	0.62***	0.53***
	(0.121)	(0.120)	(0.123)	(0.121)
Non-voter in 2017	-0.58***	-0.15	-0.40**	-0.43**
	(0.182)	(0.179)	(0.185)	(0.180)
High party knowledge	0.53***	0.43***	0.56***	0.53***
	(0.127)	(0.126)	(0.128)	(0.123)
Party trust (0–7)	-0.11***	-0.15***	-0.13***	-0.12***
	(0.036)	(0.037)	(0.036)	(0.037)
Partisanship (ref. = No party)				
Conservative	-0.29	-0.16	0.01	-0.06
	(0.256)	(0.257)	(0.260)	(0.251)
Labour	0.57**	0.61**	0.65**	0.73***
	(0.257)	(0.260)	(0.260)	(0.247)
UKIP	-2.48***	-1.83***	-2.14***	-2.31***
	(0.574)	(0.551)	(0.533)	(0.436)
Other party	0.83***	0.77***	1.08***	0.68**
	(0.280)	(0.271)	(0.288)	(0.268)
Don't know	-0.10	0.06	-0.32	-0.10
	(0.239)	(0.239)	(0.235)	(0.238)
Partisanship (ref. = Very)				
Fairly strong	-0.02	-0.10	-0.21	-0.03
	(0.204)	(0.204)	(0.208)	(0.198)
Not very strong	0.15	-0.01	0.01	0.12
	(0.224)	(0.222)	(0.228)	(0.216)
Don't know	-0.39	-1.18**	-1.05**	-0.64
	(0.387)	(0.479)	(0.412)	(0.397)
Constant	0.95**	-0.43	1.00**	0.58
	(0.383)	(0.379)	(0.389)	(0.376)
Pseudo-R^2	0.21	0.12	0.21	0.19
n	1,600	1,600	1,600	1,600

Standard errors in parentheses, ***$p<0.01$, **$p<0.05$, *$p<0.1$, pseudo-R^2 is McKelvey & Zavoina, in a survey-weighted mode

Notes

Notes to Introduction

1 In this book I use the terms 'ideals' and 'desires' interchangeably to convey what it is that citizens would ideally like to see from parties.

2 In order to disaggregate the influence of partisan cues it would be necessary to pose practically every question in relation to a specific party *and* parties in general. This means that a question such as 'In your opinion, when parties develop their policy positions, how often do they think about the following groups?' would need to be disaggregated to ask 'In your opinion, when [the Labour Party/Conservative Party/Liberal Democrat Party/Green Party/UK Independence Party/Scottish National Party/ Plaid Cymru *and* parties in general] develop their policy positions, how often do they think about the following groups?' Whilst allowing the survey to detect partisan influences, this approach is exceedingly expensive, time-consuming and repetitive. With an average survey question costing £300 for a single variation, specifying different parties would quickly escalate the cost to thousands of pounds for a single question. Moreover, questions that have seven or more variants require significant time from the respondent and due to their repetitive nature are likely to gather information of lower quality, as individuals tire of engaging with the nuances of each option. Respondents may also struggle to differentiate consistently between their views of multiple parties (many of which they may be unfamiliar with). For this reason, the Party Survey did not gather data on views of specific parties.

3 The survey was piloted twice prior to submission to YouGov in two focus groups: one with professional service staff and students at the University of Sheffield, and one with a group of stay-at-home parents. In both cases respondents were asked to complete the survey and talk through any problems they encountered and any ambiguities that arose. The conceptual meaning of questions was also examined, by asking respondents

to explain what they thought they were being asked and how this conditioned their response. In addition, the survey was piloted online with YouGov before being sent out. Fifty responses were sought and initial data was used to test the validity of scalar measures.

4   For more information on recruitment to the deliberative workshops, see Appendix 2.

Notes to Chapter 1

1   Data taken from *Eurobarometer*, 87.3 (May 2017).
2   The precise wording of the question was: 'I would like to ask you a question about how much trust you have in certain institutions. For each of the following institutions, please tell me if you tend to trust it or tend not to trust it.'
3   The question was worded as follows: 'Some people say that political parties in [country] care what ordinary people think. Others say that political parties in [country] don't care what ordinary people think. Using the scale on this card (where ONE means that political parties care about what ordinary people think, and FIVE means that they don't care what ordinary people think), where would you place yourself?'
4   Respondents were able to choose between the following options in answering this question: 'nearly all interested in votes rather than people's opinions', 'most just interested in votes', 'some just interested in votes', 'most interested in opinions' and 'nearly all interested in opinions'.
5   The precise wording of the question was as follows: 'Some people say that political parties are necessary to make our political system work in [country]. Others think that political parties are not needed in [country]. Using the scale on this card (where ONE means that political parties are necessary to make our political system work, and FIVE means that political parties are not needed in [country]), where would you place yourself?' This was asked only in the 1996–2001 module of the survey and was not included in more recent modules. The CSES database is accessible at https://www.gesis.org/en/services/data-analysis/international-survey-programs/cses (last accessed 24 February 2020).

Notes to Chapter 2

1   The possible responses included 'Don't know'. For the analysis, responses of 1 and 2 were collapsed ('Parties should use things like opinion polls to find out what the people want and then act on the results, even if this goes against what parties think is in the public interest'), as were scores

of 3 and 4 ('Parties should act on their view of what is in the public interest, even if this might go against what opinion polls suggest the public want').

2 The possible responses included 'Don't know'. Again, for the analysis, responses of 1 and 2 were collapsed ('It is more important to have parties that stick to their principles, even if this means not following public opinion'), as were scores of 3 and 4 ('It is more important to have parties that follow public opinion, even if this means not sticking to their principles').

3 The options were randomised for respondents, but kept consistent for the next question. Responses were again on a 1–4 scale (1 = Strongly disagree, 2 = Disagree, 3 = Agree, 4 = Strongly agree) and there was a 'Don't know' option.

4 The precise question wording here was: 'Thinking about different people and institutions in British politics, please use the following scale to say how much you personally trust each of the following. 0 means you do not trust them at all, and 7 means you have complete trust'. Responses reported here are for 'Political Parties' but additional institutions were also presented to respondents.

5 When it comes to modelling approaches like this, it could be that the chosen variables do not capture a very select group of people driving the result. However, this seems unlikely for two related reasons: (1) these sociodemographic and attitudinal variables are standard across multiple studies that address related issues such as voting behaviour; and (2) the overall group of dissatisfied respondents is large enough to make this improbable. This is a general issue of dissatisfaction, not one driven by highly educated partisans for instance.

6 The options were randomised for respondents, but kept consistent for the next question. Responses were on a 1–5 scale (1 = Almost never, 2 = Less than half of the time, 3 = About half the time, 4 = More than half the time, 5 = Almost all of the time) and there was a 'Don't know' option.

7 For their responses participants were asked to select one of: Very often; Sometimes; Rarely; Never. There was also a 'Don't know' option.

8 The question wording was: 'How often would you say that parties change their positions to reflect what people want?' and again for their responses participants were asked to select one of: Very often; Sometimes; Rarely; Never; 'Don't know'.

Notes

Notes to Chapter 3

1 It should be noted that the opinions gathered here concern perceptions of the participatory opportunities offered to engage with parties
themselves. This chapter does not therefore consider citizens' attitudes
towards participating in the wider political system through parties, but
instead concentrates on monitoring citizens' views of engaging with
parties themselves.

2 Supporter networks are the low-cost mechanisms by which individuals can gain rights within a party without having to sign up for full
membership.

3 There was also a 'Don't know' option.

4 The precise question wording was as follows:
> To what extent do you agree or disagree with the following
> statements?
>> When people like me get involved in political parties, we *can* really
>> have an impact on what parties say and do.
>> When people like me get involved in political parties, we *should* be
>> able to have an impact on what parties say and do.
>> There are better ways of bringing about change in society than
>> getting involved with political parties.
>> Political parties provide a way for ordinary people to come
>> together to change the country.

The order of presentation of these options was randomised for respondents. The responses were on the following scale:
> 1 = Strongly disagree, 2 = Disagree, 3 = Neither agree nor disagree,
> 4 = Agree, 5 = Strongly agree. 'Don't know' was also an option.

5 This analysis focuses on those who choose to affiliate and does not, therefore, include those with no affiliation and no interest in engaging with
parties.

6 This point became evident in survey question testing, where large
numbers of respondents selected 'Don't know'. For this reason, the
decision was taken not to interrogate general perceptions of party
participation.

7 The four-point scale was 1 = Not at all important, 2 = Not very important, 3 = Fairly important, 4 = Very important. 'Don't know' was also an
option.

8 The options were ordered as follows: (1) Get involved in a group within
a party that has shared interests; (2) Get involved with a party locally;
(3) Get involved in party activities generally; (4) Get involved with a party
nationally; (5) Get involved in a group within a party that has shared
characteristics.

Notes to Chapter 4

1 The precise question wording was as follows:
   You answered X. How well do you feel that parties today currently do these things?
   Run the country/Represent those who voted for them
   Very well
   Fairly well
   Not very well
   Not well at all
   Don't know

2 It should be noted that the number of respondents indicating a preference for judging in accordance with representation was somewhat smaller, but still large enough to allow the answers to be split.

3 The precise question wording was as follows:
   When parties are in government, which of the following statements best describes your opinion of how parties do the following things?
   Deliver promised policies
   Deliver good policy outcomes
   Manage the day-to-day running of government
   Deal with crises
   The above options were randomised across respondents. Responses were on a scale of 1–4: 1 = Parties do this extremely well and no improvements could be made, 2 = Parties mainly do this well, but small improvements could be made, 3 = Parties tend not to do this well and a lot of improvements could be made, 4 = Parties don't do this at all well and huge improvements could be made, Don't know.

4 Respondents were presented with two statements and asked to indicate where they positioned themselves on a four-point scale where 1 indicated strong agreement with the statement 'It is more important for parties to govern in the interests of the whole nation' and 2 indicated slight agreement, whereas 3 indicated slight agreement with the statement 'It is more important for parties to govern in the interests of specific groups' and 4 indicated strong agreement. 'Don't know' was also an option.

5 The precise question wording was as follows:
   When parties govern, they can make decisions by thinking about different things. Please rank these phrases to show what you think parties currently think about the most, where 1 is what parties think about the most and 3 is what parties think about the least.
   Whether a decision fits with the party's principles and objectives
   Whether a decision will gain the party votes in an election
   Whether a decision is supported by evidence and independent advice

These options were randomised across respondents, but then made to give consistent rankings of 1–3.

Notes to Chapter 5

1 Respondents were asked:

> To what extent do you agree or disagree with the following statements:
>
> > There is not much difference between what a party promises and what it actually does when it wins an election.
> >
> > Political parties are more interested in winning elections than in governing afterwards.
> >
> > Political parties spend too much time bickering with each other.

Notes to Chapter 6

1 If, for example, those with unrealised desires were all supporters of the UK Independence Party (UKIP) or of the Green Party, then it is unlikely that parties that do not want to court appeal from those groups would be interested in engaging in these ideas. In practice, however, parties across the spectrum have an interest in appealing to older voters and those with low levels of trust.

Bibliography

Abedi, A. and Lundberg, T. (2009) 'Doomed to Failure? UKIP and the Organisational Challenges Facing Right-Wing Populist Anti-political Establishment Parties', *Parliamentary Affairs*, 62(1): 72–87.

Allen, N. and Birch, S. (2011) 'Political Conduct and Misconduct: Probing Public Opinion', *Parliamentary Affairs*, 64(1): 61–81.

Allen, N. and Birch, S. (2015) *Ethics and Integrity in British Politics*, Cambridge: Cambridge University Press.

Almond, G. and Verba, S. (1965) *The Civic Culture*, Boston: Little, Brown and Co.

American Political Science Association (1950) 'Foreword', *American Political Science Review*, 44(3): v–ix.

Atkinson, M. and Mancuso, M. (1985) 'Do We Need a Code of Conduct for Politicians? The Search for an Elite Political Culture of Corruption in Canada', *Canadian Journal of Political Science*, 18(3): 459–80.

Audickas, L., Dempsey, N. and Keen, R. (2018) *Membership of UK Political Parties*, Number SN05125, 1 September, London: House of Commons Library.

Bardi, L., Bartolini, S. and Treschsel, H. (2014a) 'Responsive and Responsible? The Role of Parties in Twenty-First Century Politics', *Western European Politics*, 37(2): 235–52.

Bardi, L., Bartolini, S. and Treschsel, H. (2014b) 'Party Adaptation and Change and the Crisis of Democracy', *Party Politics*, 20(2): 151–9.

Bartels, L. (2002) 'Beyond the Running Tally', *Political Behaviour*, 24(2): 117–50.

Bartolini, S. and Mair, P. (2001) 'Challenges to Contemporary Political Parties', in L. Diamond and R. Gunther (eds), *Political Parties and Democracy*, Baltimore: John Hopkins University, pp. 327–44.

Beer, S. (1982) *Modern British Politics*, London: Faber and Faber.

Beetham, D. (2004) 'Political Legitimacy', in K. Nash and A. Scott (eds), *The Blackwell Companion to Political Sociology*, Oxford: Blackwell, pp. 107–16.

Bengtsson, Å. and Wass. H. (2010) 'Styles of Political Representation: What Do Voters Expect?', *Journal of Elections, Public Opinion and Parties*, 20(1): 55–81.

Benn. T. (2006) 'Tony Benn: You Ask the Questions', *The Independent*, 5 June, available here: https://www.independent.co.uk/news/people/profiles/tony-benn-you-ask-the-questions-481110.html, accessed 2 May 2018.

Birch, A. (1964) *Representative and Responsible Government*, London: Unwin.

Blyth, M. and Katz. R (2005) 'From Catch-All Politics to Cartelisation: The Political Economy of the Cartel Party', *West European Politics*, 28(1): 33–60.

Bolleyer, N., Little, C. and von Nostitz, F.-C. (2015) 'Implementing Democratic Equality in Political Parties: Organisational Consequences in the Swedish and the German Pirate Party', *Scandinavian Political Studies*, 38: 158–78.

Borge, R. and Santamarina Sáez, E. (2016) 'From Protest to Political Parties: Online Deliberation in New Parties in Spain', *Media Studies*, 7(14): 104–22.

Bourdieu, P. (1979) 'Public Opinion Does Not Exist', in A. Mattelart and S. Siegelaub (eds), *Communication and Class Struggle*, New York: International General, pp. 124–30.

Bowler, S. and Karp, J. (2004) 'Politicians, Scandals, and Trust in Government', *Political Behavior*, 26(3): 271–87.

Budge, I., Robertson, D. and Hearl, D. (1987) *Ideology, Strategy and Party Change: Spatial Analyses of Post-war Election Programmes in 19 Democracies*, Cambridge: Cambridge University Press.

Burke, E. (1998 [1770]) 'Thoughts on the Cause of the Present Discontents', in David Womersley (ed.), *A Philosophical Enquiry into the Origin of Our Ideas of the Sublime and Beautiful and Other Pre-Revolutionary Writings*, London: Penguin Classics, pp. 201–76.

Butler, D. and Powell, E. (2014) 'Understanding the Party Brand: Experimental Evidence on the Role of Valence', *Journal of Politics*, 76(2): 492–505.

Campbell, A., Gurin, G. and Miller, W. (1954) *The Voter Decides*, Evanston: Row Peterson.

Campbell, A., Converse, P., Miller, W. and Stokes, D. (1960) *The American Voter*, New York: Wiley and Sons.

Caramani, D. (2017) 'Will vs. Reason: The Populist and Technocratic Forms of Political Representation and Their Critique to Party Government', *American Political Science Review*, 111(1): 54–67.

Carman, C. (2006) 'Public Preferences for Parliamentary Representation in the UK: An Overlooked Link?', *Political Studies*, 54(1): 103–22.

Carter, N. (2018) *The Politics of the Environment: Ideas, Activism and Policy*, Cambridge: Cambridge University Press.

Castiglione, D. and Warren, M. (2006) 'Rethinking Democratic Representation: Eight Theoretical Issues', Paper at 'Rethinking Democratic Representation', Centre for the Study of Democratic Institutions, University of British Columbia, 18–19 May.

Centeno, M. (1993) 'The New Leviathan: The Dynamics and Limits of Technocracy', *Theory and Society*, 22(3): 307–35.

Citrin, J. (1974) 'Comment: The Political Relevance of Trust in Government', *American Political Science Review*, 68: 973–88.

Clarke, H., Sanders, D., Stewart, M. and Whiteley, P. (2009) *Performance Politics and the British Voter*, Cambridge: Cambridge University Press.

Clarke, N., Jennings, W., Moss, J. and Stoker, G. (2016) *The Rise of Anti-politics in Britain*, Southampton: University of Southampton.

Converse, P. (1964) 'The Nature of Mass Belief Systems', in D. E. Apter (ed.), *Ideology and Discontent*, London: Free Press, pp. 206–61.

Daalder, H. (2002) 'Parties: Denied, Dismissed, or Redundant? A Critique', in R. Gunther, J. R. Montero and J. Linz (eds), *Political Parties: Old Concepts and New Challenges*, Oxford: Oxford University Press, pp. 39–57.

Dahl, R. (1971) *Polyarchy: Participation and Opposition*, New Haven: Yale University Press.

Dalton, R. J. (2004) *Democratic Challenges, Democratic Choices*, Oxford: Oxford University Press.

Dalton, R. J. and Wattenberg, M. (2002) *Parties Without Partisans: Political Change in Advanced Industrial Democracies*, Oxford: Oxford University Press.

Dalton, R. J. and Weldon, S. (2005) 'Public Images of Political Parties: A Necessary Evil?', *West European Politics*, 28(5): 931–51.

Dalton, R. J., Farrell, D. M. and McAllister, I. (2013) *Political Parties and Democratic Linkage*, Oxford: Oxford University Press.

Dennison, J. and Goodwin, M. (2015) 'Immigration, Issue Ownership and the Rise of UKIP', *Parliamentary Affairs*, 68(1): 168–87.

Deschouwer, K. (1996) 'Political Parties and Democracy: A Mutual Murder?', *European Journal of Political Research*, 29: 263–78.

Deschouwer, K. (2005) 'Pinball Wizards: Political Parties and Democratic Representation in the Changing Institutional Architecture of European Politics', in A. Römmele, D. Farrell and P. Ignazi (eds), *Political Parties and Political Systems*, London: Praeger, pp. 83–99.

Diamond, L. and Gunther, R. (2001) *Political Parties and Democracy*, Baltimore: Johns Hopkins University Press.

Dogan, M. (1997) 'Erosion of Confidence in Advanced Democracies', *Studies in Comparative International Development*, 32(3): 3–29.

Dommett, K. and Flinders, M. (2014) 'The Politics and Management of Public Expectations: Gaps, Vacuums and the 2012 Mayoral Referenda', *British Politics*, 9(1): 29–50.

Dommett, K. and Pearce, W. (2019) 'What Do We Know About Public Attitudes Towards Experts? Reviewing Survey Data in the UK and EU', *Public Understanding of Science*, 28(6): 669–78.

Dommett, K. and Rye, D. (2017) 'Taking Up the Baton? New Campaigning Organisations and the Enactment of Representative Functions', *Politics*, 38(4): 411–27.

Dommett, K. and Temple, L. (2019) 'The Expert Cure? Exploring the Restorative Potential of Expertise for Public Satisfaction with Parties', *Political Studies*, online first.

Driver, S. (2011) *Understanding British Party Politics*, London: Polity Press.

Drummond, A. J. (2006) 'Electoral Volatility and Party Decline in Western Democracies: 1970–1995', *Political Studies*, 54(3): 628–47.

Dunleavy, P. (1987) 'Class Dealignment in Britain Revisited', *West European Politics*, 10(3): 400–19.

Bibliography

Duverger, M. (1954) *Political Parties: Their Organization and Activity in the Modern State*, London: Methuen.

Easton, D. (1965) *A Systems Analysis of Political Life*, New York: Wiley.

Ekman, J. and Amnå, E. (2012) 'Political Participation and Civic Engagement', *Human Affairs*, 22(3): 283–300.

Enroth, H. (2015) 'Cartelization Versus Representation? On a Misconception in Contemporary Party Theory', *Party Politics*, 23(2): 124–34.

Enyedi, Z. (2014) 'The Discreet Charm of Political Parties', *Party Politics*, 20(2): 194–200.

Epstein, L. (1967) *Political Parties in Western Democracies*, New York: Praeger.

Eulau, H. and Karps, P. (1977) 'The Puzzle of Representation: Specifying Components of Responsiveness', *Legislative Studies Quarterly*, 2(3): 233–54.

Everson, D. (1982) 'The Decline of Political Parties', *Proceedings of the Academy of Political Science*, 34(4): 49–60.

Ezrow, L., De Vries, C., Steenbergen, M. and Edwards, E. (2010) 'Mean Voter Representation and Partisan Constituency Representation: Do Parties Respond to the Mean Voter Position or to Their Supporters?', *Party Politics*, 17(3): 275–301.

Faucher, F. (2014) 'New Forms of Political Participation. Changing Demands or Changing Opportunities to Participate in Political Parties?', *Comparative European Politics*, 13: 405–29.

Fenno, R. F. (1978) *Home Style: House Members in Their Districts*, Boston: Little, Brown and Co.

Finer, H. (1949) *The Theory and Practice of Modern Government*, New York: H. Holt.

Fiorina, M. (1981) *Retrospective Voting in American National Elections*, New Haven: Yale University Press.

Fishkin, J., Luskin, R. and Jowell, R. (2000) 'Deliberative Polling and Public Consultation', *Parliamentary Affairs*, 53(4): 657–66.

Flinders, M. (2009) 'Bridging the Gap: Revitalising Politics and the Politics of Public Expectations', *Representation*, 45(3): 337–47.

Flinders, M. and Judge, D. (2017) 'Fifty Years of *Representative and Responsible Government:* Contemporary Relevance, Theoretical Revisions and Conceptual Reflection', *Representation*, 53(2): 97–116.

Font, J., Wojcieszak, M. and Navarro, C. (2018) 'Participation, Representation and Expertise: Citizen Preferences for Political Decision-Making Processes', *Political Studies*, 63(S1): 153–72.

Garland, J. and Brett, W. (2014) *Open Up: The Future of the Political Party*, London: Electoral Reform Society.

Gauja, A. (2012) 'The "Push" for Primaries: What Drives Party Organisational Reform in Australia and the United Kingdom?', *Australian Journal of Political Science*, 47(4): 641–58.

Gauja, A. (2015) 'The Construction of Party Membership', *European Journal of Political Research*, 54: 232–48.

Gauja, A. (2017) *Party Reform: The Causes, Challenges and Consequences of Organisational Change*, Oxford: Oxford University Press.

Bibliography

Gerbaudo, P. (2019) *The Digital Party: Political Organisation and Online Democracy*, London: Pluto Press.

Gibson, R. (2015) 'Party Change, Social Media and the Rise of "Citizen-Initiated" Campaigning', *Party Politics*, 21(2): 183–97.

Gidengil, E., Blais, A., Nadeau, R. and Nevitte, N. (2002) 'Changes in the Party System and Anti-party Sentiment', in W. Cross (ed.), *Political Parties, Representation, and Electoral Democracy in Canada*, Don Mills: Oxford University Press, pp. 68–86.

Goetz, K. (2014) 'A Question of Time: Responsive and Responsible Democratic Politics', *West European Politics*, 37(2): 379–99.

Grant, W. (2008) 'The Changing Patterns of Group Politics in Britain', *British Politics*, 3(2): 204–22.

Green, J. and Jennings, W. (2012) 'The Dynamics of Issue Competence and Vote for Parties In and Out of Power: An Analysis of Valence in Britain, 1979–1997', *European Journal of Political Research*, 51: 469–503.

Green, J. and Jennings, W. (2017) 'Party Reputations and Policy Priorities: How Issue Ownership Shapes Executive and Legislative Agendas', *British Journal of Political Science*, 49(2): 443–66.

Hall, E. (2018) 'Integrity in Democratic Politics', *British Journal of Politics and International Relations*, 20(2): 395–408.

Halpin, D. (2010) *Groups, Representation and Democracy: Between Promise and Practice*, Manchester: Manchester University Press.

Hansard Society (2018) *Audit of Political Engagement 15*, London: Hansard Society.

Hansard Society (2019) *Audit of Political Engagement 16*, London: Hansard Society.

Hatier, C. (2012) '"Them" and "Us": Demonising Politicians by Moral Double Standards', *Contemporary Politics*, 18(4): 467–80.

Hay, C. (2002) *Political Analysis: A Critical Introduction*, Basingstoke: Palgrave.

Hay, C. (2007) *Why We Hate Politics*, Cambridge: Polity Press.

Hibbing, J. and Theiss-Morse, E. (2002) *Stealth Democracy: Americans' Beliefs About How Government Should Work*, Cambridge: Cambridge University Press.

Himmelweit, H., Humphreys, P. and Jaeger, M. (1985) *How Voters Decide*, Milton Keynes: Open University Press.

House of Commons (2018) *Code of Conduct*, HC 1474.

Ignazi, P. (2014) 'Power and the (Il)legitimacy of Political Parties: An Unavoidable Paradox of Contemporary Democracy', *Party Politics*, 20(2): 160–9.

Ignazi, P. (2017) *Party and Democracy: The Uneven Road to Party Legitimacy*, Oxford: Oxford University Press.

Jennings, W., Stoker, G. and Twyman, J. (2016) 'The Dimensions and Impact of Political Discontent in Britain', *Parliamentary Affairs*, 69(4): 876–900.

Jerit, J. and Barabas, J. (2012) 'Partisan Perceptual Bias and the Information Environment', *Journal of Politics*, 74(3): 672–84.

Kahneman, K. (2011) *Thinking, Fast and Slow*, London: Penguin.

Katz, R. (2014) 'No Man Can Serve Two Masters: Party Politics, Party Members, Citizens and Principal-Agent Models of Democracy', *Party Politics*, 20(2): 183–93.

Bibliography

Katz, R. and Mair, P. (1994) *How Parties Organize: Change and Adaptation in Party Organizations in Western Democracies*, London: Sage.

Katz, R. and Mair, P. (1995) 'Changing Models of Party Organisation and Party Democracy: The Emergence of the Cartel Party', *Party Politics*, 1(5): 5–28.

Katz, R. and Mair, P. (1997) 'Party Organisation, Party Development and the Emergence of the Cartel Party', in Peter Mair (ed.), *Party System Change: Approaches and Interpretation*, Oxford: Oxford University Press, pp. 93–119.

Katz, R. and Mair, P. (2009) 'The Cartel Party Thesis: A Restatement', *Perspectives on Politics*, 7(4): 753–66.

Keane, M. and Merlo, A. (2010) 'Money, Political Ambition, and the Career Decisions of Politicians', *American Economic Journal: Microeconomics*, 2(3): 186–215.

Kellner, P. (2012) *Democracy on Trial: What Voters Really Think*, London: YouGov.

Keman, H. (2014) 'Democratic Performance of Parties and Legitimacy in Europe', *West European Politics*, 37(2): 309–30.

Kimball, D. and Patterson, S. (1997) 'Living Up to Expectations: Public Attitudes Toward Congress', *Journal of Politics*, 59(3): 701–28.

Kirchheimer, O. (1966) 'The Transformation of Western European Party Systems', in J. LaPalombara and M. Weiner (eds), *Political Parties and Political Development*, Princeton: Princeton University Press, pp. 177–200.

Kitschelt, H. and Wilkinson, S. I. (2009) *Patrons, Clients and Policies: Patterns of Democratic Accountability and Political Competition*, Cambridge: Cambridge University Press.

Koole, R. (1996) 'Cadre, Catch-All or Cartel?', *Party Politics*, 2(4): 507–23.

Lavezzolo, S. and Ramiro, L. (2017) 'Stealth Democracy and the Support for New and Challenger Parties', *European Political Science Review*, 10(2): pp. 267–89.

Lawson, K. (1980) *Political Parties and Linkage: A Comparative Perspective*, London: Yale University Press.

Lawson, K. (2005) *How Political Parties Work: Perspectives from Within*, London: Praeger.

Lee, B. (2014) 'Window Dressing 2.0: Constituency-Level Web Campaigns in the 2010 UK General Election', *Politics*, 34(1): 45–57.

Lees-Marshment, J. (2001) *Political Marketing and British Political Parties: The Party's Just Begun*, Manchester: Manchester University Press.

Liberal Democrats (2018) *Leading Change: Proposals to Open Up the Party*, London: Liberal Democrats.

Lilleker, D., Tenscher, J. and Štetka, V. (2015) 'Towards Hypermedia Campaigning? Perceptions of New Media's Importance for Campaigning by Party Strategists in Comparative Perspective', *Information, Communication and Society*, 18(7): 747–65.

Linz, J. (2002) 'Anti-party Sentiments in Southern Europe', in R. Gunther, J. R. Montero and J. Linz (eds), *Political Parties: Old Concepts and New Challenges*, Oxford: Oxford University Press, pp. 257–90.

Lipset, S. (1959) 'Some Social Requisites of Democracy: Economic Development and Political Legitimacy', *American Political Science Review*, 53(1): 69–105.

Bibliography

Majone, G. (1996) *Regulating Europe*, London: Routledge.

Mair, P. (1997) *Party System Change: Approaches and Interpretation*, Oxford: Oxford University Press.

Mair, P. (2009) 'Representative Versus Responsible Government', MPIfG Working Paper 09/8, Cologne: Max Planck Institute for the Study of Societies, available here: http://www.mpifg.de/pu/workpap/wp09-8.pdf, accessed 24 January 2020.

Mansbridge, J. (2003) 'Rethinking Representation', *American Political Science Review*, 97(4): 515–28.

Margetts, H., John, P., Hale, S. and Yasseri, T. (2015) *Political Turbulence: How Social Media Shape Collective Action*, Princeton: Princeton University Press.

Martin, A. (2014) 'The Party Is Not Over: Explaining Attitudes Toward Political Parties in Australia', *International Journal of Public Opinion Research*, 26(1): 1–17.

Mayne, Q. and Hakhverdian, A. (2017) 'Ideological Congruence and Citizen Satisfaction: Evidence From 25 Advanced Democracies', *Comparative Political Studies*, 50(6): 822–49.

McAllister, I. (2000) 'Keeping Them Honest: Public and Elite Perceptions of Ethical Conduct Among Australian Legislators', *Political Studies*, 48(1): 22–37.

Milazzo, C. and Mattes, K. (2016) 'Looking Good For Election Day: Does Attractiveness Predict Electoral Success in Britain?', *British Journal of Politics and International Relations*, 18 (1): 161–78.

Miller, A. (1974) 'Political Issues and Trust in Government: 1964–1970', *American Political Science Review*, 68(3): 951–72.

Morgan, D. (1996) 'Focus Groups', *Annual Review of Sociology*, 22(1): 129–52.

Morgeson, F. (2013) 'Expectations, Disconfirmation, and Citizen Satisfaction with the US Federal Government: Testing and Expanding the Model', *Journal of Public Administration Research and Theory*, 23(2): 289–305.

Mudde, C. (2004) 'The Populist Zeitgeist', *Government and Opposition*, 39(4): 541–63.

Mudge, S. and Chen, A. (2014) 'Political Parties and the Sociological Imagination: Past, Present, and Future Directions', *Annual Review of Sociology*, 40(1): 305–30.

Müller, J-W. (2017) *What Is Populism?*, London: Penguin.

Naurin, E. (2011) *Election Promises, Party Behaviour and Voter Perceptions*, Basingstoke: Palgrave Macmillan.

Norris, P. (2011) *Democratic Deficit: Critical Citizens Revisited*, Cambridge: Cambridge University Press.

Önnudóttir, E. H. (2016) 'Political Parties and Styles of Representation', *Party Politics*, 22(6): 732–45.

Pastorella, G. (2016) 'Technocratic Governments in Europe: Getting the Critique Right', *Political Studies*, 64(4): 948–65.

Pattie, C. and Johnston, R. (2012) 'The Electoral Impact of the UK 2009 MPs' Expenses Scandal', *Political Studies*, 60(4): 730–50.

Pattie, C. and Johnston, R. (2013) 'Personal Mobilization, Civic Norms and Political Participation', *Geoforum*, 45: 178–89.

Pedersen, K. and Saglie, J. (2005) 'New Technology in Ageing Parties: Internet Use in Danish and Norwegian Parties', *Party Politics*, 11(3): 359–77.

Pharr, S. J. and Putnam, R. (eds) (2000) *Disaffected Democracies: What's Troubling the Trilateral Countries?*, Princeton: Princeton University Press.

Pharr, S. J., Putnam., R. and Dalton, R. (2000) 'Trouble in the Advanced Democracies? A Quarter-Century of Declining Confidence', *Journal of Democracy*, 11(2): 5–25.

Pickard, J. (2015) 'Jeremy Corbyn Debuts His New Style of People's PMQs', *Financial Times*, 16 September, available here: https://www.ft.com/content/c599a046-5c67-11e5-9846-de406ccb37f2, accessed 24 January 2020.

Pitkin, H. (1967) *The Concept of Representation*, Berkeley: University of California Press.

Poguntke, T. and Scarrow, S. (1996) 'The Politics of Anti-party Sentiment: Introduction', *European Journal of Political Research*, 29(3): 257–62.

Popkin, S. (1991) *The Reasoning Voter: Communication and Persuasion in Presidential Campaigns*, Chicago: University of Chicago Press.

Rehfeld, A. (2009) 'Representation Rethought: On Trustees, Delegates and Gyroscopes in the Study of Political Representation and Democracy', *American Political Science Review*, 103(2): 214–30.

Reiter, H. (1989) 'Party Decline in the West: A Skeptic's View', *Journal or Theoretical Politics*, 1(3): 325–48.

Römmele, A. (2003) 'Political Parties, Party Communication and New Information and Communication Technologies', *Party Politics*, 9(1): 7–20.

Rothstein, B. (2009) 'Creating Political Legitimacy: Electoral Democracy Versus Quality of Government', *American Behavioral Scientist*, 53(3): 311–30.

Sarewitz, D. (2001) 'Science and Environmental Policy: An Excess of Objectivity', in R. Frodeman (ed.), *Earth Matters: The Earth Sciences, Philosophy and the Claims of Community*, Upper Saddle River: Prentice Hall, pp. 79–98.

Särlvik, B. and Crewe, I. (1983) *Decade of Dealignment*, Cambridge: Cambridge University Press.

Sartori, G. (1976) *Parties and Party Systems: A Framework for Analysis*, Cambridge: Cambridge University Press

Sartori, G. (2005) 'Party Types, Organisation and Functions', *West European Politics*, 28(1): 5–32.

Scarrow, S. (2014) *Beyond Party Members*, Oxford: Oxford University Press.

Scarrow, S., Webb, P. and Poguntke, T. (2017) *Organizing Political Parties: Representation, Participation and Power*, Oxford: Oxford University Press.

Schofield, K. (2016) 'More Than 3,000 Voters "Purged" from Labour's Leadership Election', Politics Home website, 7 September, available here: https://www.politicshome.com/news/uk/political-parties/labour-party/news/78748/revealed-more-3000-voters-purged-labour-leadership, accessed 28 June 2019.

Seyd, B. (2015) 'How Do Citizens Evaluate Public Officials? The Role of Performance and Expectations on Political Trust', *Political Studies*, 63(S1): 73–90.

Seyd, P. (2020) 'Corbyn's Labour Party: Managing the Membership Surge', *British Politics*, 15(1): 1–24.

Simmons, K., Silver, L., Johnson, C. and Wike, R. (2018) 'In Western Europe, Populist Parties Tap Anti-establishment Frustration But Have Little Appeal Across Ideological Divide', Washington, DC: Pew Research Center, available here: https://www.pewresearch.org/global/2018/07/12/in-western-europe-populist-parties-tap-anti-establishment-frustration-but-have-little-appeal-across-ideological-divide/, accessed 9 January 2019.

Spoon, J. and Klüver, J. (2014) 'Do Parties Respond? How Electoral Context Influences Party Responsiveness', *Electoral Studies*, 35: 48–60.

Stanley, L. (2016) 'Using Focus Groups in Political Science and International Relations', *Politics*, 36(3): 236–49.

Stoker, G. (2006) *Why Politics Matters: Making Democracy Work*, Basingstoke: Palgrave Macmillan.

Stoker, G., Hay, C. and Barr, M. (2016) 'Fast Thinking: Implications for Democratic Politics', *European Journal for Political Research*, 55(1): 3–21.

Stokes, D. (1992) 'Valence Politics', in D. Kavanagh (ed.), *Electoral Politics*, Oxford: Clarendon Press, pp. 141–64.

Taggart, P. (1996) *The New Populism and the New Politics: New Protest Parties in Sweden in a Comparative Perspective*, London: Macmillan.

Tilley, J. and Hobolt, S. (2011) 'Is the Government to Blame? An Experimental Test of How Partisanship Shapes Perceptions of Performance and Responsibility', *Journal of Politics*, 73(2): 316–30.

Urbinati, N. and Warren, M. (2008) 'The Concept of Representation in Contemporary Democratic Theory', *Annual Review of Political Science*, 11: 387–412.

van Biezen, I. (2008) 'The State of the Parties: Party Democracy in the 21st Century', *European Review*, 16(3): 263–9.

van Biezen, I. (2014) 'The End of Party Democracy as We Know It? A Tribute to Peter Mair', *Irish Political Studies*, 29(2): 177–93.

van Biezen, I. and Poguntke, T. (2014) 'The Decline of Membership-Based Politics', *Party Politics*, 20(2): 205–16.

van Biezen, I. and Saward, M. (2008) 'Democratic Theorists and Party Scholars: Why They Don't Talk to Each Other, and Why They Should', *Perspectives on Politics*, 6(1): 21–35.

van Biezen, I., Mair, P. and Poguntke, T. (2012) 'Going, Going … Gone? The Decline of Party Membership in Contemporary Europe', *European Journal of Political Research*, 51: 24–56.

Vivyan, N. and Wagner, M. (2015) 'What Do Voters Want From Their Local MP?', *Political Quarterly*, 86(1): 33–40.

Vliegenthart, R., Boomgaarden, H. G. and Boumans, J. W. (2011) 'Changes in Political News Coverage: Personalization, Conflict and Negativity in British and Dutch Newspapers', in K. Brants and K. Voltmer (eds), *Political Communication in Postmodern Democracy*, London: Palgrave Macmillan, pp. 92–110.

Wattenberg, M. (1986) *The Decline of American Political Parties: 1952–1984*, Cambridge: Harvard University Press.

Bibliography

Webb, P. (1995) 'Are British Political Parties in Decline', *Party Politics*, 1(3): 299–322.

Webb, P. (2002) 'Political Parties and Democratic Control in Advanced Industrial Societies', in Paul Webb, David M. Farrell and Ian Holliday (eds), *Political Parties in Advanced Industrial Democracies*, New York: Oxford University Press, pp. 438–60.

Webb, P. (2013) 'Who Is Willing to Participate? Dissatisfied Democrats, Stealth Democrats and Populists in the United Kingdom', *European Journal of Political Research*, 52(6): 747–72.

Werner, A. (2016) 'Party Responsiveness and Voter Confidence in Australia', *Australian Journal of Political Science*, 51(3): 436–57.

White, J. and Ypi, L. (2010) 'Rethinking the Modern Prince: Partisanship and the Democratic Ethos', *Political Studies*, 58(4): 809–28.

Whitely, P. (1984) 'Perceptions of Economic Performance and Voting Behaviour in the 1983 General Election in Britain', *Political Behaviour*, 6(4): 395–410.

Whiteley, P. (2009) 'Where Have All the Members Gone? The Dynamics of Party Membership in Britain', *Parliamentary Affairs*, 62(2): 242–57.

Zaller, J. (1992) *The Nature and Origins of Mass Opinion*, Cambridge: Cambridge University Press.

Zaller, J. and Feldman, D. (1992) 'A Simple Theory of the Survey Response: Answering Questions Versus Revealing Preferences', *American Journal of Political Science*, 36(3): 579–616.

Index

Note: 'n.' after a page reference indicates the number of a note on that page.

Index

Facebook 85
fans 99, 100
Farage, Nigel 209
Farrell, D. M. 36
finance 151
financial crisis 160
first-past-the-post electoral system
    131, 151
Five Star Movement 34
focus groups 9, 12, 20, 21, 72, 87,
    114, 134, 213
forums 21, 101, 204, 208
France 31, 213

Garland, J. 158
Gauja, A. 203
gender issues 76, 145
general elections 34, 35, 114, 131
    see also elections
Gerbaudo, P. 206
Germany 31
Gidengil, E. 215
Goetz, K. 127
governance 111–38
    governing functions 115–20
    overview 24, 111–12, 137–8
    parties and governance 112–15
    party conduct 155–6, 159, 161, 162
    party motivations 132–7
    party performance 120–6
    public attitudes 36, 37, 39, 41, 44
    responsiveness or responsibility
        127–32
    value of parties 4, 5
    what citizens want from parties
        174, 175, 177, 178–9, 181, 184,
        186, 187
Green, J. 111, 120
Green Party 35, 98, 137, 190, 209,
    239n.1
Greenpeace 85
Gunther, R. 38

Halpin, D. 39
Hansard Society 32

Hay, C. 43, 209
Hibbing, J. 83
honesty 44, 153, 158, 167, 168, 175,
    180, 187

ideal parties 151–2
ideals *see* citizens' desires/ideals
ideological parties 123, 133–4
Ignazi, P. 34, 37, 43, 113–14, 143
immutable attitude 73, 74
impact of participation 89–92, 174,
    177, 181
inclusiveness 154, 163–5, 166, 175,
    180, 181, 182–5
independent advice 135, 136, 138,
    174, 177, 207
inert attitude 73, 74
information availability 156
information transparency 155
integrity 154, 167–9, 175, 180
interest groups 82, 124
international comparative analysis
    213–14
internet 105, 107, 208
issue campaigning 97
Italy 31, 213

Jennings, W. 42, 111, 120, 141
journalism 207

Katz, R. 39, 40, 121
Keman, H. 113, 185
Kimball, D. 36
Kirchheimer, O. 38
Klüver, J. 72

Labour Party
    challenges faced 190
    general and specific parties 15, 25
    participatory opportunities 91
    party response 198, 199, 200, 201,
        202, 205
    public attitudes 13, 15, 35
    re-educating citizens 207–8
    representative source 63

Index

Index

Index

Index

CPSIA information can be obtained
at www.ICGtesting.com
Printed in the USA
JSHW011042100720
6569JS00006B/53